Introduction to Data Management Functions and Tools

IDMA 201 COURSE TEXTBOOK

Insurance Data Management Association (IDMA) Associate Insurance Data Manager (AIDM) Designation Program

Technics Publications
BASKING RIDGE, NEW JERSEY

Published by:

2 Lindsley Road
Basking Ridge, NJ 07920 USA

https://www.TechnicsPub.com

Cover design by Lorena Molinari

Edited by the Insurance Data Management Association (IDMA)

First Edition

First Printing 2017

Copyright © 2017 Insurance Data Management Association, Inc. (IDMA)

ISBN, print ed.   9781634622424
ISBN, Kindle ed.   9781634622431
ISBN, PDF ed.   9781634622455
ISBN, Enterprise ed.   9781634622462

Library of Congress Control Number: 2017908148

Contents

Introduction

Founded in 1983, IDMA is an independent nonprofit professional association dedicated to increasing the level of professionalism, knowledge, and visibility of insurance data management through education, research, annual forums, local chapter meetings, news bulletins, and peer-to-peer networking. It serves individuals employed in any aspect of insurance data management. This includes individuals engaged in any of the following enterprise information governance activities within various functional areas of insurance companies, regulatory bodies, statistical/rating organizations, industry consulting firms, professional associations and learned societies, and technology research and services providers:

- data definition
- data collection
- data administration
- data standards
- data processing
- data analysis
- internal and external data reporting
- data quality

The main objective of IDMA is the administration of an educational program designed to increase professional proficiency and to provide a professional designation in the data management discipline. Additionally, IDMA provides an ongoing forum for the discussion of issues and innovations in data management through technical seminars, educational workshops, and publications.

IDMA courses, workshops, and forums are highly recommended for a broad audience including new hires, IT and data modeling professionals who want to broaden their knowledge of the business side of insurance data management, anyone who manages and governs data in the industry (statistical, or management information data), and anyone who needs to use or communicate good quality data/information – from actuaries to underwriters, and claims and analytics professionals.

Students who complete the four IDMA-developed courses and successfully pass the examinations are awarded an *Associate Insurance Data Manager (AIDM®)* designation. The IDMA courses may be taken in any order; there are no prerequisites. However, the courses are numbered to indicate a recommended sequence.

Students who complete additional course work from other selected insurance industry educational organizations and successfully pass the specified examinations receive the *Certified Insurance Data Manager (CIDM®)* designation.

For details on the designation requirements, please refer to the IDMA website at www.IDMA.org or call our office at +1 (201) 469-3069.

Using this Textbook

Introduction to Data Management Functions and Tools is the assigned textbook for the IDMA 201 course in the IDMA *Associate Insurance Data Manager (AIDM®)* designation program. This course defines data management, describes the functions of data managers, provides the business case for data management and introduces the student to concepts and tools used by data managers.

Data management skills bring tremendous value, affecting the very viability of many aspects of an enterprise. Disciplined and well-trained data management professionals are essential in helping their organizations save money, increase revenue, increase customer satisfaction, and protect one of the enterprise's most valuable assets – its data.

As you read the material presented in this course, keep in mind that what you are reading is not intended to be representative of any particular entity. That is a key value of data management skills: they fit in many places in an organization and are critical skills for professionals to possess. Whether you are an actuary, a claims professional, business analyst, or almost any of the other key functions, knowledge of data management can help you do your job better and help you prepare, understand, and protect the raw material—the data—so critical to your organization.

Due to the nature of data management and the many areas that are impacted by it, you may see information and terms repeated as you move through the various assignments and courses. You may also see a few slight differences in definitions or concepts. This occurs due to the topics being presented, the context in which they are presented, and the author's understanding or perception of their subject matter. For this course, students should apply definitions and concepts as presented in the course material.

Important Note Applicable to All IDMA Course Material: IDMA strives to keep all of its course material current. The information provided is up to date at the time of publication. The timing and pace of industry changes and the constraints of publication can at times result in a lag in updates being included. IDMA regularly reviews content to ensure that it is current and will publish updates as necessary and appropriate.

Exam Information

IDMA exams are given online, consist of one hundred (100) multiple-choice and true/false type questions, and are three hours long. Unofficial scores are tabulated and issued immediately after the exam completion. Official scores are mailed to students within 15 business days after the conclusion of the exam cycle. Passing score is 70%.

Students are allowed to take more than one course exam during an exam cycle. Students are also allowed to retake an exam within the same exam cycle if they were not successful on their first try.

Exams are conducted with no reference materials, papers, books, or other aids permitted in the room. No student may communicate with another during the exam. Students are not allowed to maintain copies of their exam. All exam materials are considered the property of IDMA.

Exam Registration Information and Requirements

IDMA does not contract with testing centers (such as Prometric, Pearson, Kryterion, etc...) to host its exams onsite. IDMA exams are given, so far as possible, at the student's worksite with cooperation of the human resources or education department in locating a proctor and site.

NOTE: Students are responsible to locate a proctor and provide IDMA with the proctor's contact information. A proctor could be anyone from your HR department, your boss, or staffer. A week prior to the exam, IDMA will email your proctor a "proctor package" explaining the exam process. You will also receive your exam pass via email around the same time.

Purchase of the study guide for the present IDMA course does not automatically register a candidate for the examination. As you proceed with your studies, be sure to arrange for your exam.

- Visit our website at www.IDMA.org to access and print the exam registration form, which contains information and forms needed to register for your exam.
- Plan to register with IDMA well in advance of your exam. Late fees apply two weeks prior to the start of the exam cycle.
- Coordinate with your proctor the date and start time of your exam.

How to Study for IDMA Exams

Use the assigned study materials (textbook and course guide). Focus your study on the Educational Objectives presented at the beginning of each course guide assignment. Thoroughly read the textbook and any other assigned materials, and then complete the course guide exercises. Choose a study method that best suits your needs; for example, participate in traditional class, or informal study group; or study on your own.

IDMA recommends that you begin your studies for the exam at least two months prior to your scheduled exam date.

Student Resources

For more information on any of the IDMA publications, course examinations, and other services:

- Visit our website at www.IDMA.org
- Call us in and outside of the U.S. at +1 (201) 469-3069
- Email our executive director, Farouk Yassine, at fyassine@idma.org
- Fax us at +1 (201) 748-1690
- Write to us at Insurance Data Management Association (IDMA), 545 Washington Boulevard, 16th Floor, Jersey City, NJ 07310

Contributors

IDMA owes a debt of gratitude to the following individuals for their help in developing the content of this course:

Hema Chaurasia, CPCU, CIDM

Lucy DeCaro, WCP, FIDM

Nora FitzGerald, FIDM

Larry Gehrke, CPCU, CIDM, FLMI, FIDM

Julie Gonzalez, AIDM, AU

Pamela Lyons, CPCU

Peter Marotta, AIDM, FIDM

Josef Martin, CPCU, CIDM

Richard Morales, PMP, CPCU, CIDM

Aimee Siliato, FIDM

Ellen Sonkin, CPCU, CIDM, APA, FIDM

Tracy Spadola, CPCU, CIDM, FIDM

Richard Sullivan, CPCU, CIDM

Farouk Yassine, CPCU, CIDM

Jane Zawistowski, AIDM, FIDM

Data, Information, and Knowledge

Today, more than ever, the world runs on data. They represent significant assets to individuals, organizations, and society as a whole. As the pace of change accelerates, data and the information derived from them are essential for strategic, tactical, and operational decision making. The quality of the data on which these decisions are based is crucial. Maintaining high quality data can be challenging for a number of reasons, but careful management of the data lifecycle helps to protect and maintain data quality. Well organized and managed data support the efficient creation and use of information throughout an organization, although the legacy systems used by many insurers present some challenges. One traditionally unrecognized source of a wealth of data and information is referred to as organizational memory.

Educational Objectives

Upon completion of this assignment, you should be able to:

1. Define data, information, and knowledge. Describe the relationship between them.
2. Explain why data and information are assets, and why this is important to both society and organizations.
3. Describe how managers use information and what they do in the absence of information.
4. Describe the role of information in organizational change.
5. Describe why data quality is so important to today's organization.
6. Explain why high data quality is so difficult to maintain.
7. Describe the data lifecycle.
8. Define data architecture.
9. Describe how data architecture and legacy systems impact an organization's ability to obtain the information needed.
10. Define organizational memory and explain its importance.
11. Describe the components of organizational memory.

Data, Information, and Knowledge

Although they are closely related, the terms data, information, and knowledge are not synonymous. **Data** are facts about, or attributes of, entities, those things about which an organization wishes to collect or create data. Entities can be organizations, customers, employees, products, objects, activities, or processes. Data can be expressed in a variety of forms including numbers, characters, symbols, or images. On their own, without analysis or context, data are meaningless and are often referred to as "raw".

Each specific piece of data (a datum) has attributes of its own and can be described in a variety of ways. These "data about data" are referred to as **metadata** and, in addition to identifying what the data mean or represent, they can include:

- The reason the datum is collected;
- The way in which it is collected;
- Its source;
- How it is stored;
- How it is accessed;
- How it is made available to users (i.e. access restrictions); and
- The frequency with which it is updated.

Information is data that have been analyzed, processed, or organized for a particular purpose and presented in a form and context that are relevant and meaningful. For example, an automobile's Vehicle Identification Number (VIN) is a seventeen-position code that includes letters and numbers. While it uniquely identifies a particular vehicle, it provides no obvious information about that vehicle. A VIN is data. However, examination of the specific sequence of letters and numbers that comprises a VIN reveals a variety of information about the vehicle, including:

- The country in which it was manufactured;
- The manufacturer;
- The model, body style, engine type, and transmission;
- The year in which it was manufactured; and
- The plant in which it was assembled.

As another example, a claims adjuster reviews and analyzes a variety of data in order to determine the value of a covered loss. The amount of the claim settlement reflects the information derived from those data.

Knowledge is the ability, based on experience and understanding, to use information in a competent, productive way. For example, it is an underwriter's knowledge that allows him or her to use vehicle information, in conjunction with details about its operator, to assess the likelihood of the vehicle being stolen or involved in an accident. Knowledge allows an underwriter to provide appropriate coverage and to charge an adequate premium. Consistent application of this knowledge over time can lead to profitable results for the insurer. Figure 1.1 illustrates the relationships between data and information, and information and knowledge.

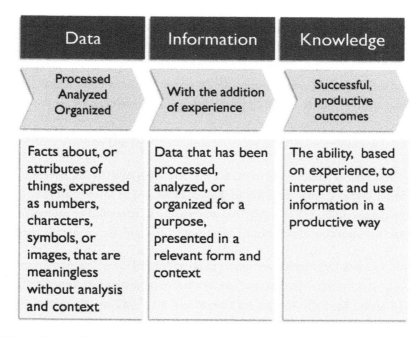

Figure 1.1 Data and information, and information and knowledge

As another example, a monthly sales figure of $125,000 for a particular product is data. Out of context, the number is meaningless. Knowledge is what enables a sales manager to transform that raw data into information by comparing that month's sales with those of previous months and asking appropriate questions. Are sales increasing? Are sales decreasing? Is a change in sales the result of normal seasonal fluctuations? What factors may be causing the increase or decrease? What additional data are required to more accurately evaluate the company's sales performance?

Data and Information as Assets

Individuals, families, organizations, communities, and governments all use data and information in a variety of ways. For example, individuals and families use Consumer Reports to make purchasing decisions. Corporations use financial statements to measure actual performance against goals. Insurers use policy and claim data to develop rates and premiums. Communities use demographics as an aid to urban planning. Governments use statistical information to support the development of laws and regulations.

In the past, data and information were not typically considered assets. When a family or an organization valued its assets, it focused on money in the bank, investments, and things like real estate, vehicles, or inventory that could be sold relatively quickly. However, one current definition of the term "asset" highlights the value of data. An **asset** is "A resource with economic value that an individual, corporation, or country owns or controls with the expectation that it will provide future benefit."[1]

---

[1] http:www.investopedia.com/terms/a/asset.asp (accessed November 18, 2015).

As the technology for collecting, storing, manipulating, and disseminating data has advanced, the demand for data and information has increased as has their use. Today, data and information are generally recognized as among the most valuable of an organization's assets because of the benefits they provide. For example, insurers analyze loss data obtained as part of the claims adjusting process to determine the rates upon which future premiums will be based. Those same data, analyzed differently, can help identify opportunities to cross-sell products to existing customers, develop innovative new products and services, or target niche markets. The availability of data has a very direct impact on an organization's ability to serve its customers well and improve profits.

Organizations that are best able to collect, organize, access, and analyze data can have a significant competitive advantage. They can bring higher quality products to market faster and at lower cost than their competitors. This can benefit not only the organization, but its customers and society in general. For example, safer vehicles protect not only their owners and operators but also the other motorists with whom they share the road.

For some organizations, data and information are assets in an additional way. These organizations collect data and manipulate them to create new information that is of use to other organizations. Information is the product that they sell. In the insurance industry, there are several such organizations. Some are controlled by governments and/or regulatory bodies and some are privately or publicly owned.

Like all assets, data require management. Corporations, non-profit organizations, government departments, social services, schools, hospitals—in fact, any organization that manages data well—can enhance service, reduce costs, and add value for stakeholders. Information derived from data can provide managers with a cohesive view of an organization's activity and a basis on which to make better decisions. For corporations, well-managed data can ultimately increase value for shareholders.

Like any asset, data need to be secured. Security is an important element of effective data management. Data need to be protected from unauthorized use, and from being mistakenly or deliberately changed, deleted, or misused. The more data organizations acquire, and the more they rely on those data, the greater a potential security risk the data represent. For example, if a hospital's patient records were compromised in any way, the risk to patients and to the hospital itself could be significant.

How Managers Use Information

In organizations of any size, there are generally three levels of management. At the top are the senior executives including, for example, the chief executive officer (CEO), chief financial officer (CFO), and chief information officer (CIO). Executives are responsible for directing the organization as a whole. They are not involved in managing day-to-day operations.

Middle managers report to the executives. They have responsibility for a distinct sub-section of the organization, such as a department, a region, or a plant. In an insurance company, middle managers include the underwriting manager, claims manager, information systems manager, marketing manager, and regional managers. Middle managers are responsible for achieving the goals established by senior executives.

Reporting to the middle managers are the first-level, or front-line, managers, such as supervisors, crew leaders, or office managers. They are responsible for the organization's day-to-day operations and for directly supervising its employees. Effective employee supervision helps ensure that middle management's plans are successfully implemented to achieve the executives' goals.

At each of these levels, managers perform a variety of functions. The most commonly cited functions of all managers are planning, organizing, leading, and controlling. In all of these, information is essential.

Planning

Managers at different levels within an organization engage in different types of planning. Two areas in which senior executives are involved are business modeling and strategic planning. In business terminology, a **business model** is a simple statement of how an organization will generate income. For example, the business model for a commercial insurer might be to sell property and liability insurance to commercial customers in a specified region. A restaurant's business model might be to serve scratch-made Tex-Mex food to customers at three locations within a major center.

Over time, both internal and external factors may cause senior executives to revisit the business model and make changes to it. The insurer may expand its services to include risk management consulting and loss control. The restaurant may add catering services or market a line of sauces and condiments to create additional income sources.

In the absence of adequate information and market research, an organization's business model, or changes to it, may be flawed. The insurer may find it is not able to compete effectively with an already established loss control provider. The cost to the restaurant of producing a branded line of products may prove to be prohibitive. Decisions made without sufficient, accurate information can damage an organization's bottom line.

Strategic planning is more involved than business modeling. It takes a long-term view, often three or more years into the future, and articulates senior management's vision for the organization at that point. It defines how the executives would like to see the organization positioned, and establishes objectives to help it reach that goal based on both internal and external considerations.

One tool commonly used in strategic planning is referred to as **SWOT analysis** (i.e. Strengths, Weaknesses, Opportunities, Threats). SWOT analysis involves recognizing and evaluating an organization's internal strengths and weaknesses relative to its competitors and identifying external opportunities on which it might capitalize and external–threats against which it should guard. To be able to do so, senior executives require considerable amounts of information about both the internal and external environments.

SWOT analysis is often represented by a simple matrix, as seen in Figure 1.2.

Middle managers engage in **tactical planning**. Tactical planning involves identifying, selecting, and scheduling the activities an organization must complete in order to achieve its strategic objectives. For example, if an organization has a strategic objective of increasing sales by twenty-five percent over the next three years, a supporting tactical objective might be to hire and train four additional salespeople during the current year, or to develop and launch a sales incentive program for company employees.

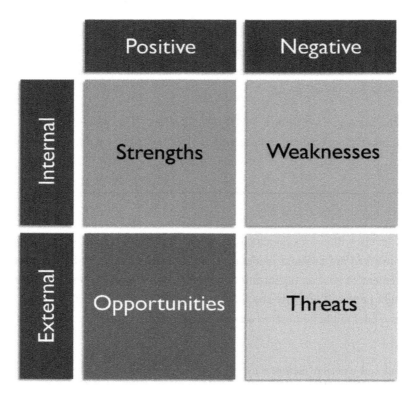

Figure 1.2 SWOT analysis, used by senior executives in the strategic planning process

Supervisors, unit managers, crew leaders, and other front-line managers are involved in **operational planning**. Just as tactical planning supports the goals established in strategic planning, operational planning facilitates completion of the activities identified in tactical planning. In support of a tactical plan to hire and train four additional sales people during the current year, a sales supervisor may plan to reorganize or renovate the office to accommodate the additional staff.

Information supports decision-making at all three levels within an organization. For example, workflow statistics help front-line managers improve resource allocation. Mid-level managers use information to perform cost-benefit analyses and evaluate which potential projects would best help achieve the organization's strategic goals. Executives use aggregate internal information combined with external data to establish and guide the organization's strategic focus.

Organizing

Organizations can be structured in a variety of ways. For example, one may be centralized with multiple departments, each of which deals with a single aspect of the organization's business. Another may be decentralized with regional offices that handle all aspects of the business within a given territory. Choosing the structure that best supports an organization's strategic goals is referred to as **organizational design**. An organizational chart is a visual representation of organizational design. Senior executives determine the overall structure of an organization, but middle managers and even front-line managers also make decisions about organizational design and resource allocation within their region, department, office, or team.

Job design is another aspect of organizing. Managers determine which individual job functions can be grouped together into a single job description, and how many different job descriptions are needed to complete all the tasks required to achieve the organization's goals. As changes occur in either the external or internal environment, managers may make changes in job design; for example, focusing job descriptions to create specialists in certain areas, or organizing employees into functional teams.

Decisions about organizational design and job design rely on information about both the internal and external environments. As changes occur in those environments, organizational design or job design may change as well. For example, changes in taxation practices in a jurisdiction may lead to the sale, closure, or relocation of a subsidiary located there. Internal financial data may indicate that outsourcing certain operations is more cost effective than continuing to perform those operations in-house. Changes in worker health and safety regulations may necessitate changes in job descriptions. Escalating employee turnover may lead to job design changes intended to enhance employee satisfaction through increased empowerment or flexible work schedules.

Leading

One important aspect of management is the ability to lead. Effective managers have interpersonal skills, motivational skills, and leadership skills. In addition to those skills, they need sufficient information to clearly understand the organization's strategic vision, its objectives, processes, and the environment in which it operates. They also need detailed, accurate and timely information about the actual performance of both the organization and its employees. Information and performance monitoring allow managers to identify strengths, weaknesses, opportunities and threats, and to respond appropriately.

Controlling

To help ensure that an organization meets its goals, managers complete the following tasks:

- Establish performance benchmarks;
- Compare actual performance to those benchmarks; and
- Take action to correct shortfalls in performance.

Performance benchmarks are established at every level. Strategic planning sets goals for the organization as a whole. Tactical plans include performance benchmarks for regions, departments, branch offices, or business units. Operational plans establish performance objectives for teams and offices. Managers negotiate performance goals with individual employees.

Managers need information about actual performance in order to measure it against benchmarks. Depending on the type of organization and the benchmark involved, that information may come from a variety of sources including client satisfaction surveys, financial statements, audits and inspections, workflow statistics, production and inventory levels, sales and expense reports, or employee turnover statistics.

Accurate information, provided in a timely manner and appropriate format, helps managers determine the reason for any deviation from objectives and decide on appropriate corrective action. For example, a sudden increase in an insurer's property insurance claims may be the result of deteriorating underwriting effectiveness. However, it could also be the result of a catastrophe such as a hurricane. The appropriate response to the increase in losses would differ depending on the cause of the increase.

Information not only allows managers to take corrective action when objectives are not met; it also allows them to monitor the effectiveness of the corrective action they have taken. This is essential to verifying that the cause for the shortfall has been accurately identified and that the corrective action settled on is appropriate and effective. Should an organization exceed its objectives, information allows managers to determine the reason, adjust its objectives appropriately, or identify emerging opportunities.

In the Absence of Information

Information is essential to all four management functions: planning, organizing, leading, and controlling. Insufficient, inaccurate, poorly presented, outdated, or untimely information forces decision makers to rely solely on experience, perceptions, and insights which may or may not be correct. When there is an issue or problem to resolve, they may ask questions or look for precedents. Often, they settle on the first reasonable solution they discover rather than searching for the optimal one. In fact, in the absence of high quality information, a manager's decision is often simply a "best guess". Fortunately, technology and the increasing availability of business information tools allow managers and executives to make better-informed and justified decisions.

Organizational Change

Organizations operate in dynamic environments. Competitors' products and services change. Laws and regulations change. Customer needs, tastes, and expectations change. Methods of doing business change. Technologies change. To remain viable, or to take advantage of the opportunities these changes present, organizations must change as well.

Organizational change[2] is the process of using an organization's resources, people, technology, and financial assets to reach a desired future outcome. To do so successfully, organizations need information to:

- Identify gaps between desired and actual performance;
- Establish goals that are challenging but realistic; and
- Determine how best to close any identified gaps between actual and desired performance.

Organizational change may occur in one or more of the following areas:

- Strategic focus
- Business model
- Organizational design

---

[2] Adapted from IDMA Curriculum Dictionary of Key Terms and Concepts, copyright 2015, p.111.

- Technologies
- Work processes
- Human resource practices
- Corporate culture
- External relationships

For example, consider a relatively simple organization, a book distributor. Before the Internet became fully commercialized in the United States of America (U.S.A.) in the mid-1990s, some book distributors adopted a mail-order business model. These distributors purchased customer mailing lists from a variety of sources. They printed catalogues with a list of titles and a brief description of each book, as well as a customer order form, and mailed the catalogues to potential customers. A customer wishing to purchase a book completed the order form and mailed it back to the company. An employee at the book distributor's facility input the customer information, order details, and payment information into the company's order and accounting systems. Once payment was received—the customer's check cleared the bank or the credit card information was confirmed—other employees at the distributor's central warehouse fulfilled the order. The process could take weeks and the distributor had relatively little information about its customers.

To enter the realm of e-commerce and compete successfully with Amazon.com when it first began operations as an online bookstore in 1995, a mail-order book distributor would have had to make significant changes to its business model, organizational design, technologies, and work processes. To remain competitive, it would have had to continue to evolve strategically, technologically, and operationally. Amazon's present order fulfillment system is very sophisticated. It allows the organization to acquire and manage large amounts of customer data and to target individual purchasers with products and special offers based on their purchasing history. It also allows customers to make more informed purchasing decisions by giving them access to product reviews written by other customers. This adds value not only for Amazon's customers but for its suppliers as well.

The ability to automate routine tasks, coupled with increased management effectiveness through greater access to information, has changed the way organizations are structured and the processes they use. For example, in the past, personal lines insurers' underwriting departments were often divided into regional teams of underwriters and support staff. Each insurance application was reviewed by an underwriter and risks were evaluated on an individual basis. Today, many insurers use expert systems to underwrite the majority of applicants with only the exceptional files being reviewed by an underwriter. Information systems allow the underwriter to evaluate and manage the insurer's exposure to risk on a portfolio basis rather than on a risk-by-risk basis. The organizational design and operational processes of the underwriting function have changed significantly, and insurers have been able to reduce staffing costs.

The need for flexibility has even led to the evolution of new organizational structures. One example is adhocracy. Unlike a traditional bureaucracy, an adhocracy is flexible, adaptive, and integrative with few hierarchical layers. It is appropriate for use in a highly dynamic environment. An adhocracy is formed for a particular purpose, often to solve a specific problem or to develop a new product or service, and is populated by experts with decision-making authority. During the first years of its existence, the National Aeronautics and Space Administration (NASA) operated as an adhocracy.[3]

---

[3] http://www.britannica.com/EBchecked/topic/1887627/adhocracy (accessed November 24, 2015).

Information's Role in Organizational Change

Information and communication technologies have made considerable advancements since the 1990s and continue to do so. They have become closely integrated into the management and operations of essentially all industries. Organizations are increasingly working with clients or suppliers to share information and create a cooperative environment, and this trend is reflected in the insurance industry. The Internet allows even relatively small organizations to compete globally and it makes massive quantities of previously inaccessible data accessible. As organizations' ability to acquire data and to create information has grown, competition has escalated both in terms of products and services as well as the time required to develop and deliver them. In an environment in which the pace of change is accelerating, organizations that can adapt are more likely to succeed.

Information provides a catalyst for organizational change. As an organization acquires more data and uses them more effectively it becomes more agile. It is better able to understand its environment and to adjust its focus, structure, processes, and relationships to respond to environmental changes. This is particularly true when an organization's business strategy, organizational design, and information management capabilities are aligned.

Data Quality

If information supports an organization's strategic, tactical, and operational decisions, and information is derived from data, then the quality of those data is critical. The Insurance Data Management Association (IDMA) defines **data quality** as "The degree to which data are fit for their intended uses; data are of high quality if they are fit for their intended uses in operations, decision making, and planning."[4]

To be fit for use, data must have certain characteristics. Accuracy is essential. A customer's name, mailing or shipping address, email address, and telephone number must be correct and without typographical errors. An error in a shipping address can result in a customer not receiving an order. In addition to causing customer dissatisfaction, which can be costly in terms of lost future sales, this creates additional costs for the organization because the time employees spend discovering and correcting the error is time they are not spending on other revenue-generating activities.

Data must be complete. For example, an insurer needs specific details about vehicles and their operators in order to provide automobile insurance coverage. In the absence of any of these data, an insurer is unable to issue a policy. Obtaining the missing data takes time, slows customer service, and increases the insurer's expenses.

It is important that data be timely, meaning they are up-to-date and immediately accessible when required. Particularly in a dynamic environment, timely data are essential for decision makers. They are important for an organization's operations as well. For example, if a supplier's sales representative changes, an organization's purchasing staff need to know the name and contact information for the new representative promptly. Accessibility is also key. It is of little benefit to have large quantities of high-quality data if they are not readily accessible when required.

---

[4] IDMA Curriculum Dictionary of Key Terms, Insurance Data Management Association, 2011, p. 37.

Data must also be consistent with an organization's business rules. For example, if a car rental agency has a business rule that each customer can rent only one vehicle at a time, and must return one vehicle before renting another, the organization's system must be able to capture, for each customer, each vehicle rental and each vehicle return.

Finally, data must be relevant. Different contexts require different types of data. For example, the chief financial officer analyzes financial data. Marketing managers make decisions based on customer and sales data. Operations managers plan and schedule based on inventory, processing, resource, and order data. The way in which data are presented can enhance their relevance. Forms, tables, graphs, charts, or diagrams can be effective methods of presenting data in a meaningful way.

The Cost of Poor Quality Data

In 1992, George Labovitz and Yu Sang Chang developed the 1-10-100 rule to illustrate the cost of poor quality[5]. In manufacturing, quality professionals use the 1-10-100 rule to describe the increasing cost of correcting errors as a product moves from initial design through manufacturing and on to the customer. A problem identified and corrected in the design phase costs relatively little, whereas one identified and corrected during production may cost ten times as much, and one identified after the product has reached the marketplace costs far more. For example, the cost of a product recall can be significant, both financially and in terms of an organization's reputation.

The 1-10-100 rule applies to data quality as well. The cost of correcting a data entry error at the moment it is made is small, perhaps $1. The cost of correcting that same error later increases to perhaps $10. The cost of not correcting the error is greater still.

For example, an insurance brokerage may send its personal lines clients a monthly electronic newsletter with tips on safety, maintenance, and loss prevention, and explanations of coverages and other policy provisions. The newsletter helps the brokerage maintain relationships and provides a vehicle for cross-selling existing clients. Brokerage employees contact each personal lines client to obtain an email address and enter it into the agency management system. The cost of verifying and correcting an email address at the point it is initially entered is negligible; it takes a moment or two of the employee's time. This is referred to as the **cost of prevention**. If an electronic newsletter bounces back because the client's email address was input incorrectly, an employee would have to look up the client's telephone number, call to obtain the correct email address, and input it into the system. This would take time and keep the employee from serving other clients or performing other tasks. This is the **cost of correction**. If the client's email address is not corrected, he or she will not receive the newsletters, which could result in a loss of cross-selling opportunities and perhaps loss of the client's loyalty. This is the **cost of failure**.

In a 2011 article in the *Journal of Industrial Engineering and Management* entitled *The Cost of Poor Quality Data*, authors Anders Haug, Frederik Zachariassen and Dennis van Liempd illustrated how poor quality data can affect an organization both operationally and strategically. Their illustration is reproduced in Figure 1.3. In addition to direct

---

[5]Why Data Should Be a Business Asset – The 1-10-100 Rule, Mary Doyle, viewed at http://www.business2community.com/big-data/data-business-asset-1-10-100-rule-0967242 (accessed April 7, 2016).

measurable costs, there are also hidden costs such as the value of lost opportunities, the loss of knowledge through employee turnover, or business losses resulting from inappropriate strategic decisions.

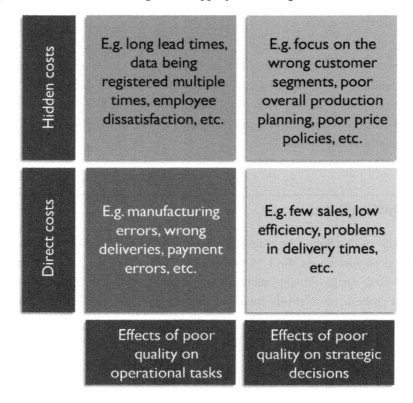

Figure 1.3 From the Journal of Industrial Engineering and Management entitled The Cost of Poor Quality Data, http://bit.ly/2elU5Sn (accessed November 28, 2014)

The cost of bad data can be significant. The Data Warehousing Institute (TDWI) has estimated that the consequences of poor data quality cost businesses in the United States more than $800 billion a year. In addition, a survey conducted by Demand Gen indicated the following:

"Sample findings:

Many organizations rely on marketing/prospect data that is 20%-40% inaccurate

30% of companies currently have no strategy to update inaccurate or incomplete data

8 out of 10 companies indicated that dirty data are hindering their lead generation campaigns"

Poor quality data, sometimes called "dirty data", can also lead to increased scrutiny by regulators. This is particularly true in industries that are highly regulated such as the financial services industry. For example, state insurance departments monitor insurer solvency, and insurers are required to submit detailed financial statements annually. Inaccuracies in these statements, either self-disclosed or identified by external auditors, could cause regulators to investigate and take action. As well, under the terms of the Sarbanes-Oxley Act, senior executives in many organizations are personally responsible for ensuring that financial data are accurate, and that the company has adequate controls in place to protect the integrity of its financial information.

Challenges in Maintaining High Data Quality

High quality data are difficult to maintain for any number of reasons. Clearly one source of bad data is unintentionally inaccurate data entry, or typographical errors. Sometimes, however, incorrect data are entered intentionally. For example, a cashier serving a customer in a grocery store may not remember the Universal Product Code (UPC) for a tangerine. Rather than look it up, he or she may simply input the UPC for an orange instead. Done frequently enough, this sort of intentional error can cause problems in the store's inventory and ordering systems, and potentially a loss in profits.

If required data are not clearly defined, there can be inconsistencies. For example, an "Address" field may require either a mailing address or a shipping address; the two may not be the same. A customer's mailing address could be a post office box whereas the shipping address would be a physical location. If staff is not properly trained as to which address is required, or if fields in online customer entry forms are not clearly labeled, customer address data will be inconsistent.

Input fields may not be long enough resulting in truncation of the data. Fields may not accept the type of data that needs to be entered. For example, an online retailer in the U.S.A. may have a ZIP Code field that accepts only numbers. This would preclude customers in Canada from entering their postal code, which is a series of numbers and letters.

Organizations, particularly large ones, may have more than one customer with the same name. If one customer's information needs to be updated and the employee making the change neglects to verify that he or she is updating the correct customer's file, both customer's files will subsequently have incorrect data.

The passage of time is another source of bad data. For example, colleges and universities acquire a variety of data about their students including their address, telephone number, and email address. After graduation, these data could help the institution's alumni association keep in contact with graduates and solicit donations for the school. However, graduates move to take jobs; their addresses and telephone numbers change; their email addresses change. The quality of the institution's data about its graduates deteriorates over time.

Another source of bad data comes from the fact that many organizations have multiple systems that are not well-integrated. Data may be duplicated across those systems. For example, a customer's name, address, and telephone number may appear in both an organization's accounting system and its marketing system. When a change occurs, perhaps the customer moves, both systems must be updated and this does not always occur.

Increasingly, organizations obtain data from a variety of outside sources. Suppliers share data with manufacturers. Customers input data into companies' systems when they make online purchases. Organizations purchase data, for example customer lists, from other businesses. There is no way for an organization to easily verify the quality of the data it obtains from other sources.

Another potential source of bad data is **data conversion**. As organizations update systems, they move existing data from an older system to the new one. This can be challenging because the two systems may require different data in different formats, organized in different ways. The process of converting data from the old format and structure to the new one can introduce errors into previously good quality data. For example, if an older system includes a customer's city and state in a single field, and the new system has two separate fields for city and state, converting customer addresses may be problematic.

Another consideration with respect to data quality relates to the processes they undergo. Data are acquired, stored, selected and retrieved, transformed and manipulated, aggregated, and presented. Errors can occur in any one of these processes. For example, a hardware failure in a storage device can result in the loss of data that are not backed up. The transformations and manipulations data undergo to create information must be appropriate, correct, and documented; otherwise the result is misleading information that does not accurately reflect the underlying data.

Whatever the reason for poor quality data, there are steps organizations can take to improve and maintain data quality. An understanding of the data lifecycle helps organizations achieve this goal.

The Data Lifecycle

The Data Management Association International (DAMA) published the first edition of the *DAMA Guide to the Data Management Body of Knowledge (DAMA-DMBOK)* in 2009. DMBOK provides a comprehensive set of guidelines for effective data management and outlines the data lifecycle in terms of the following steps:

1. Plan
2. Specify
3. Enable
4. Create and acquire
5. Maintain and use
6. Archive and retrieve
7. Purge

Figure 1.4 illustrates the data lifecycle.

Planning is the first step in any successful project or undertaking. Careful analysis of an organization's structure, business processes, business rules, and operational functions identifies the types of data it requires. A detailed, well-documented plan helps create strategic and tactical roadmaps, and a structure within which to work.

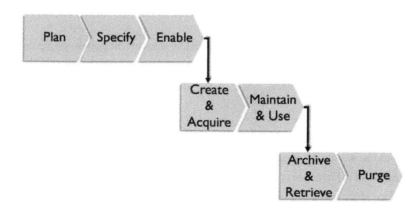

Figure 1.4 The data lifecycle

Specification involves deciding on, and documenting, a wealth of details including the following:

- What the source or sources of data will be;
- How data will be formatted, organized and stored;
- Who will have authority to enter, access, change, or delete data;
- How data will be shared among different groups within the organization; and
- How data will be kept secure and confidential.

Enabling involves overlaying these specifications onto a technological platform that allows the organization to complete the next two steps in the data lifecycle: create and acquire data, and maintain and use data. These two steps are the operational portion of the data lifecycle. This is where prospects are identified and entered into the system, sales contacts are made, products are sold and shipped, invoices are sent, and records are updated. This is where data are used to achieve the organization's goals. Success, or failure, at this stage is directly determined by how effectively the first three steps—plan, specify, and enable—were executed.

Archiving and retrieval occur when data are no longer required operationally, but are still necessary for query, analysis, or reporting purposes. For example, once an insurance claim has been settled and the claimant has signed a release, the claim file is no longer required in day-to-day operations. However, some of the data it contains are important for use in establishing the rates that will form the basis for calculating future insurance premiums. Those data need to be retained. In addition, laws and regulations specify how long certain types of data, for example financial information, must be kept. Compliance requires that organizations be able to do so cost-effectively without overburdening operational systems.

The DAMA Dictionary of Data Management defines **archive** as "1. A copy of a database or documents preserved in a secondary, lower cost storage location, for infrequent historical reference and/or recovery; 2. Verb. To move stored data (structured or unstructured) to a secondary, less readily accessed location, at lower storage costs, for historical reference and/or recovery."[6]

One important aspect of data archiving is that data must be stored in a format that will make them readily accessible when required. For example, data archived in the past on a floppy disk would be inaccessible from most desktop computers today. The form in which archived data are stored must be kept current. In addition, sufficient data should be retained to ensure subsequent analysis yields meaningful information. Archiving past customers' accounting data, but not their purchasing data, would result in far less information for sales analysis.

When it is not necessary to retain data, or when data have become obsolete, they can be purged from the system and discarded. Because purged data cannot be retrieved, and because errors in purging can cause damage to a system, typically only specific individuals within an organization are authorized to purge data.

---

[6] The DAMA Dictionary of Data Management, First Edition 2008, Mark Mosley Editor, Technics Publications LLC, New Jersey, copyright 2008 DAMA International, p. 12.

Defining Data Architecture

Data architecture is the collection of "Models, policies, rules, or standards that govern which data are collected, and how it is stored, arranged, and put to use in a database system, and/or in an organization."[7] A **data architect** is a person responsible for the design, structure, organization, and maintenance of data for a particular company or project. Just as an architect carefully designs the blueprints for a building, a data architect carefully maps out the structure and organization of the relevant data for a company or project. He or she can work for a single company and focus entirely on internal data or work for a database group and assist multiple companies with their data.

Understanding Data Architecture

Data architecture is integral to the planning and specifying stages of the data lifecycle. It identifies what data are needed, how they should be collected and stored, and how they will be used. In addition, it highlights the interactions and relationships between data from different sources and the various users of those data. It develops a comprehensive framework for defining and organizing data and information efficiently within the organization as a whole.

When developing systems, data architects work with business analysts and operational units to catalogue all required data. They first identify all of the entities about which the organization wishes to collect or create data. For each entity, they determine the specific data to be collected. For example, for the entity "customer" an organization may want to collect a name, address, email address, and telephone number. These data about the entity "customer" are called **attributes**. Depending on operational requirements, attributes may also include past purchases, or important dates such as a birthday or anniversary.

Data architecture also identifies data created and used by multiple functional units to ensure that data interactions are documented and accounted for during system design. As an example, consider the entity "employee." Human resources may assign this entity the attributes name, age, address, current position, educational background, job history, and hire date. Payroll will also have an "employee" entity, and may assign it the attributes name, address, hire date, hourly rate of pay or salary, and hours worked. Operational units may also have an "employee" entity with a different set of attributes.

All three departments need access to data about the organization's employees. Without an understanding of the organization's business needs, developers could create separate application systems for all three departments. Each system would have its own version of the entity "employee" and they would all be different. In this case, it is the data architect's role to identify that the "employee" entity is important to all three departments, define all of the attributes required, and determine how these data will be shared among the departments.

---

[7] http://www.businessdictionary.com/definition/data-architecture.html (accessed April 7, 2016).

Tapping Organizational Memory

Some of an organization's knowledge is in a structured format that is readily accessible, for example data and information stored in databases and operated upon by business process systems. However, the majority of data and information are unstructured. Unstructured data include such things as documents, emails, photographs, electronic calendars, even hand-written sticky notes stuck on computer monitors. Some estimate that up to 80 percent of an organization's data are unstructured.

Advancements in technology have made it easier for organizations to acquire, store, retrieve, and mine unstructured data. Data mining is a technique for analyzing data captured by business transactions and gathered from other sources.[11] However, capturing and tapping the tacit knowledge of an organization's human assets, and the knowledge embedded in its processes and culture, is more challenging. Yet this knowledge has significant value. Understanding what decisions were made in the past, and the reasons for which they were made, helps organizations make better current decisions. As well, the ability to access organizational memory makes organizations more efficient and flexible, helps them respond better to changes in their environment, and helps avoid "reinventing the wheel" when a previously solved problem or issue resurfaces.

Summary

Data are attributes of entities. Analyzed, processed, or organized for a particular purpose and presented in a form and context that are relevant and meaningful, data reveal information. Experience and understanding help turn information into knowledge. Data and information can be considered assets because they can be used to produce value. Managers at all levels use information to plan strategically, tactically and operationally; to organize; to lead; and to control. In the absence of good quality information, management decisions are little more than "best guesses". Because in today's fast-paced environment information is essential, and information is derived from data, high-quality data are critical. However, data quality can be difficult to maintain for a variety of reasons. Careful management of the data lifecycle can help an organization protect the quality of its data. Data architecture is an essential element of managing the data lifecycle. Many insurers currently rely on legacy systems with different data architectures which make integration of these systems challenging. One previously unrecognized source of knowledge worthy of attempts to capture and tap is the knowledge contained in organizational memory, which not only includes explicit knowledge, but tacit and embedded knowledge as well.

Bibliography

Insurance Data Management Association Dictionary of Terms, Key Terms and Concepts Used In The IDMA Certification And Introductory Courses Copyright 2015 by the Insurance Data Management Association.

[11] Adapted from the IDMA Curriculum Dictionary of Key Terms and Concepts, copyright 2011, p. 37.

IDMA Data Management Value Propositions, Insurance Data Management Association.

The DAMA Dictionary of Data Management, First Edition 2008, Mark Mosley Editor, Technics Publications LLC, New Jersey, copyright 2008 DAMA International.

The DAMA Guide to the Data Management Body of Knowledge (DAMA-DMBOK) First Edition, DAMA International, Technics Publications LLC, New Jersey, copyright 2009 DAMA International.

Fundamentals of Database Management Systems, 2nd Edition, Mark L. Gillenson, Fogelman College of Business and Economics, University of Memphis, published by John Wiley & Sons, Inc., printed and bound by RR Donnelley, copyright 2012, by John Wiley & Sons, ISBN 978-0-470-62470-8.

Data Architecture from Zen to Reality, Charles D. Tupper, Elsevier, Morgan Kaufman imprinter of Elsevier, 30 Corporate Drive, Suite 400, Burlington, MA 01803, USA, copyright 2011 Elsevier Inc.

An Overview of Business Intelligence Technology, Surajit Chauddhuri, Umeshwar Dayal and Vivek Narasayya, Communications of the ACM, 08/2011 Vol 54 No 8, page 88.

ACM Tech Pack on Business Intelligence/Data Management October 2013, BI/DM Tech Pack Committee, Pat Cupoli, DAMA, ICCP, Tech Pack Committee Co-Chair Barry Devlin, 9sight Consulting Raymond Ng, University of British Columbia Stephen Petschulat, SAP, Tech Pack Committee Co-Chair, Copyright © ACM 2013.

Data as an Asset, David Pratt, November 17, 2010, Data Management Wonk (accessed November 16, 2015).

ISO Mitigation Online, About ISO (accessed November 18, 2015).

Reference for Business, Encyclopedia of Business 2nd edition, Management Levels viewed at http://bit.ly/1kmtRPM (accessed November 19, 2015).

Reference for Business, Encyclopedia of Business 2nd edition, Management Functions viewed at http://bit.ly/1zKo4Vz (accessed November 19, 2015).

What is a SWOT Analysis, Tim Berry, BPlans, viewed at http://bit.ly/1lK9tVa (accessed November 19, 2015).

Strategic Planning Tools, Bill Dann, Professional Growth Systems, viewed at http://bit.ly/2rASiTR (accessed November 20, 2015).

Role of Information Technology in Managing Organizational Change and Organizational Interdependence, Global Risk Management Network, LLC, Cornell Business and Technology Park, Ithaca, NY 14852-4892, U.S.A., viewed at http://bit.ly/2sIVM6d (accessed November 20, 2015).

The Role of Networks in Organizational Change, Robert L. Cross, Salvatore Parise & Leigh M. Weiss viewed at http://bit.ly/2sb5cGt (accessed November 20, 2015).

Process Innovation: Reengineering Work Through Information Technology, (Google eBook), Thomas H. Davenport, Harvard Business Press, Dec 30 2013 (accessed November 21, 2015).

Lesser-Spotted Framwork-11 DMBOK (Data Management Body of Knowledge) (accessed November 22, 2015).

Types of Organizational Change, CliffsNotes, Houghton Mifflin Harcort, viewed at http://bit.ly/2sCrnXH (accessed November 23, 2015).

Timeline History Amazon.com, Amazon Genius (accessed November 24, 2015).

Chapter 1 of the paper "Defining Business Rules ~ What Are They Really?", produced by the Business Rules Group, viewed at http://bit.ly/2txiR8H (accessed November 26, 2015).

Three Tips for Improving Your Organization's Data Quality, Gadi Eichhorn, viewed at http://bit.ly/2rB3uzu (accessed November 26, 2015).

"Data Quality Management, The Most Critical Initiative You Can Implement", Jonathan G. Geiger, Intelligent Solutions Inc., Boulder CO (accessed November 26, 2015).

Data Quality, IBM, viewed at https://ibm.co/2txjajW (accessed November 27, 2015).

What is 1-10-100 Rule?, Total Quality Management February 25, 2009, viewed at http://bit.ly/2txpDeA (accessed November 28, 2015).

The Cost of Poor Quality Data, Anders Haug, Frederik Zachariassen and Dennis van Liempd, *Journal of Industrial Engineering and Management 2011* (accessed November 25, 2015).

The Real Cost of Bad Data: The 1-10-100 Rule, Bud Walker, viewed at http://bit.ly/2txysW1 (accessed November 28, 2015).

The Real Cost of bad Data, Six Simple Steps to Address Data Quality Issues viewed at http://bit.ly/2szj4Lp (accessed November 28, 2015).

The Unseen Cost of Bad Data, economia, viewed at http://bit.ly/2sbbjL8 (accessed November 28, 2015).

Why Data Should Be a Business Asset – The 1-10-100 Rule, Mary Doyle, Business2 Community viewed at http://bit.ly/2txLKl4 (accessed November 28, 2015).

The cost of bad data: stats, Ben Davis, Econsultancy, viewed at http://bit.ly/1pGeeju (accessed November 28, 2015).

Clean Up Your (Data) Act, Customer Communications Group Inc, viewed at http://bit.ly/2rBlKsR (accessed November 28, 2015).

Assessing the Impact of Dirty Data on Sales & Marketing Performance, demand Gen Report, viewed at http://bit.ly/2txHdzl (accessed November 28, 2015).

How Does Bad Data Happen?, SpringCreek Systems, May 27, 2013 (accessed November 30, 2015).

Where Is Your Bad Data Coming From, published June 18, 2012 by Ben Gallagher in address Validation, Bad data, Data quality, Matching, viewed at the clean data blog at http://bit.ly/2rBdGbk (accessed November 30, 2015).

Database Archiving for Long-term Data Retention, Craig S. Mullins, adapted from the second edition of Database Administration: The Complete Guide to DBA Practices and Procedures, Addison-Wesley (2013), Information Life (accessed December 1, 2015).

Lifecycle Data Management Planning, Michigan State University Library (accessed December 1, 2015).

Regulatory Compliance Demystified: An Introduction to Compliance for Developers, Microsoft Developer Network, 2006, viewed at http://bit.ly/2rB24Fc (accessed December 1, 2015).

JD Edwards EnterpriseOne Applications Procurement Management Implementation Guide, Section 24 Purging Data, Oracle, viewed at http://bit.ly/2sCPHZu (accessed December 2 2015).

Organizational Memory and Knowledge Repositories, Alan Frost M.Sc., 2010, KMT, viewed at http://bit.ly/2szNYmK (accessed December 2, 2015).

Designing Organizational Memory: Preserving Intellectual Assets in a Knowledge Economy, Jeff Conklin, Ph.D. viewed at http://bit.ly/2sJ6QAx (accessed December 2, 2015).

Knowledge Management, Alan Frost M.Sc, KMT, viewed at http://bit.ly/1iQljLA (accessed December 3, 2015).

Knowledge management and "organizational memory" – remembrance and recollection in a knowledge-intensive firm, Dan Kärreman, Lund University Department of Business Administration, 220 07 Lund Sweden, E-mail: DanKärreman@fek.lu.se viewed at http://bit.ly/2rpr7Y1 (accessed December 3, 2015).

Understanding organizational memory from the Integrated Management Systems (ERP), Gilberto Perez &, Isabel Ramos, JISTEM - Journal of Information Systems and Technology Management On-line version ISSN 1807-1775, JISTEM J.Inf.Syst. Technol. Manag. vol.10 no.3 São Paulo Dec. 2013, viewed at http://bit.ly/2sIJ9s3 (accessed December 3 2015).

Considering an Organization's Memory, Mark S. Ackerman (Information and Computer Science, University of California, Irvine, Irvine, CA 92697 USA, ackerman@ics.uci.edu) ; Christine Halverson (IBM, T.J. Watson Research Center, P.O. Box 704, Yorktown Heights, NY 10598 USA, krys@watson.ibm.com) (accessed December 3, 2015) at http://bit.ly/2tczPKq (accessed December 3, 2015).

Are Your Cores Systems Running Out of Time, Robbins Gioia, viewed at http://bit.ly/2rABxrO (accessed December 3, 2015).

Data, Legacy Systems, and the New Age of Real-Time Architecture, Loraine Lawson, IT Business Edge, viewed at http://bit.ly/2rFU8hm (accessed December 3, 2015).

Accidental Architectures and the Future of Intelligent Networks, Eric Kavanagh, September 24, 2013, Inside Analysis, viewed at http://bit.ly/2rB2jjA (accessed December 3, 2015).

The Joy of Legacy Data, Scott Wambler, Agile Data, viewed at http://bit.ly/2slnHXi (accessed December 3, 2015).

When Companies Become Prisoners of Legacy Systems, Adam Schneider, principal and chief advisor for Deloitte Center for Financial Solutions, viewed at http://bit.ly/1LJYxZH (accessed December 3, 2015).

Legacy Systems Continue to Have a Place in the Enterprise, John Lamb, Computer Weekly viewed at http://bit.ly/XeUQ5M (accessed December 4, 2015).

Big Banks' Legacy IT Systems Could Kill Them, Karl Flinders, viewed at http://bit.ly/1fEWMfZ (accessed December 4, 2015).

Issues and Challenges Facing Legacy Systems, Frederico Zooufaly, Developer.com, viewed at http://bit.ly/2j7UQn4 (accessed December 4, 2015).

Data Quality Management (DQM), The Challenge: Ensuring ETL Transforms Don't Mask Data Quality Problems (accessed December 4, 2015).

Chapter 10 - Access to Legacy Applications and Data, Microsoft Developer Network, viewed at http://bit.ly/2txzpgO (accessed December 4, 2015).

Easier Access to Mainframe Data: The Key to the Pursuit of Application Innovation, Tyler Allman   in Enterprise Executive on June 11, 2013, Enterprise Media, viewed at http://bit.ly/2txFOIZ (accessed December 4, 2015).

Legacy Evolution to SOA: Introduction, The Open Group (accessed December 4, 2015).

IEEE Nuts & Bolts: Karl Wiegers and Dave Card, editors kwiegers@acm.org / card@computer.org Legacy Information Systems: Issues and Directions, Jesus Bisbal, Dierdre Lawless, Bing Wu, and Jane Grimsom, Trinity College Dublin http://bit.ly/2skIDhd (accessed December 4, 2015).

White Paper: The Trouble with Legacy Systems, An Insurance Executive's Challenges and Options viewed at http://bit.ly/2skRBLc (accessed December 5, 2015).

Why Data Should Be a Business Asset – The 1-10-100 Rule, by Mary Doyle, August 6, 2015, viewed at http://bit.ly/2tcoidQ (accessed April 7, 2016).

http://bit.ly/2sIkALM (accessed November 15, 2015).
http://bit.ly/1sBm3uX (accessed November 15, 2015).
http://bit.ly/2rG3DwN (accessed November 15, 2015).
https://cfx.ws/2rATpD1 (accessed November 15, 2015).
http://bit.ly/1v65ADc (accessed November 15, 2015).
http://bit.ly/2txHEJZ (accessed November 15, 2015).
http://bit.ly/1vVfcge (accessed November 18, 2015).
http://bit.ly/1oD4AS9 (accessed November 19, 2015).
http://bit.ly/2rFIzqq (accessed November 19, 2015).
http://bit.ly/2rB3W0M (accessed November 22, 2015).
http://bit.ly/2szLCVk (accessed November 24, 2015).
http://bit.ly/2sCUgTN (accessed December 4, 2015).
http://bit.ly/2tc5nzV (accessed November 24, 2015).
http://bit.ly/2sIMbfK (accessed December 2, 2015).
http://bit.ly/2tcqkuJ (accessed December 3, 2015).

Introduction to Data Management

Data management is a discipline focused on enhancing the value of data and information. Effective data management benefits an organization in a number of ways. There are ten key data management functions that involve a variety of individuals with different expertise. Data management is most effective when implemented consistently across an entire organization. However, at the enterprise level it can be challenging. Data managers can include a variety of information technology and business professionals located in various areas within an organization. They require strong technical and interpersonal skills to successfully fulfill their roles.

Educational Objectives

Upon completion of this assignment, you should be able to:

1. Define data management.
2. Describe the goals of data management.
3. Provide the business case for data management.
4. Describe the data management functions key to meeting the goals.
5. Describe the roles of individuals in data management.
6. Describe the roles of various organizational units in data management.
7. Explain why successful data management requires an understanding of both organizational behavior and IT.
8. Define enterprise data management.
9. Describe the core functions and key roles in enterprise data management.
10. Describe the challenges to implementing enterprise data management.
11. Describe the purpose of the data manager.
12. List the key data manager functions.
13. Describe where in an organization data managers can be located.
14. Describe the interactions between data managers and business analysts, front line managers, executives, and IT professionals.
15. Describe the critical skills of successful data managers.
16. Describe the data manager's role at different phases of the Data Lifecycle.
17. Describe the role of professionalism in data management and explain why it is integral to success.
18. List and describe data management best practices.

Data Management

Data management is the process of planning, defining, organizing, maintaining, and managing access to digitally created, stored, and transmitted data that are of relevance and use to an organization.

The business function of data management focuses on achieving a number of goals:

- Understanding the data
- Enhancing data quality
- Ensuring data security
- Maintaining data integrity
- Increasing data integration
- Improving access to information

To use data effectively, it is important to understand what they signify. Each piece of data needs to be clearly defined in terms of what it means, how it is represented, how it is acquired or created, and how it is to be used.

As was discussed in the first chapter, data quality is the extent to which data are accurate, complete and timely, meet the needs of the organization, and are relevant for their intended use. **Data security** is the degree to which data are kept confidential and protected from unauthorized access, use, or alteration.

Data integrity is related to both data quality and data security. It refers to the accuracy, uniformity, and reliability of the values used to store and manipulate data. Data that have integrity conform to established standards, formats, and business rules. For example, an insurer may specify that each automobile policy issued have a unique policy number eight digits long beginning with the letter A. If the insurer's data have integrity, all policy numbers will be in the correct format and there will be no duplication. Implied in the concept of data integrity is that data are the same when retrieved as they were when acquired or created. Data can become corrupted in a variety of ways. For example, hardware failures or programming errors can cause accidental, unintended changes to data. Malicious attacks by hackers can also seriously compromise the integrity of an organization's data. Data can become "orphaned" when some part of the pathway through which they are accessed is deleted.

Data integration combines data from a variety of sources to create useful information. It is "the planned and controlled transformation and flow of data across databases, for operational and/or analytical use."[12] Data integration supports data quality and integrity by reducing inconsistencies in data formats and specifications across systems, and helps to reduce data redundancy. Data integration and data access can be accomplished through the use of a data warehouse or data federation. A **data warehouse** is "an integrated, centralized decision support database and the related software programs used to collect, cleanse, transform, and store data from a variety of operational sources."[13] **Data federation** achieves the same goal as data warehousing but in a different way. It aggregates data from different sources in a virtual database."

---

[12] The DAMA Dictionary of Data Management, First Edition 2008, Mark Mosley Editor, Technics Publications LLC, New Jersey, copyright 2008 DAMA International, p. 38.

[13] Ibid, p. 47.

HOW DATA MANAGEMENT ADDS VALUE[14]
The Data Management discipline adds value in several ways:

Overall Process

- Reduces the cost of collecting, storing, and dispersing data
- Participates in the creation of an enterprise data vision
- Monitors data quality
- Provides an additional enterprise communication channel for new products, services, programs, and technologies
- Provides expertise in process improvement
- Provides project management expertise
- Helps to develop and maintain Information Technology (IT) systems to support many of the data functions
- Works with users to provide data specifications for users and IT
- Acts as an intermediary between business areas and IT on matters of data content

Data Acquisition and Quality Assurance

- Maintains internal coding instructions, tables, and documentation
- Maintains external statistical plans and requirement documents
- Assists data users in defining the data requirements for existing and new products
- Determines data interfaces for acquisitions and new trading partners
- Manages vendors who provide data services
- Defines the company standards for acquiring data
- Defines the data
- Defines corporate data dictionary content
- Establishes data quality standards
- Monitors compliance with the data and data quality standards
- Assists industry organizations in defining data standards
- Assists in populating metadata repositories that store information about data
- Reconciles business and financial data

Data Storage

- Provides quality controls
- Provides expertise on the availability and location of data
- Assists in the creation and population of data warehouses

Data Disbursement

- Develops data specifications for internal and external reporting
- Develops and maintains data reporting tools
- Disburses data to internal users
- Reports data to advisory organizations, research organizations, and regulators
- Ensures compliance with data reporting laws and regulations
- Provides analysis of data
- Protects the privacy and confidentiality of data

---

[14] IDMA Data Management Value Proposition, copyright 2015.

There is a compelling business case to be made for effective data management. By enhancing data quality, ensuring data security, maintaining data integrity, and increasing data integration the data management function improves access to information. Decision makers have better information faster, which increases the likelihood that the organization will succeed strategically, tactically, operationally, and competitively.

Effective data management can also result in operational efficiencies, for example by consolidating data from several legacy systems. It can allow an organization to respond more quickly to change. It can improve an organization's effectiveness by identifying sales opportunities or enhancing customer satisfaction. It can allow an organization to tailor products and services for individual customers. It can improve an organization's ability to comply with regulatory requirements. Finally, it can help ensure that an organization's information technology (IT) is closely aligned with its business goals and strategies.

Data Management Functions

There are ten data management functions that help organizations achieve the goals of defining data, enhancing data quality, ensuring data security, maintaining data integrity, increasing data integration, and improving access to information:

1. Data Governance
2. Data Architecture Management
3. Data Development
4. Data Operations Management
5. Data Security Management
6. Reference and Master Data Management
7. Data Warehousing and Business Intelligence Management
8. Document and Content Management
9. Metadata Management
10. Data Quality Management

Data Governance

Data governance relates to an organization's high-level data strategy and defines how authority and control will be exercised with respect to the organization's data. It should be the foundation for all other data management activities. **Data governance** is "the exercise of authority, control and shared decision making (planning, monitoring, and enforcement) over the management of data assets."[15]

The *DAMA-DMBOK* outlines the goals of data governance:

---

[15] The DAMA Dictionary of Data Management, First Edition 2008, Mark Mosley Editor, Technics Publications LLC, New Jersey, copyright 2008 DAMA International, p. 38.

- To define, approve, and communicate data strategies, policies, standards, architecture, procedures, and metrics.
- To track and enforce regulatory compliance and conformance with data policies, standards, architecture, and procedures.
- To sponsor, track, and oversee the delivery of data management products and services.
- To manage and resolve data related issues.
- To understand and promote the value of data assets.[16]

Data Architecture Management

Data architecture management is the process of analyzing an organization's strategies, structures and processes to identify all of the data it requires and then developing a theoretical framework within which to meet those requirements. Data architecture management is most effective when implemented at the enterprise level, meaning that it is undertaken for the organization as a whole, including all of its component parts.

The first step in defining an organization's data architecture is to develop an **enterprise data model**, which is "a common consistent view and understanding of data elements and their relationships across the enterprise."[17] It is important that the enterprise data model aligns with the organization's other **business models**. In the context of data management, a business model is "a current or future state representation of some aspect of an enterprise, typically from a process, data, geographic, event, organizational, or financial perspective." [18] Data architecture management ensures that the architecture of the enterprise's databases; the integration of its systems; and the design of its data warehouse support its enterprise data model and business models.

Data Development

Data development is an important phase in the system development life cycle (SDLC)[19] both in the initial phases and as part of system maintenance. Figure 2.1 illustrates the SDLC.

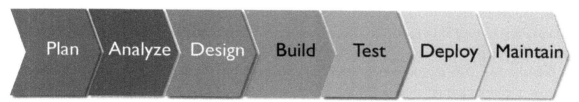

Figure 2.1 The system development life cycle (SDLC)

---

[16] The DAMA Guide to the Data Management Body of Knowledge (DAMA-DMBOK) First Edition, Mark Mosley Editor, Technics Publications LLC, New Jersey, copyright 2009 DAMA International, p. 37.

[17] The DAMA Dictionary of Data Management, First Edition 2008, Mark Mosley Editor, Technics Publications LLC, New Jersey, copyright 2008 DAMA International, p. 57.

[18] Ibid, p. 19.

[19] The DAMA Guide to the Data Management Body of Knowledge (DAMA-DMBOK) First Edition, DAMA International, Technics Publications LLC, New Jersey, copyright 2009 DAMA International, p 4.

Individuals from the organization's business side define the requirements for data and information. Data architects, analysts, and database administrators design and integrate databases to meet the defined business information needs. Software architects and developers determine how the system will capture and use data, and design the user interface. Included in data development are testing of the system, documentation and training, preparing for deployment of the system, and installation and deployment.

Data modeling is part of data development. A **data model** is a graphical representation of data and the relationships among them. It helps analysts define data requirements and design data structures to meet those requirements. For example, a data model would highlight the fact that each customer may have one or more insurance policies. The system would need to be able to link multiple policies to a single insured.

Data Operations Management

Data operations management is "planning, control, and support for structured data assets across the data lifecycle, from creation and acquisition through archival and purge."[20] It involves managing the day-to-day operation of the organization's systems and focuses on database performance, and data integrity and availability.

Data operations management comprises database support and data technology management. **Database support** includes activities such as monitoring and tuning the performance of the organization's databases; planning and implementing procedures for data backup and recovery; data archiving, retention, and purging; and supporting specialized databases.

Data technology management involves evaluating, selecting, and implementing hardware and software solutions to meet the organization's needs.

Data Security Management

Data security management is another key data management function. Confidential information about customers, employees, and others needs to be protected. Information proprietary to the organization itself needs to remain secure. Organizations need to be compliant with government privacy, confidentiality, and security regulations. For example, the Sarbanes-Oxley Act requires that organizations have adequate controls in place to protect the integrity of their financial data. Data security management is the process of developing, implementing, and monitoring the effectiveness of policies and procedures that protect data and information. It ensures that data and information are accessible for appropriate use and inaccessible for inappropriate use.

Reference and Master Data Management

Master data are data about things that are important to the organization, such as customers, employees, regional offices, products, accounts, or a fleet of trucks. Within an organization, these data are typically used by multiple

---

[20] The DAMA Guide to the Data Management Body of Knowledge (DAMA-DMBOK) First Edition, DAMA International, Technics Publications LLC, New Jersey, copyright 2009 DAMA International, p. 130.

systems. For example, an individual customer's data can exist in an underwriting system, a claims system, and an accounting system. Unfortunately, these data can differ from system to system. The goal of master data management is to determine which data in each system are most correct and create a consolidated record of the most accurate and complete data. Those data are then integrated for use by all systems.

Reference data are data used to categorize other data and can include such things as codes and flags. For example, a code may indicate that a claim has been received but not yet assigned to a claims adjuster. In some cases, organizations define their own reference data. In others, reference data are defined by outside sources. For example, the United States Postal Services have defined a standard two-letter code for each state. Like master data, reference data may vary among an organization's various internal systems. However, standardized reference data support integration and the sharing of information. The goal of master and reference data management is "ensuring consistency with a 'golden version' of data values."[21]

Data Warehousing and Business Intelligence Management

Data warehousing and business intelligence management are two closely related elements of data management. A data warehouse is a database used to support decision-making within an organization. Data are extracted from the organization's operational systems and cleansed. Cleansing, or "data scrubbing", is the process of "making data more accurate and consistent; in other words, 'cleaning them up'. It refers to eliminating duplicate records, correcting misspellings and errors in names and addresses, ensuring consistent descriptions, punctuation, syntax and other content issues."[22] The data are transformed from their original format to the format required by the data warehouse and then they are loaded into the database. This is referred to as "extract-transform-load" (ETL) and software programs perform the ETL processes. Data warehousing may also involve the creation of **data marts**. These are subsets of the data warehouse that focus on a particular subject area enabling quicker response times and facilitating use by limiting data selection options.

Data warehousing enhances an organization's ability to access and analyze its data. Software tools, called query tools, allow managers to request specific information from the database, organized in a particular way, and to generate reports. This ability to query an organization's stores of data allows managers to gain a greater insight into an organization's operations and performance. This is referred to as **business intelligence (BI)** and it supports strategic, tactical, and operational planning.

Document and Content Management

For the purposes of data management, a document is essentially any unstructured way of presenting information. Examples include printed manuals, written correspondence, emails, scanned copies of paper documents, and photographs. Conceptually, **document management** is like a library. It is a collection of systems used to maintain,

---

[21] The DAMA Dictionary of Data Management, First Edition 2008, Mark Mosley Editor, Technics Publications LLC, New Jersey, copyright 2008 DAMA International, p.104.

[22] http://www.pcmag.com/encyclopedia/term/40838/data-scrubbing (accessed April 14, 2016).

classify, organize, and retrieve electronic documents. It focuses on the document as a whole rather than on the content it contains.

Content management is more sophisticated than document management. **Content management** is "the organizing, categorizing, and structuring of information resources so that they can be stored, published, and reused in multiple ways. A content management system is used to collect, manage and publish information content, storing the content either as components or whole documents, while maintaining the links between components. It may also provide for content revision control. Content management is a critical data management discipline for non-tabular data found in text, graphics, images, video and audio recordings."[23]

Document and content management also involves determining how unstructured data will be backed up and retrieved when necessary, and when these data should be archived or purged from the system.

Metadata Management

Metadata management involves "planning, implementation, and control activities to enable easy access to high quality, integrated meta-data."[24] Metadata are often referred to as "data about data". They provide information about the data themselves, where they come from, the processes they undergo and the relationships among them. High quality metadata can serve as a roadmap, assisting business users to find and understand the specific data they need to make informed decisions.

The goals of metadata management are to ensure that metadata terminology and practices are consistent and clearly understood across the organization; to integrate metadata from various sources within the organization; to facilitate access to metadata; and to ensure the quality and security of the organization's metadata.

Data Quality Management

The last of the ten data management functions is **data quality management (DQM)**. Data quality management is ongoing; it is an iterative process. However, the need for DQM can often arise out of changes within the organization itself. For example, corporate mergers and acquisitions can necessitate the blending of data from different sources, some of which may not be of an acceptable quality.

Data quality management involves four stages, which are illustrated in Figure 2.2: plan, deploy, monitor, and act.

In the planning stage, the DQM team develops a plan to assess the organization's data, identify the target level of data quality required to meet business needs, establish standards or benchmarks for measuring data quality, and create business rules to support high quality data.

---

[23] The DAMA Dictionary of Data Management, First Edition 2008, Mark Mosley Editor, Technics Publications LLC, New Jersey, copyright 2008 DAMA International, p. 29.

[24] The DAMA Guide to the Data Management Body of Knowledge (DAMA-DMBOK) First Edition, DAMA International, Technics Publications LLC, New Jersey, copyright 2009 DAMA International, p. 260.

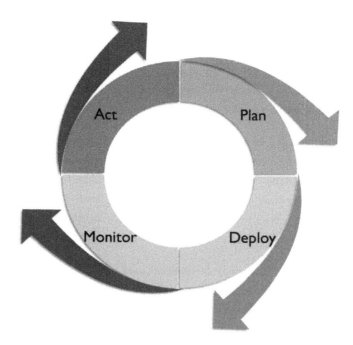

Figure 2.2 The data quality management (DQM) cycle

In the deploy stage, the DQM team compares actual data quality with the standards established in the planning phase, identifies the sources of data quality problems, and implements solutions. It is important to monitor data quality to ensure that the corrective measures implemented have been successful. If data quality meets established benchmarks no further action is immediately required. However, if data quality remains unchanged or deteriorates, the DQM team will work to identify the cause or causes and take corrective action.

Roles of Individuals in Data Management

Although the key data management functions are generally performed in all successful organizations, assignment of responsibility for them within a given organization will depend to some extent on its size, structure, focus, and culture. Data management roles and accountabilities can vary, even among similar organizations. However, a successful data management program requires the sponsorship and support of a data management executive who is responsible for overseeing data governance and data stewardship, developing data management staff, and interceding where necessary in data management projects.

Data management comprises a variety of roles and responsibilities:

- **Data architects** develop and maintain the enterprise data model and ensure that data warehouses and data marts are appropriately integrated and not redundant.
- **Data modelers/consultants** determine data requirements, integrate the various data components into data models, identify the means of capturing the data, develop or approve the business rules associated with the data, and define data quality requirements.
- **Business intelligence analysts** design and maintain the business intelligence user environment and train users in its application.

- **Data/reporting analysts** document, interpret, and maintain controls on the data, and develop or assist in the development of external and internal reports.
- **Database administrators** select or design the appropriate software, implement the software, and control its use to ensure a proper structure for the data.
- **Data security administrators** ensure controlled access to classified data.

These responsibilities may be spread across multiple functional areas within an organization. For example, database and data security administrators may be members of an IT unit. However, the other functions may reside in operational areas, such as finance or actuarial. Where these data management functions reside, and how they will be performed, depend to a great extent on the size of the enterprise. In a small organization, a single person may fill many roles. A particular role may be filled by an individual whose primary function is unrelated to data management. However, an enterprise with an effective data management structure supports all of these functions.

In addition to these internal functions, there may be external data management relationships. **Collaborators** are groups with whom organizations develop data sharing agreements. **Data brokers** supply data processing and metadata support by subscription. As well, in the insurance industry, government and regulatory bodies define data management requirements for financial and regulatory reporting, and confidentiality.

In addition to these more technical functions, individuals throughout an organization may participate in data stewardship activities. **Data stewardship** is "the formal, specifically assigned and entrusted accountability for business (non-technical) responsibilities ensuring effective control and use of data and information assets."[25]

Business data owners are individuals involved in an organization's various operational areas and they are often responsible for the primary creators, acquirers, and users of data. They work with data stewards to ensure that essential data are identified, defined, used, and managed so as to support operational functions.

Business data stewards are subject matter experts (SMEs) who are responsible for a particular segment of the organization or a specific subject area. A business data steward's role is to identify and define data and metadata requirements; draft data model specifications; define business rules and data quality requirements; identify and help resolve data issues; and assist in evaluating and improving the quality of the organization's data. They are usually members of one or more data stewardship teams.

A **data stewardship team** is "a temporary or permanent focused group of business data stewards collaborating on data modeling, specification, and data quality improvement, typically in an assigned subject area, led by a coordinating data steward and facilitated by a data architect."[26] Data stewardship teams are led by **coordinating data stewards**. These individuals recruit business data stewards; serve on data stewardship steering committees; work to ensure that the organization's requirements for quality data are met; and review data quality audits.

Technical data stewards are members of the IT department who focus on the organization's technical data requirements.

---

[25] The DAMA Dictionary of Data Management, First Edition 2008, Mark Mosley Editor, Technics Publications LLC, New Jersey, copyright 2008 DAMA International, p.45.

[26] Ibid, p. 46.

Executive data stewards exercise stewardship at the most senior level. This is "a role held by a senior manager sitting on the data governance council, accountable for the data quality and data practices within a department, for planning and oversight of data management programs, and appointment of other data stewards."[27]

Groups Involved in Data Management

Several formal groups are commonly involved in an organization's data management and data stewardship activities:

- Data management services
- Data governance council (DGC)
- Data stewardship steering committee
- Data governance office (DGO)

These groups may have different names in different organizations. Their importance lies not in their name but in the functions they perform and the individuals they involve.

Data Management Services is a unit or group of units responsible for data management. Frequently, they are part of IT, but they may reside in other departments. The team or teams include a variety of data management professionals, such as data architects, analysts, security specialists, metadata specialists and decision-support specialists. When data management services are centralized into one unit with responsibility for the organization as a whole, the unit is sometimes referred to as an enterprise information management center of excellence. A center of excellence supports and coordinates with the organization's operations; offers guidance in terms of standards and methodologies; encourages training and certification; and supports effective data governance.

A **data governance council (DGC)** is another group commonly involved in data management. A DGC is a cross-functional group with members from both IT and the organization's operational side. Members of the DGC generally include the chief information officer (CIO), the data management (DM) leader, and a business executive who acts as chief data steward. It is not uncommon for this group to include executives representing other functions, such as actuarial, underwriting, and claims. The DGC makes high level, strategic decisions about data governance as an integrated function within the organization.

A **data stewardship steering committee** is a group comprising members from both IT and multiple operational or business functions. It is responsible for overseeing data management initiatives identified by the DGC. The steering committee is made up of coordinating data stewards.

The last group, typically found in larger organizations, is the **data governance office (DGO)**. Facilitators in the DGO act as coordinators, scheduling data governance and stewardship meetings; preparing agendas and minutes; ensuring that data modeling and data architecture activities include representatives from the operational side of the organization; and assisting in other data stewardship initiatives.

---

[27] Ibid, p. 61.

Organizational Behavior and Data Management

Organizational behavior refers to the way in which individuals and groups behave and interact within an organization. The study of organizational behavior includes elements of psychology, anthropology, sociology, and economics. Organizational behavior theory suggests that a variety of factors can affect the way in which individuals perform within an organization. These factors include the organization's structure and culture, the leadership style of its managers, the characteristics of the teams within the organization, and the ways in which the organization communicates both internally and externally.

Organizational behavioral theorists have described five different frameworks within which organizations can operate. These are illustrated in Figure 2.3. Few organizations operate solely within one of these. Generally there is some overlap across multiple frameworks, particularly in international organizations operating in countries with different cultures.

The **autocratic** framework is the traditional business model in which managers' focus is on authority. Employees are expected to perform as required and little thought is given to employees' needs. Beyond their wages or salary, employees receive little. Typically, in this type of environment, employees' performance tends to meet minimum standards.

	Autocratic	Custodial	Supportive	Collegial	System
Model Basis	Power	Economic	Leadership	Partnership	Community Understanding
Manager Focus	Authority	Money	Employee Support	Teamwork	Compassion
Employee Focus	Obedience	Security & Benefits	Performance & Participation	Responsibility & Self-discipline	Ownership
Need Met	Subsistence	Security	Status & Recognition	Self-Actualization	Wide Range
Performance	Minimal	Passive Cooperation	Awakened Drives	Moderate Enthusiasm	Passion & Commitment

Figure 2.3 Organizational frameworks, adapted from http://bit.ly/2sCJNYy (accessed December 14, 2014)

In an organization with a **custodial** framework, management's orientation is financial. Employees are focused on benefits and security, and those are the only employee needs that are met. In this framework, employees tend to do their jobs but little more.

In a **supportive** framework, managers are concerned with leadership and supporting employees to encourage and enhance performance. Employees seek status and recognition, and work to improve their own job performance.

In a **collegial** organization, management focuses on partnership and teamwork, empowering employees to participate more actively. This approach encourages employees to take responsibility. They feel more fulfilled in their jobs and enthusiastic about achieving organizational goals.

The **system** framework focuses on building a culture of community in which employees take ownership and are passionately committed to the organization's success.

It is important that data management professionals understand organizational behavior because it can have a significant impact on the success of data management initiatives. Individuals and organizations are often resistant to change, even when it is in their best interests. New technologies, and the changes in business processes and operational roles associated with them, can be daunting for non-technical members of the organization. Technological changes implemented to help achieve strategic objectives will generally earn a greater return on investment if all of the organization's employees embrace those changes. Effective data management requires commitment and participation through all levels and across all functional areas within the organization. Data management professionals who understand organizational behavior are better able to create a culture that promotes commitment, cooperation, and participation in data management activities at all levels.

Enterprise Data Management

Enterprise data management, often referred to as enterprise information management (EIM), is essentially "data management performed with an enterprise-wide mandate"[28]. Successful EIM initiatives can help eliminate information silos and allow for timely access to high quality data by users across the entire enterprise. It can lead to increased integration and alignment among the functional areas, resulting in less organizational fragmentation and enhanced operational focus on enterprise-wide strategies. Effective EIM initiatives can result in additional benefits:

- Improved data quality in terms of accuracy and consistency
- Enhanced strategic and tactical decision making at the enterprise level
- Consolidated data architecture to optimize information delivery
- Standardized processes and guidelines for ensuring data security
- Flexibility and agility to meet the needs of a rapidly changing environment

However, EIM differs from traditional data management in terms of both scope and complexity. There are significant challenges associated with EIM. For example, consider an insurance enterprise with a property and casualty division, a life and health division, and a risk management and loss control division all operating internationally. The enterprise provides a variety of products and services in several languages. Its business processes vary from division to division. It is subject to different regulatory and reporting obligations in multiple jurisdictions. It has most likely entered the global market through mergers and acquisitions, leaving it with a complex assortment of legacy systems. Its IT function is most likely distributed, and the skill and expertise of its data managers and IT professionals may differ significantly from location to location. It is unlikely that the corporate culture would be homogeneous across the enterprise.

Successful implementation of an EIM strategy requires careful planning, strong leadership, a considerable investment, and significant technical expertise. It may also require the organization to restructure itself, its business processes, and its internal and external relationships. Often, an enterprise's approach to data management is fragmented because the organization itself is fragmented. It is not enough to focus on data, systems, and technology when implementing an EIM initiative; a successful EIM implementation requires consideration of the enterprise as

---

[28] Ibid, p. 58.

a whole. And EIM professionals need to develop the soft skills necessary to recognize and manage the organizational behavior and cultural issues that are critical success factors in any significant organizational change.

EIM faces challenges and opportunities in a number of areas. EIM initiatives are more likely to succeed when there is an EIM champion at a senior level within the organization. This individual's role would be to ensure that an EIM focus is integrated into all data management activities and that senior executives understand the relevance of EIM and the competitive advantage it can deliver. EIM relies heavily on effective data governance, which in turn relies on executive commitment and support. An organization requires clearly defined data governance and stewardship roles, responsibilities, and processes to ensure that governance can be sustained over the long term.

Accounting practices cannot currently measure changes in business value that result directly from improved data management. Organizations need to find a way to measure how EIM affects their bottom line. To determine the success of any initiative an organization needs performance metrics, benchmarks against which actual performance is measured. Because it is not currently possible to measure the financial benefits of EIM, other metrics are required. It is important to find meaningful ways to measure the impact of implementing EIM.

The ability to manage metadata are essential to EIM. However, the cost of managed metadata environments (MME) may be prohibitive for some organizations. A cost-effective approach to metadata management could improve EIM capabilities. However, the initial metadata repository focus was on capturing and integrating metadata rather than on making them accessible. Metadata administrators can enhance the value of an enterprise's data and its metadata by making the metadata more easily accessible.

An enterprise's information architecture and enterprise data model typically consist of a number of components. It is important that all of these be integrated and consistent. EIM professionals can support integration and consistency by ensuring that consideration of the enterprise's information architecture is an integral part of such things as business planning and IT planning.

Data Managers

Data managers are individuals whose primary day-to-day role is to provide business managers with the information they need to accomplish the objectives of the organization. Effective data managers:

- Understand the needs of their customers;
- See their task from the customer's perspective; and
- Have cross-functional expertise and training.

Whether working in the insurance industry or in another industry, a data manager is a professional who specializes in one or more data management functions: data governance, data architecture management, data development, data operations management, data security management, reference and master data management, data warehousing and BI management, document and content management, metadata management, and data quality management.

Data managers analyze an organization's data and information needs and assist in the development, implementation, and maintenance of the technical solutions required to meet those needs. In addition, data managers typically perform the common management functions of planning, organizing, leading, and controlling. These include tasks such as budgeting; evaluating, prioritizing and managing projects; and monitoring performance.

Data managers engage in a variety of activities requiring technical skills. One of these is business process modeling. A **business process model** is a tool for understanding and graphically describing the processes within an organization. Business process modeling can document current operations and workflows, and help identify ways in which they can be improved. Associated with business process modeling is data modeling, which explores and documents the attributes of, and relationships among the data an organization acquires and uses. Once business processes are optimized and data requirements are clearly understood, systems can be designed to best support the organization's business operations and information requirements.

Data managers participate in the development of the enterprise data strategy and enterprise data model that supports the strategy. They conduct data analysis and work with data stewards and others to enhance and maintain data quality. They develop data standards. They are responsible for database administration, "the function of managing the physical aspects of data resources, including database design and integrity, backup and recovery, performance and tuning."[29]

Depending on the size, structure, and culture of an enterprise, data managers may be located in a variety of areas. Some organizations centralize the data management function, for example in an enterprise information management center for excellence or similar group. Others distribute data management responsibilities across multiple units. Still others embed at least some data management responsibilities in operational units in the form of data stewards.

Because of their role as a technical facilitator, data managers interact with a wide variety of individuals within the organization. They work with executives to establish data governance policies, and to develop strategic plans for data and information systems that are aligned with the organization's operational strategies. They work with business analysts to understand, document, and optimize the organization's business processes and systems. They work with front-line operational managers to provide technical support, training, and business intelligence capabilities. And they work with a variety of IT professionals to develop, deploy, and maintain the organization's various technological solutions.

Skills of Successful Data Managers

Effective data managers have a variety of skills and abilities. They have a thorough understanding of the business operations of the enterprise that has entrusted them with the management of its data. They understand the business environment in which the organization operates as well as its strategic and tactical focus. Successful data managers have comprehensive technical knowledge about the systems, policies, and procedures the organization uses to acquire, manipulate, disseminate, use, and store data. They keep current with new technologies and techniques for managing data effectively.

In addition to technical skills, successful data managers also have well-developed interpersonal skills. They are active listeners and effective communicators, able to make often complex technical concepts comprehensible to

---

[29] Ibid, p. 48.

non-technical members of the organization. They are able to convince others of the value of data management initiatives and to secure their commitment and participation. They are skilled mentors. And they are able to work well independently or as part of a team.

Data Managers and the Data Lifecycle

At each stage in the data lifecycle, data managers use both their technical and interpersonal skills to enhance and maintain the accuracy, completeness, timeliness, consistency, and relevance of the organization's data and information. They develop strategic and tactical plans for meeting operational requirements. They develop policies and procedures for ensuring data quality, security, and integration. They monitor and optimize the functioning of the organization's databases. They work to find cost-effective solutions that make current data readily available and archived data accessible.

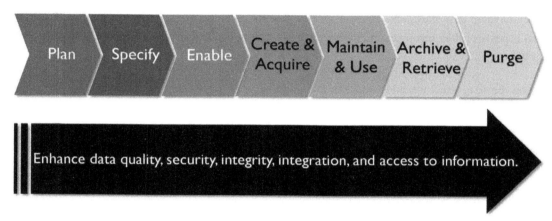

Figure 2.4 The Data Manager's Role in the Data Lifecycle

Professionalism

Successful data managers maintain a level of professionalism. The Insurance Data Management Association's (IDMA's) *Standards for Professionalism for Insurance Data Managers* highlights the importance of professionalism and outlines commitments and guidelines to assist data managers in enhancing their professional competence.

IDMA's Standards for Professionalism for Insurance Data Managers
Insurance data managers are responsible for the insurance industry's most valuable asset – data. The purpose of the Standards of Professionalism for Insurance Data Managers is to define for data managers the high level of professional conduct and ethical standards this responsibility demands. The discipline evolves rapidly, driven by many forces, including technological progress, regulatory change, and legislative mandate. Data managers must, as professionals, continually upgrade their skills and awareness.

Commitment 1 – Professional Integrity

- An insurance data manager should perform professional duties honestly, with integrity and competence, and in a manner that fulfills the profession's responsibility to the public.
- Guideline 1.1 – An insurance data manager should observe and obey all laws, regulations, and conventions which bear on issues of honesty and fair dealing and avoid all conduct that causes unjust harm to others.
- Guideline 1.2 – An insurance data manager should neither engage in nor uphold conduct that is or may be detrimental to the insurance data management profession.
- Guideline 1.3 – An insurance data manager should act with honesty and integrity in representing her/his work product. In particular, s/he should not willfully mislead others relative to the definition or the quality of any data for which s/he has management responsibility.
- Guideline 1.4 – An insurance data manager should act to protect the confidentiality of any proprietary or sensitive information to which s/he has been granted access, except when disclosure is required by law or regulation.

Commitment 2 – Continuing Education

- An insurance data manager should pursue learning and professional growth as an ongoing activity.
- Guideline 2.1 – An insurance data manager should seek continually to improve professional knowledge, skills, and competence, either through traditional educational means, or by participation in meaningful industry or discipline-related activity.
- Guideline 2.2 – An insurance data manager should pursue continuing education in one or more of the following activities: passing professional or academic courses related to the insurance industry; participating in insurance industry meetings, seminars, or forums; writing professional articles; developing curriculum materials for IDMA or other insurance organizations; participating on industry committees or work groups; participating with other industry organizations (ACORD, ASWG, CAS, IAIABC, IASA, LOMA, NAIC, RIMS, SOA, WCIO, etc.); or, participating with organizations outside the industry that promote the profession (ANSI, DAMA, UN/CEFACT, etc.).

Commitment 3 – Cross Functional Training and Awareness

- An insurance data manager should seek an understanding of other disciplines and functions, and in turn should seek to convey an understanding of the data management discipline to other professionals.
- Guideline 3.1 – An insurance data manager should seek extensive knowledge of insurance company operations and functions to effectively provide service to a wide range of information users.
- Guideline 3.2 – An insurance data manager should endeavor to understand a task from the viewpoint of the users of data.
- Guideline 3.3 – An insurance data manager should recognize and work with other professionals who possess knowledge and skills relevant to the task at hand.

<u>**Commitment 4 – Foster Professionalism in the Insurance Data Management Discipline**</u>
- An insurance data manager should seek to increase and encourage professionalism in the data management discipline.
- Guideline 4.1 – An insurance data manager should encourage entry of qualified individuals into the data management profession.
- Guideline 4.2 – An insurance data manager should strive to continually improve her/his knowledge and skills.
- Guideline 4.3 – An insurance data manager should not misrepresent her/his expertise as extending beyond her/his actual level of accomplishment.
- Guideline 4.4 – An insurance data manager should join and maintain membership in the Insurance Data Management Association, Inc. (IDMA), and should encourage participation and membership in IDMA among her/his colleagues.

Data Management Best Practices

Insurance Services Office (ISO) publishes *Data Management Best Practices* specifically targeted at the insurance industry. The following highlights have been excerpted from that publication, the entire version of which can be provided to you at no cost through IDMA.

ISO's data management best practices include:

- *Data Stewardship*: Establish a corporate data stewardship program. Responsibilities for the program do not necessarily need to reside with one person or department, as each business unit could have stewardship over the data it manages. But your company should direct stewardship from a corporate perspective.
- *Data and Data Quality Standards*: To promote consistency, increase efficiency, and maximize utility, foster the development and adoption of data and data-quality standards that will serve as models for data development and acquisition.
- *Organizational Issues*: Structure the organization to promote good data management and data quality.
- *Operations and Processes*: Establish processes to maximize data quality and usefulness.
- *Data Element Development and Specification*: Design and maintain data, systems, and reporting mechanisms in a manner that promotes good data management and data quality.
- *Data Management and Data Quality Tools*: Develop tools that promote and foster good data management quality.
- *Measurement:* Establish data quality as a performance metric.
- *Individual Support*: You must support data management and data quality on an individual level, as well as the organizational level.
- *Privacy Issues*: In general, privacy should apply to raw data as specified by source and derived data as specified by the entity that derived the data.

Summary

Data management focuses on enhancing data quality, ensuring data security, maintaining data integrity, increasing data integration, and improving access to information. Effective data management supports decision making, operational efficiency, and regulatory compliance, and creates a competitive advantage. It is most effective when undertaken on an enterprise-wide basis, although EIM implementation is not without challenges.

Data managers include a variety of IT and data professionals as well as business data stewards. They can be located in various areas within an organization and require technical skills, interpersonal skills, and an understanding of organizational behavior. Because of the importance and complexity of their role, data managers require a high degree of ethics and professionalism. The ten key data management activities include:

1. Data Governance;
2. Data Architecture Management;
3. Data Development;
4. Data Operations Management;
5. Data Security Management;
6. Reference and Master Data Management;
7. Data Warehousing and Business Intelligence Management;
8. Document and Content Management;
9. Metadata Management; and
10. Data Quality Management.

Bibliography

The DAMA Dictionary of Data Management, First Edition 2008, Mark Mosley Editor, Technics Publications LLC, New Jersey, copyright 2008 DAMA International.

The DAMA Guide to the Data Management Body of Knowledge (DAMA-DMBOK) First Edition, DAMA International, Technics Publications LLC, New Jersey, copyright 2009 DAMA International.

Fundamentals of Database Management Systems, 2nd Edition, Mark L. Gillenson, Fogelman College of Business and Economics, University of Memphis, published by John Wiley & Sons, Inc., printed and bound by RR Donnelley, copyright 2012, 2005 by John Wiley & Sons, ISBN 978-0-470-62470-8.

ACM Tech Pack on Business Intelligence/Data Management October 2013, BI/DM Tech Pack Committee, Pat Cupoli, DAMA, ICCP, Tech Pack Committee Co-Chair Barry Devlin, 9sight Consulting Raymond Ng, University of British Columbia Stephen Petschulat, SAP, Tech Pack Committee Co-Chair, Copyright © ACM 2013.

Insurance Data Management Association Data Management Value Proposition, IDMA, 545 Washington Boulevard, Jersey City New Jersey, www.IDMA.org.

Data Management Responsibilities, DAMA International Foundation, Why Data Management viewed at http://bit.ly/2rpPVyN (accessed December 10, 2015).

An Oracle White Paper on Enterprise Architecture May 2011, Enterprise Information Management: Best Practices in Data Governance, viewed at http://bit.ly/1QD6YBx (accessed December 10 2015-12-10).

CMMI Institute Unveils the Data Management Maturity Model, Katie Tarara, 05/28/2015, CMMI Institute viewed at http://bit.ly/2txkvHJ (accessed December 10, 2015).

What is Data Integrity? Learn How to Ensure Database Data Integrity vie Checks, Tests & Best Practices Veracode, Michael Teeling, May 14 2012, viewed at http://vera.cd/1nuHcbU (accessed December 10, 2015).

Data Integrity, Microsoft Developer Network, http://bit.ly/2sIJ5IA.

Oracle Database Online Documentation, 10g Release 2 (10.2), Database Concepts, Data Integrity viewed at http://bit.ly/2sCUWsi (accessed December 11, 2015).

Five Benefits to Integrating All Your Enterprise Data, Angela Guess, Web Analytics, Updated: February 10th 2012 (accessed December 11, 2015).

The Benefits of Data Integration, Jacob Bainton, May 27, 2010 viewed at http://bit.ly/2rpKErg (accessed December 11, 2015).

Data Integration, IBM, viewed at https://ibm.co/2sldcDp (accessed December 11, 2015).

360DegreeView, LLC, White Paper, The Data integration Strategy "Take Aim Before You Shoot" viewed at http://bit.ly/2tcyhQp (accessed December 11, 2015).

The Business Case for Information Management, An Oracle Thought Leadership White Paper, December 2008, viewed at http://bit.ly/1NLPiWX (accessed December 11, 2015).

Business Case Analysis, David Bowman's Information Management Checklist (accessed December 11, 2015).

Data Governance: The Basic Information, The Data Governance Institute, The Data Manager's Public Library viewed at http://bit.ly/2slndAr (accessed December 12, 2015).

2.7 What Is Data Development?, Data Development Overview, viewed at http://bit.ly/2slau0N (accessed December 12, 2015).

Data Modeling 101, Scott W, Ambler, Agile Data, viewed at http://bit.ly/XALNgy (accessed December 12, 2015).

What Is Master Data?, Semarchy The Data Convergence Company, viewed at http://bit.ly/2tcmrps (accessed December 16, 2015).

Definitions of Data Categories, Danette McGilvray and Gwen Thomas, viewed at http://bit.ly/2sbl5wZ (accessed December 16, 2015) Source: Excerpted from Executing Data Quality Projects: Ten Steps to Quality Data and Trusted Information published by Morgan Kaufmann Publishers.

Database design with UML and SQL, 3rd edition, Tom Jewitt, viewed at http://bit.ly/2sIliZs (accessed December 16, 2015).

How To - Quick Study: ETL, Marc L. Songini, Computer World viewed at http://bit.ly/2rBnrGv (accessed December 17, 2015).

What is Document Management (DMS)?, Association for Information and Image Management International (AIIM), viewed at http://bit.ly/1mfUkyl (accessed December 17, 2015).

What is Enterprise Content Management (ECM)?, Association for Information and Image Management International (AIIM), viewed http://bit.ly/1dpqFMU (accessed December 17, 2015).

A Gentle Introduction to Metadata, Jeff Good, University of California-Berkley (accessed December 17, 2015).

Technical versus business metadata – classification, Dan E. Linstedt, Denver University, B-eye Network, viewed at http://bit.ly/2rGncFc (accessed December 17 2015).

The benefits of metadata and implementing a metadata management strategy, Alex Berson and Larry Dubov, TechTarget, SearchIT Channel, viewed at http://bit.ly/2sD1aIm (accessed December 17, 2015).

Who Needs Business Metadata? Posted on July 10, 2012 by Roger Nolan, Perspectives The Informatica Blog, viewed at http://infa.media/2rpHXpt (accessed December 18, 2015).

Paper 125-26, Metadata: Everyone Talks About It, But What Is It?, John E. Bentley, First Union National Bank, viewed at http://bit.ly/2rFQZhA (accessed December 18, 2015).

What is a Center of Excellence, October 29, Agile Elements, viewed at 2008 http://bit.ly/2rpXyFo (accessed December 18, 2015).

Defining Organizational Structures, Gwen Thomas, The Data Governance Institute, The Data Manager's Public Library viewed at http://bit.ly/2txCP3i (accessed December 12, 2015).

Leadership, How to Successfully Implement Organizational Change, Mary Vaughn, President Metargy, Monday, August 20, 2012, Sand Hill viewed at http://bit.ly/2txBidG (accessed December 21, 2015).

What Is Organizational Culture? And Why Should We Care? Michael Watkins, May 15, 2013, Harvard Business review, viewed at http://bit.ly/1vHLNUo (accessed December 21, 2015).

What Is the Importance of Organizational Behavior?, wiseGEEK, viewed at http://bit.ly/2sl9Y2F (accessed December 21, 2015).

Source: Boundless. "What is Organizational Behavior?." Boundless Management. Boundless, 25 Nov. 2015. Retrieved 21 Dec. 2015 from http://bit.ly/1P90M3o.

Enterprise Information Integration: Successes, Challenges and Controversies; Alon Y. Halevy (Editor), Naveen Ashish, Dina Bitton, Michael Carey, Denise Draper, Jeff Pollock, Arnon Rosenthal, Vishal Sikka; Copyright 2002 Association for Computing Machinery (accessed December 22, 2015).

Putting the Enterprise into the Enterprise System, Thomas H. Davenport, Harvard Business Review (accessed December 22, 2015).

Mind the Enterprise Search Gap: Smartlogic Sponsor MindMetre Research Report viewed at http://bit.ly/2sJ5Pbp (accessed December 31, 2015).

Manage Data with Organizational Structure, by Thomas C. Redman, November 26, 2012, Harvard Business Review viewed at http://bit.ly/2txN2MW (accessed December 31, 2015).

Leadership and Organizational Behavior (accessed December 31, 2015).

Suggested citation: Friese, S., Tout, K. & Kirby, G. (2015). Best Practices in Ensuring Data Quality in Quality Rating and Improvement Systems (QRIS). OPRE Research Brief #2015-47. Washington, DC: Office of Planning, Research and Evaluation, Administration for Children and Families, U.S. Department of Health and Human Services (accessed January 2, 2016).

business process modelling, business process modelling explanation - diagrams, definitions, examples viewed at http://bit.ly/1gt6zVk (accessed January 2, 2016).

Building Successful Master Data Management Teams - The role and importance of partnerships between business and IT in MDM strategy White Paper sponsored by Aligning Business and IT to Improve Performance, © Copyright viewed at http://bit.ly/2sIFwlD (accessed January 4, 2016).

Better data, better decisions, The case for independent enterprise data management viewed at http://pwc.to/2slffao (accessed January 4, 2016).

Data Standards

Standards are important because they provide a foundation for success. They facilitate communication, support quality and consistency in products and services, and allow for technological innovation and collaboration. Standards development organizations (SDOs) create voluntary standards in an open, consultative manner. There are thousands of SDOs worldwide that develop and maintain standards. Organizations of significance to the insurance and financial services industry include the International Organization for Standardization (ISO), the American National Standards Institute (ANSI), the Association for Cooperative Operations Research and Development (ACORD), the International Association of Industrial Accident Boards and Commissions (IAIABC) and the Workers Compensation Insurance Organizations (WCIO). SDOs develop data standards to allow for data sharing among different systems within a single organization, or across a variety of different organizations. One example of the implementation of data standards is in electronic data interchange (EDI) which allows different systems to interact without human involvement. Standards in data naming support EDI as well as other data sharing and data management initiatives.

Educational Objectives

Upon completion of this assignment, you should be able to:

1. Define standards.
2. Explain why standards matter and what standards do.
3. Describe the role of standards development organizations (SDOs).
4. Identify the purpose of the major SDO's, including the International Organization for Standardization (ISO), the American National Standards Institute (ANSI), the Association for Cooperative Operations Research and Development (ACORD), the International Association of Industrial Accident Boards and Commissions (IAIABC), and the Workers Compensation Insurance Organizations (WCIO).
5. Identify organizations other than SDOs that impact or define standards.
6. Discuss the rationale for data sharing.
7. Define electronic data interchange (EDI).
8. Define the structure and rules for standard data element names.
9. Name the "representation" or "class words" for data elements.

Standards

The existence and application of standards are reflected everywhere. Standards are the reason that:

- The plug on a lamp cord fits into the electrical outlet on the wall;
- Manufacturers can assemble products using parts from various suppliers;
- Buildings are structurally sound;
- Children's toys are safe;
- Food and drinking water are fit for consumption;
- Cell phones can communicate; and
- The Internet exists.

A **standard** is a document that provides requirements, specifications, guidelines, or characteristics that can be used consistently to ensure that materials, products, processes and services are fit for their purpose.[30]

Standards matter because of what they do:

- Facilitate product development
- Enhance service delivery
- Reduce costs
- Improve quality
- Ensure health and safety
- Accelerate communication
- Support innovation
- Provide ready-made solutions
- Protect the environment
- Promote international trade

Facilitate Product Development

Many products are designed for use with other products. Standardization ensures that, for example, a garden hose will attach to an exterior residential water faucet, or that a printer manufactured by one company will operate properly when used with a competitor's computer. The use of standards facilitates product development because it reduces the number of decisions required during the design process and imposes a set of building blocks that help ensure product compatibility and interoperability. This helps get new products to market more quickly.

Enhance Service Delivery

Standards can enhance the delivery of services in a number of ways. Many professions have standards of practice, or codes of conduct, that require individuals to provide a high level of service in an ethical and professional

---

[30] What is a Standard? ISO, viewed at http://www.iso.org/iso/home/standards.htm (accessed April 16, 2016).

manner. Individual organizations establish internal service standards. For instance, an insurer may offer customers direct access to claims adjusters 24 hours a day, seven days a week. The electronic standards that allow cell phones and the Internet to function have made a variety of services accessible anywhere, any time. For example, an individual can use his or her cell phone to deposit a check into a bank account.

Reduce Costs

Standardization places limits on the number of product alternatives made available. This can help reduce costs for both producers and consumers. For example, while many commercial insurance policies are customized for particular insureds, for any given insurer the majority of personal lines policies are standardized. This standardization simplifies underwriting, policy issuance and claims handling, and facilitates process automation. This in turn reduces operating costs for the insurer and premiums for its insureds.

Improve Quality

Establishing standards is an effective way of maintaining or improving the quality of a product or service. However, for quality standards to be effective, an organization must have a system in place to measure actual performance to the standard so that any deviation can be identified and addressed.

Ensure Health and Safety

Standards protect consumers and users of goods and services in a variety of ways. For example, the United States Food and Drug Administration (USFDA) sets standards to ensure food quality and the safety and effectiveness of drugs and medical devices. The United States Consumer Product Safety Commission (CPSC) establishes standards to ensure that consumer products are safe for their intended use.

Various organizations publish standards relating to such things as occupational health and safety, equipment and vehicle safety, and the labeling of hazardous materials. Standard, language-independent signs like those illustrated in Figure 3.1 help inform individuals and protect them from potential dangers.

Figure 3.1 Standard, language-independent signs

Accelerate Communication

The electronic standards that form the foundation for the Internet have significantly accelerated the speed with which individuals and organizations communicate. With traditional postal service, it can take days or even weeks to exchange information. With email, that same exchange can take place in moments.

Support Innovation

Within an organization, across an industry, or across borders, collaboration and the sharing of information lead to new products and services. Standard terminology facilitates communication. When individuals and organizations share a common technical vocabulary, they can exchange ideas and collaborate more easily, facilitating technology transfer and innovation.

Provide Ready-Made Solutions

Standard policies and procedures offer ready-made answers to the question "How do I . . .?". For example, standard protocols allow medical professionals to provide patients with treatment immediately rather than taking time to consider, and weigh the benefits of, a variety of treatment options.

Protect the Environment

Organizations in many countries and internationally have established standards intended to protect the environment. For example, the United Nations Environmental Programme (UNEP) includes voluntary standards and product labeling conventions to make information about products' environmental impact and sustainability available to consumers. The United States Environmental Protection Agency (EPA) issues a variety of standards designed to protect air and water quality.

Promote International Trade

Standards promote international trade because goods manufactured in one part of the globe can be compatible with goods manufactured in another part. Organizations wishing to export to a particular market can consult the applicable design and regulatory standards from that market and ensure their products are in compliance.

Standards in the Insurance Industry

There are a variety of standards within the insurance industry. Some are imposed by regulators; some reflect traditional business practices; some have been developed by industry groups through open discussion and consensus. Areas in which standards exist include the following:

- Terminology
- Coverage and forms
- Accounting practices
- Solvency requirements
- Market conduct
- Rating and pricing
- Business processes
- Data quality and consistency
- Data exchange

Standards Development Organizations (SDOs)

Individual organizations often have internal, proprietary standards, but many use industry standards as well. These are typically developed by subject matter experts in a particular field. For example, the National Fire Protection Association (NFPA) issues "more than 300 consensus codes and standards designed to minimize the possibility and effects of fire and other risks."[31] The Institute for Electrical and Electronics Engineers (IEEE) publications include software and systems engineering standards, and a glossary of software engineering terminology.

There are two general approaches to standards creation. Some standards are regulatory, drafted and enforced by government agencies. Others are voluntary and are developed through collaboration and negotiation. Organizations that create standards in this open, consultative manner are referred to as **standards development organizations** (SDOs).

Standards are not static; their development is an iterative process. As technology, business processes, consumer demands, and the regulatory environment change, standards need to change in response. In addition to developing new standards, SDOs spend considerable time maintaining current standards and attempting to coordinate them with other existing standards. The process of standards development and maintenance is illustrated in Figure 3.2.

Thousands of SDOs operate globally in essentially every aspect of endeavor including agriculture, education, engineering, financial services, manufacturing, medical and social services, and others. Some important organizations in the area of standards development include the following:

International Organization for Standardization (ISO)[32]
American National Standards Institute (ANSI)
Association for Cooperative Operations Research and Development (ACORD)
International Association of Industrial Accident Boards and Commissions (IAIABC)
Workers Compensation Insurance Organizations (WCIO)

---

[31] National Fire Protection Association (NFPA), Codes and Standards, viewed at http://www.nfpa.org/codes and standards (accessed January 9, 2015).

[32]**Note:** Insurance Services Office, an organization discussed later in this chapter, also uses the acronym ISO. These two organizations are not affiliated in any way and should not be confused.

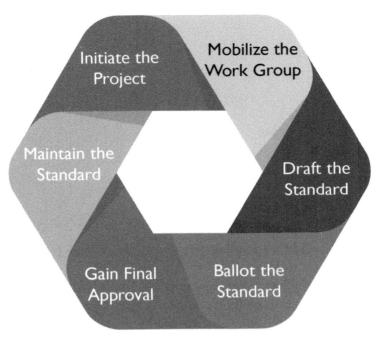

Figure 3.2 The standards development lifecycle, adapted from IEEE Standards Association http://bit.ly/2txI4Qq (accessed January 20 2015)

International Organization for Standardization (ISO)

The **International Organization for Standardization (ISO)** is the world's largest SDO. Because it is international, and its acronym would vary by language, the organization chose ISO from the Greek word "isos" meaning "equal". Its vision is "To be the world's leading provider of high quality, globally relevant International Standards through its members and stakeholders."[33]

ISO is a non-governmental body that was founded in 1947. It has member organizations from over 160 countries and each is the primary SDO in its home country. The organization works to create standards that reflect international consensus with input from countries in the developing and transitional regions of the world as well as from developed countries. In fact, more than three quarters of ISO members are from developing countries.[34]

ISO standards are crafted by technical committees populated by subject matter experts from industry, non-governmental organizations, government agencies, and others who have been recommended by ISO members. In addition to subject matter experts, ISO solicits input from consumers as well. Each year, ISO's Committee on Consumer Policy (COPALCO) identifies areas in which consumer participation would be desirable, for example in developing standards relating to the safety of toys or household appliances. Consumers wishing to become involved can do so by contacting their national consumers' association, the ISO member organization in their country, or Consumers International.

---

[33] ISO Strategic Plan 2011 – 2015, viewed at http://www.iso.org/iso/iso_strategic_plan_2011-2015.pdf (accessed January 6, 2016).

[34] http://www.iso.org/iso/home/standards-development//who-develops-iso-standards.htm (accessed January 6, 2015).

As of June 2017, ISO offered 21,686 voluntary international standards categorized as follows:

- Engineering technologies (27.8%)
- Materials technologies (22.9%)
- Electronics, information technology, and telecommunications (17.2%)
- Transport and distribution of goods (10.1%)
- Generalities, infrastructures, sciences, and services (9.1%)
- Agriculture and food technologies (5.6%)
- Health, safety, and environment (4.3%)
- Construction (2.3%)
- Special technologies (0.7%)

ISO has developed a number of standards relating to data management and data interchange. The ISO 8000 standard focuses on data quality.

One important element of implementing ISO standards is **conformity assessment**. This is the process of determining whether an organization's products or services actually comply with the requirements outlined in a particular ISO standard. There are three methods of assessing conformity: certification, testing, and inspection. Although ISO itself does not certify or accredit organizations using its standards, its Committee on Conformity Assessment (CASCO) has published guidelines related to the certification process. Independent, third parties use these guidelines to certify the products and services of organizations that use ISO standards.

The American National Standards Institute (ANSI)

The mission of the **American National Standards Institute (ANSI)** is "To enhance the global competitiveness of U.S. business and the U.S. quality of life by promoting and facilitating voluntary consensus standards and conformity assessment systems, and safeguarding their integrity." [35]

ANSI is a private, nonprofit organization founded in 1918. ANSI is the United States' representative to the ISO and is one of its founding members. It is affiliated with a number of other standards development and accreditation organizations including the International Electrotechnical Commission (IEC), which develops international standards for electrical, electronic, and related technologies. ANSI membership includes government agencies, academic institutions, organizations, businesses, and international groups.

ANSI is not an SDO as such. Instead, ANSI accredits SDOs that develop voluntary consensus standards according to the policies and procedures specified in the *ANSI Essential Requirements: Due process requirements for American National Standards*, which reflect globally accepted standardization principles. The ANSI *Essential Requirements* can be summarized as follows:

- The process should be open to participation by anyone directly affected.
- No single interest group should dominate the process.
- An attempt should be made to involve diverse groups to achieve a balance of interests.
- Efforts should be made to resolve conflicts between standards.

---

[35] About ANSI, viewed at http://bit.ly/1TTcu9l (accessed January 12, 2015).

- Appropriate notice should be given to allow for participation by interested parties.
- Written views and objections of all participants should be considered promptly.
- Evidence of consensus should be documented.
- An appeals process should be put in place, well documented and readily accessible.
- The process should follow written procedures available to all interested parties.
- All accredited SDOs are required to comply with ANSI policies and procedures.

ANSI evaluates standards developed by accredited SDOs to determine whether they qualify to be approved as American National Standards (ANS). As of December 2015, there were over 240 ANSI accredited SDOs in the United States and approximately 10,000 ANS.[36] In support of global standardization efforts, ANSI promotes the use of ANS internationally, and the use of international standards domestically when appropriate. ANSI has ISO authority to accredit third parties performing assessments of conformity to ISO standards. ANSI also accredits members of United States technical advisory groups (TAGs) to ISO technical committees. While ISO and ANSI develop standards for use in a variety of areas, there are a number of SDOs that focus specifically on the insurance industry. These include the:

- Association for Cooperative Operations Research and Development (ACORD);
- International Association of Industrial Accident Boards and Commissions (IAIABC); and
- Workers Compensation Insurance Organizations (WCIO)

Association for Cooperative Operations Research and Development (ACORD)

The **Association for Cooperative Operations Research and Development (ACORD)** is a nonprofit organization founded in 1970. Its original name was the Agent-Company Operations Research and Development organization, and it was formed by insurers and producers seeking to streamline insurance transactions. Today the organization's members include insurers, reinsurers, agents and brokers, software vendors, and others.

Forms were the primary means of capturing, storing, and retrieving data when ACORD was originally founded. Prior to ACORD's formation, many insurers issued proprietary application, endorsement, and claims reporting forms. Producers needed to stock and use a variety of these proprietary forms, which resulted in inefficiencies and errors. ACORD's initial thrust was to standardize insurance forms. The organization subsequently broadened the scope of its activities to include the development and implementation of data standards that facilitate the exchange of insurance information.

Mission
ACORD (Association for Cooperative Operations Research and Development) is a global, nonprofit organization serving the insurance and related industries. ACORD facilitates the development of open consensus data standards and standard forms, and works with its member and partner organizations to drive implementation of those standards. From http://bit.ly/2slfkuI (accessed January 15, 2015)

---

[36] Domestic Programs (American National Standards) Overview, viewed at http://bit.ly/2sDMXen (accessed January 15, 2015).

ACORD forms and data standards are used in many sectors of the insurance industry including life and health, property and casualty, and reinsurance. In each of these areas, the use of ACORD data standards results in a number of benefits:

- Improved data quality
- Increased operational efficiency
- Increased profitability

ACORD offers a variety of products and services in addition to forms and data standards. ACORD's Framework provides a flexible basis for standards development. It comprises five models (a Business Glossary, Capability Model, Information Model, Data Model, and Component Model), that can be used individually to develop perspectives on specific areas of insurance. The Framework models can also be used together to help understand the industry's **value chain**, which is an end-to-end set of activities initiated by a request from a customer (external or internal) and resulting in a benefit delivered to that customer. ACORD also offers implementation guides, tailored advisory services, educational materials, seminars, the ACORD Certified Expert (ACE) program, videos and workshops, and a facility for testing and certifying ACORD standards-based implementations.

International Association of Industrial Accident Boards and Commissions (IAIABC)

The **International Association of Industrial Accident Boards and Commissions (IAIABC)** is a nonprofit trade association founded in 1914. Its membership includes agencies charged with the administration and regulation of workers' compensation; workers' compensation professionals, insurers, medical providers, law firms, and organizations involved in the electronic exchange of workers' compensation data.

Mission
The mission of the IAIABC is to advance the efficiency and effectiveness of workers' compensation systems throughout the world. To do this, the IAIABC will strive to: • Ensue the IAIABC is the expert resource for the latest research, policies, best practices, standards, and information through   • Increasing outreach and connectivity on a global basis.   • Identifying and communicating the most current issues in workers' compensation.   • Provide a forum for regulators, stakeholders and experts to share information and discuss issues and solutions.   • Assist jurisdictions in identifying opportunities for reducing costs and improving delivery of benefits.   • Develop, analyze, and promulgate standards and uniform practices.   • Ensure that the IAIABC membership includes every facet of the health, safety, and workers' compensation communities.

IAIABC provides a variety of resources for its members including research information, best practices, model laws and rules, handbooks, treatment guidelines, and policy guides. In addition, the IAIABC's Electronic Data Interchange Project develops and maintains consensus standards that support the electronic exchange and reporting of workers' compensation information.

Workers Compensation Insurance Organizations (WCIO)

Workers' compensation insurers report specific data to rating and advisory organizations. The **Workers Compensation Insurance Organizations (WCIO)** develops and maintains standards for the electronic transmission of these data. Its members are managers from workers' compensation rating or advisory organizations in a number of jurisdictions. The WCIO sponsors several workgroups that focus on particular areas, such as data standards and XML (extensible markup language) messaging standards. The organization publishes a Data Reporting Handbook, a Data Specifications Manual, as well as other documents and tools for use by member organizations and workers' compensation insurers.

Other SDOs

Internationally, thousands of organizations develop and/or promote the use of standards for personnel, business processes, products and services, and the electronic exchange of data and information. Some focus on the insurance and financial services sector. For example, Polaris is an organization in the United Kingdom, owned by insurers and brokers, that develops business process models and data standards.

The Centre for Study of Insurance Operations (CSIO) is a Canadian standards development organization with representation from property and casualty insurers, brokers, and software vendors. In Germany, BiPRO is an association of insurers, brokers and software suppliers that develops open insurance industry standards.

Discussion of all of the various groups that develop and/or promulgate standards relating to insurance is beyond the scope of this text. Some are true SDOs, others are professional associations, and others are educational organizations. Several that may be of interest to data management professionals working in the insurance industry include the following:

Casualty Actuarial Society (CAS)	www.casact.org
Data Interchange Standards Association (DISA)	www.disa.org
Data Management Association (DAMA)	www.dama.org
Data Interchange Standards Association (DISA)	www.disa.org
Depository Trust & Clearing Corporation (DTCC)	www.dtcc.com
Enterprise Data Management (EDM) Council	www.edmcouncil.org
Health Level 7 (HL7)	www.hl7.org
Insurance Data Management Association (IDMA)	www.idma.org
Insurance Industry Committee on Motor Vehicle Administration (IICMVA)	www.iicmva.com
International Association for Information and Data Quality (IAIDQ)	www.iaidq.org
International Association of Insurance Supervisors (IAIS)	www.iaisweb.org
National Association of Insurance Commissioners (NAIC)	www.naic.org
National Insurance Producer Registry (NIPR)	www.nipr.com
Object Management Group (OMG)	www.omg.org
Organization for the Advancement of Structured Information Standards (OASIS)	www.oasis-open.org
Society of Actuaries (SOA)	www.soa.org
United Nations Centre for Trade Facilitation and Electronic Business (UN/CEFACT)	www.unece.org/cefact/

SDOs are not the only developers of standards. For example, individual organizations, professional membership groups, industry associations, labor unions, consumer groups, regulators, and international organizations all create standards.

Reporting and Sharing Data

The insurance industry is arguably more data-driven than many others, and data are exchanged across a network of different parties. Applicants provide data to insurance producers, or directly to insurers via telephone or on-line application forms. Producers provide applicant data to insurers and coverage and pricing information to their customers. Insurers share data with producers, reinsurers, regulators, advisory organizations, law enforcement, fraud prevention organizations, and industry associations. Insurers obtain data from government agencies, independent claims services, valuation and loss control organizations, and advisory groups.

In fact, the insurance industry could not function in our current world without the exchange of large volumes of data.

Insurance Regulation

The insurance industry is more highly regulated than many other industries. In addition to applicable federal laws, insurers within the United States are subject to direct regulation by state insurance departments, each of which is a member of the National Association of Insurance Commissioners (NAIC). The primary reason for insurance regulation is to protect consumers. In order to ensure that appropriate coverage is available and reasonably priced, and that legitimate claims are fairly and promptly paid, regulators focus on three areas:

- Insurer solvency;
- Market conduct; and
- Ratemaking.

To meet their obligations to policyholders, insurers must be solvent. Regulators establish financial standards that insurers are required to meet, for example minimum capitalization. They review insurers' financial statements and perform tests to identify insurers with potential solvency problems. Insurers are required to complete and submit the NAIC Annual Statement which provides regulators with information on written premiums, expenses, losses, reserves, and other financial details. The statutory accounting principles (SAP) used in its completion differ from generally accepted accounting principles (GAAP) and are prescribed by state insurance regulators.

To deter insurers from engaging in unfair business practices, regulators periodically review their underwriting and claims settlement procedures, and verify that the rates and forms used are those that have received regulatory approval where such approval is required.

Regulators focus on insurers' ratemaking activities largely because of the unique nature of insurance pricing. In most industries, vendors know the exact cost of their product before they bring it to market. For example, a manufacturer knows the price of its raw materials, its production costs, and other overheads. The manufacturer simply adds a profit margin to its costs to arrive at the sale price of its goods. However, at the point that they sell a policy, insurers never know how much that policy is likely to cost them in future claims payments. Essentially, insurers estimate current pricing based on past loss experience.

This unique characteristic of insurance pricing, coupled with competitive pressure, has resulted in the creation of the **underwriting cycle** or insurance cycle. In the underwriting cycle, the desire for increased market share drives some insurers to relax underwriting standards and lower rates. To remain competitive, other insurers follow suit, and consumers find insurance coverage easy to obtain at acceptable premiums. This is referred to as a "soft market". In the short term, a soft market may increase some insurers' profits by increasing the amount of business they write. However, ultimately this inadequate pricing results in underwriting losses. Insurers respond by tightening underwriting standards and increasing rates. Consumers may find coverage difficult to obtain at an affordable price. This portion of the cycle is referred to as a "hard market". Figure 3.3 illustrates the underwriting cycle.

If left unchecked, the insurance cycle could be potentially harmful to consumers. Soft markets could lead to insurer insolvencies, leaving policyholders without the coverage for which they have paid. Hard markets could find some consumers unable to afford coverage, or to obtain coverage at any price. As a result, regulators strictly monitor insurance ratemaking activities.

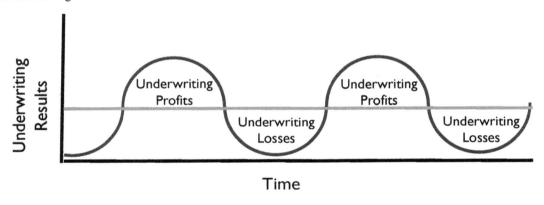

Figure 3.3 The underwriting cycle. Competitive pressures lead to lower rates and relaxed underwriting, referred to as a "soft market". The result of a soft market is underwriting losses. These losses lead to a tightening of underwriting and rate increases referred to as a "hard market".

Insurance rate regulation focuses on achieving three goals:

- Rates should be adequate to maintain insurer solvency so as to protect consumers.
- Rates should not be excessive; coverage should be reasonably affordable.
- Rates should not discriminate unfairly, although they may vary based on risk factors.

In order to properly evaluate rates across the industry, regulators require insurers to submit detailed statistical information at regular intervals. **Data collection organizations (DCOs)** are authorized to collect and submit the required data on behalf of insurers.

Electronic Data Interchange (EDI)

One implementation of a data standard is in **electronic data interchange (EDI)**. EDI is a "standards-driven technology for high volume B2B (business to business) e-business transaction exchange, linking application systems across enterprises, so that a transaction on one system at one company generates a like transaction on a system at another company."[37]

Figure 3.4 illustrates the difference between a traditional transaction and an EDI-based transaction. In a traditional transaction, a purchaser identifies the items an organization needs, completes an order form and enters it into the company's system. He or she then mails, faxes, or emails the order to the company's supplier. At the supplier's office, employees enter the order information into the company's production, shipping, and accounting systems. When the order is fulfilled, an employee at the supplier's office generates an invoice, which is mailed, faxed or emailed to the purchaser. The purchaser enters receipt of the goods in the company's inventory system and the invoice in the accounting system. The process is time-consuming; it involves a number of steps and delays; and each time data are manually entered, the possibility for errors is introduced.

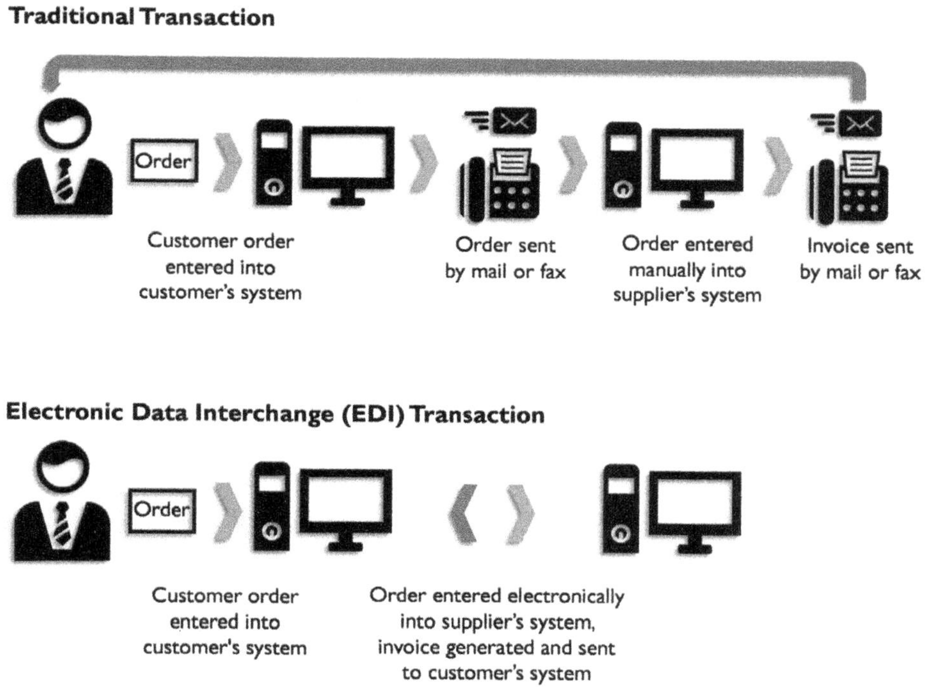

Traditional Transaction

| Customer order entered into customer's system | Order sent by mail or fax | Order entered manually into supplier's system | Invoice sent by mail or fax |

Electronic Data Interchange (EDI) Transaction

Customer order entered into customer's system

Order entered electronically into supplier's system, invoice generated and sent to customer's system

Figure 3.4 Traditional transaction vs. electronic data interchange (EDI) transaction

In an EDI-based transaction, different systems at different organizations, or within the same organization, can "talk" to each other in a common format, eliminating the need for human involvement at multiple stages in the process. This reduces errors and inefficiencies.

---

[37] The DAMA Dictionary of Data Management, First Edition 2008, Mark Mosley Editor, Technics Publications LLC, New Jersey, copyright 2008 DAMA International, pp. 55-56.

An analogy of an EDI transaction would be a situation in which a Spaniard and a German, neither of whom speaks the other's language, communicate in English, a second language common to them both. Figure 3.5 illustrates the concept of EDI in an insurance environment.

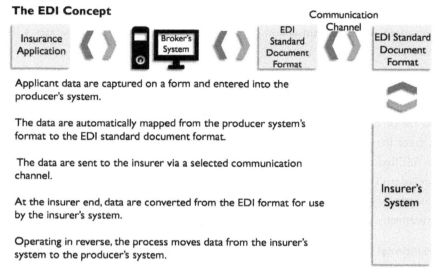

Figure 3.5 EDI in an insurance environment

When an insurance producer keys applicant data into his brokerage management software, the data are organized and stored in the format required by that software. To transmit the insurance application to the insurer, the data are automatically mapped from the producer system format to the EDI standard document format. **Data mapping** is the "assignment of source data elements to target data elements."[38] The EDI document is then sent to the insurer via whatever communication channel the producer and insurer have agreed upon. EDI standards are independent of software programs and communication technologies. At the insurer end, the data are converted from the EDI document format to whatever format is required by the insurer's system. Operating in reverse, the process moves data from the insurer's system to the producer's system.

A variety of EDI standards exist. The traditional ones are the United Nations UN/EDIFACT and the American National Standards Institute (ANSI) X12 standard. Other standards used in the financial services industry include ISO 20022 XML, NACHA, BA12, SAO IDOC, Microsoft Excel, SWIFT MT/FIN, FIX XML, FpMl, and ISO 15022.[39]

Standard Data Element Names

Standards for naming and defining data elements support EDI as well as other data sharing and data management activities. A **data element** is an item of information, such as a date of birth or risk classification. Essentially, a data

---

[38] IBID, p. 41.

[39] Document Standards Used, The Financial Services Industry, EDI by Industry, EDI Basics, viewed at http://www.edibasics.com/edi-by-industry/the-financial-services-industry/ (accessed January 22, 2015).

element represents a specific characteristic of a person, thing, process, transaction or concept. Examples of data elements include the following:

- The insured's given name
- The insured's family name
- The insured's street address
- The insured's state
- The insured's ZIP code
- The insured's gender

A **domain** is a set of values all of the same data type. For the data element indicating the insured's gender, the domain may be M signifying male, F for female, or U for unknown.

Each data element is given a unique name, usually based on the common or business term for that piece of data. Using common words and business terms in data element names makes it easier to understand what data are represented by each data element. Data element names are made up of multiple words, which are presented in order from most general to most specific. For example, the name for the insured's gender data element would be "Insured Gender". The first word indicates that the data element relates generally to the entity "insured", and the second indicates that it is the specific attribute, "gender", that the data element represents.

By convention, data element names are presented in title case, with the initial letter of each word capitalized, and they are always singular. While names may include adjectives, for example "monthly", they are typically strings of nouns. Verbs are not used.

Data element names commonly include three parts:

1. Object
2. Property term
3. Representation or class term

The initial word is referred to as the **object**. It identifies the entity—for example the person, place, thing, process, or concept—that has the attribute in question. In the data element name "Employee ID Number", "Employee" is the object.

The second part of a data element name can be referred to as the **property term**. It specifies the property, or characteristic, of the entity to which the data element refers. In the data element name "Insured Address State Code", "Address" is the property term.

The third part of a data element name can be referred to as the **representation** or **class term**. A class term is used to categorize a data element into a particular data type. It represents the general purpose or use of the data element and should always be the last word in a data element name. In the name "Transaction Effective Date", "Date" is the representation term. Representation terms may include modifiers to provide additional detail. For example, in "Sales Total Monthly Amount", "Monthly" is a representation modifier.

Not all data elements have all of these components as they can contain only two words, or more than three words. Following is a listing of class words. For the most part, their meanings are self-evident, but "Indicator" has a very specific meaning.

Representation or Class Terms			
Address	Cost	Identifier	Percentage
Age	Count	Indicator *	Period
Amount	Date	Length	Rate
Area	Day	Modifier	Ratio
Code	Description	Month	Time
Constant	Factor	Name	Total
Control	Group	Number	Year
* Indicator can only have two values, such as "yes" or "no".			

Data element names are recorded in **data dictionaries**. A data dictionary typically includes the data element names, a description of the information provided by each data element, and any associated business and/or technical metadata required by internal and external users of the system.

Standard Data Element Rules

In the early 1980s, an all-insurance industry committee met and developed the Standards and Guidelines for Data Elements. The purpose in creating these rules was to satisfy information needs in the most efficient manner and to promote data quality. The document was accepted and promulgated by both the Insurance Services Office (ISO), and the National Council on Compensation Insurance (NCCI), though the two versions may contain slightly differing examples of the rules. Following is a condensation of material contained in the text Insurance Data Quality.

Rule 1—Code as Rated

Wherever possible, the "code as rated" concept should be followed, with the coded information corresponding to the rate manuals, applications, or rating work sheet. This rule addresses a basic concept of all statistical plans, that codes be captured primarily for ratemaking purposes. To that end, it follows that there be a direct correlation between rating and coding, with a key element being a display of appropriate codes in rating manuals. The rule is qualified to the extent there is recognition that the code as rated concept cannot always be followed.

Rule 2—Common Usage Across Jurisdictions

Codes are to be common across jurisdictions where the information being captured is common. Class codes are to be common for all states for the same classification definition.

Rule 3—Zeroes and Blanks

Zero or blank must not be used as a code. This does not apply where a zero or blank is part of a code value or interspersed within the code or to claim count.

Rule 4—Required/Non-Required Items

A code must not be required in a field where the field is not applicable to the type of business or state being reported; however, when a field is optional or not required in certain cases, blanks, zeroes or valid codes (if applicable) are to be allowed.

Rule 5—Reuse of Old Codes

A discontinued code value must not be reused until such time as the data reported under the discontinued code are run off.

Rule 6—Use of Specific Alpha Codes

If alpha coding is used, avoid the use of certain alphabetic characters that are easily mistaken for numbers.

Rule 7—Use of Common Abbreviations

If abbreviations are employed, they are to reflect common usage.

Rule 8—Non-Variable Field Lengths

Fields must not be variable in length.

Rule 9—Consistency Among Reporting Requirements

Reasonable consistency of rules, codes, and coding structure must be sought when the same data element is required on different reports. However, the establishment of a code must not be determined based on limitations of the different requirements. Commonality is a goal to work toward, but should not be a constraint.

Rule 10—Responsiveness to Company and (Bureau) Systems/Resources

Code structures and coding must be designed to reflect the usage of company reporting systems and (bureau) internal systems, and to separately address different levels of users and the resources available to them for the data collection and reporting function. Reporting must not require the use of data processing capabilities that are not available to the users.

Rule 11—Need for Flexibility

The statistical plan and coding structures must be flexible and responsive to a changing environment.

Rule 12—Data Quality

Data Quality must be maintained. Codes are to be designed to achieve an acceptable level of credibility for the information collected by using simple language and the avoidance of complex coding structures. When the best possible configuration of fields or codes is considered not conducive to quality data, procedures must be improved to enhance quality.

Rule 13—One Data Item for One Information Use

Fields must represent, to the extent possible, one data element only. Each field must not have two different definitions, but rather only one definition, with more fields added if necessary, thereby using two separately coded fields rather than one multiplicatively coded field. This may be a long-range goal, but is to be considered and applied wherever feasible when establishing codes.

Rule 14—Adequate Field Size

Field size must be based on current and future requirements, as well as periodic redefinition, and be adequate to accommodate future expansion of the element defined. For example, if 75 codes are needed in a field, the field should probably be three positions, instead of two positions. Also, record layouts are to contain an adequate amount of columns for future expansion.

Rule 15—Values versus Codes

On an individual, element-by-element basis, consideration is to be given to capturing values rather codes.

Rule 16—Alpha/Numeric Coding

Codes within a field are to be numeric or alphabetic, with alphanumeric fields being avoided whenever possible.

Rule 17—Avoidance of Redundancy

New data elements must not be developed to identify specific classes of risk/coverages, which are uniquely identified by other elements. Also, there is to be no redundant coding of information in two or more data elements.

Rule 18—Avoidance of Items Not Used in Ratemaking

Data elements not used directly in ratemaking must be resisted strongly. Items incorporated for research purposes are to have a fixed life span with regular reports made and dates established to evaluate the need to continue.

Rule 19—Mappability

Wherever feasible and cost-effective, new codes are to be mappable back to the old codes to ensure continuity of usable data.

Rule 20—Conversion and Combination of Data

Code structures must enable conversion and combination of data to develop experience to meet current needs.

Rule 21—Reevaluation of Data Elements

Data elements are to be reevaluated on an ongoing scheduled basis.

Rule 22—Reevaluation of Standards and Guidelines

Standards and guidelines are to be totally reevaluated on an ongoing scheduled basis.

Rule 23—Enforcement of Standards and Guidelines

Standards and guidelines must be followed at all times. Recognizing that financial and regulatory considerations may prohibit immediate compliance, reasons must be documented and steps taken to implement correct solutions within appropriate established procedures.

Rule 24/25—Justification of Violations and Historical Record of Violations

The violation of any rule must also be presented with reasons for the violation. A statement must be included on how the correct solution will be incorporated. An historical record of violations must be maintained for reference.

Summary

Standards facilitate product development, enhance service delivery, reduce costs, improve quality, ensure health and safety, accelerate communication, support innovation, provide ready-made solutions, protect the environment, and promote international trade. Within the insurance industry, standards exist in the areas of terminology, coverage and forms, accounting practices, solvency requirements, market conduct requirements, rating and pricing, business processes, data quality, and consistency. SDOs develop and maintain standards in an open, collaborative fashion, considering the needs of all stakeholders. In addition to ISO, ANSI, ACORD, IAIABC, and WCIO, there are several other SDOs that are important for the insurance and financial services industry. Standards can be developed by organizations other than SDOs as well, for example government agencies, professional associations, labor unions, and consumer groups. Data standards support data sharing, which is important in any industry but particularly so in a highly regulated one such as the insurance industry. One implementation of data standards is reflected in EDI, which allows different systems to exchange data directly without the need for human involvement. EDI transactions reduce errors and inefficiencies. Standards for naming and defining data elements support EDI as well as other data sharing and data management initiatives.

Bibliography

http://bit.ly/2sD3y23 (accessed January 6, 2015).

Participating in the Standards System – What are Standards? Office of Consumer Affairs, viewed at http://bit.ly/2sltIn2 (accessed January 6, 2015).

The value of Standards Development Organizations, National Fire Protection Association, viewed at http://bit.ly/2rB45kW (accessed January 6, 2015).

ISO Strategic Plan 2011 – 2015, viewed at http://bit.ly/2szF60y (accessed January 6, 2015).

Using Levels of Abstraction to Name Data Elements, Judith Newton, Published: December 1, 1998, The Data Administration Newsletter, viewed at http://bit.ly/2rpxhax (accessed January 6, 2015).

Rapidly On-Board Critical Business Data and Reduce ACORD Insurance Integration Costs, ACORD Insurance integration, viewed at http://infa.media/2rFUIvi (accessed January 6, 2015).

Insurance fraud data sharing hub to be explored next year, Out-Law.com viewed at http://bit.ly/124Wqdl (accessed January 6, 2015).

What is EDI (Electronic Data Interchange)?, EDI Basics, viewed at http://bit.ly/1A1tuMc (accessed January 7, 2015).

Benefits of EDI, EDI Basics, viewed at http://bit.ly/2rFJPd8 (accessed January 7, 2015).

Discover ISO, Why standards matter, International Organization for Standardization, viewed at http://bit.ly/2szPmFY (accessed January 8, 2015).

Why Standards Matter viewed at http://bit.ly/2txNj2q (accessed January 8, 2015).

TryStandards, Global Standards Education and Standards Search, Frequently Asked Questions, viewed at http://bit.ly/2sCCCPX (accessed January 9, 2015).

WSC, World Standards Cooperation, Newsletter No. 03 - October 2011, The Benefits of Standards for National Economies, by Professor Knut Blind, viewed at http://bit.ly/2sbpsYG (accessed January 9, 2015).

Insurance in a digital world: the time is now, viewed at https://go.ey.com/2rpSSiZ (accessed January 10, 2015).

Standards and Labels, United Nations Environmental Programme (UNEP) viewed at http://bit.ly/2tcnlSV (accessed January 12, 2015).

Trade and International Labor Standards, Globalization101, a project of Suny Levin Institute, viewed at http://bit.ly/2rq0p1p (accessed January 12, 2015).

ANSI Seeks Organizations to Support International Standards Development Work on Industrial Data Information Interchange, Apr 23, 2014, ANSI News and Publications, viewed at http://bit.ly/2tcNOje (accessed January 12, 2015).

ANSI Essential Requirements: Due process requirements for American National Standards, Edition: January 2015 viewed at http://bit.ly/1AqG8Yp (accessed January 12, 2015).

An Overview of the UDEF, The Universal Data Element Framework (UDEF), viewed at http://bit.ly/2sDcG6F (accessed January 13, 2015).

ISO in Brief, International Standards for a Sustainable World, viewed at http://bit.ly/2skZ7WE (accessed January 14, 2015).

What is conformity assessment?, viewed at http://bit.ly/2sl4S6v (accessed January 14, 2015).

Who Develops ISO Standards?, viewed at http://bit.ly/1Ni5Ow0 (accessed January 14, 2015).

Data and Information Integrity

Business managers need to have confidence in the information on which they base strategic and operational decisions. They need to feel that the information is trustworthy. Data integrity is the foundation of information integrity. Good database design can promote data integrity. However, data can still become corrupted, which can lead to a variety of problems. Maintaining data integrity helps avoid these problems and ensures that the information on which managers rely is accurate, complete, consistent and valid.

IT professionals use a variety of techniques to support and enhance data integrity. However, even when these techniques are implemented, organizations can still be left with information silos of disparate, or heterogeneous, data. Organizations need to make the best use of their data, but information silos can make this difficult. One effective approach to eliminating silos is to integrate all of an enterprise's data resources using a common data architecture.

Educational Objectives

Upon completion of this assignment, you should be able to:

1. Define data integrity and information integrity.
2. Describe the basic components of a relational database.
3. Describe the problems lack of data integrity can cause an organization.
4. Describe the goals of maintaining data integrity.
5. Explain the principles of transaction management.
6. Explain the strategies, generations, and functions of maintaining data integrity.
7. Identify the types of integrity constraints that should be considered prior to data validation.
8. Describe the phenomenon of disparate data and the cycle that perpetuates it.
9. Describe how the cycle of disparate data can be broken.
10. Explain the concepts of an integrated data resource and common data architecture.

Data and Information Integrity

The concept of data integrity was introduced earlier in this course. **Data integrity** is the extent to which data are trustworthy, meaning that they are complete, accurate, consistent, and uncorrupted. Data integrity can be enforced, to some degree, through database design and structure. However, even when data are initially input or captured completely, accurately, and consistently, they can become corrupted in a variety of ways. For example, hardware failures, software bugs, power outages, human error, or attacks by hackers can significantly compromise the integrity of an organization's data.

Information is created by analyzing, processing, or organizing data and presenting them in a meaningful way. **Information integrity** is the extent to which information is accurate, complete, consistent, and valid. At best, information is only as good as the data from which it is derived. If the data are of poor quality or lack integrity, then the information will also be of poor quality and lack integrity.

Even when underlying data are of good quality and have a high degree of integrity, the information derived from them may still be flawed. This can occur when the analysis, processing, organization, or presentation of the data is performed inaccurately, incompletely, inappropriately, or incorrectly. This can result in misleading information that does not accurately reflect the underlying data. Figure 4.1 illustrates the relationship between data integrity and information integrity.

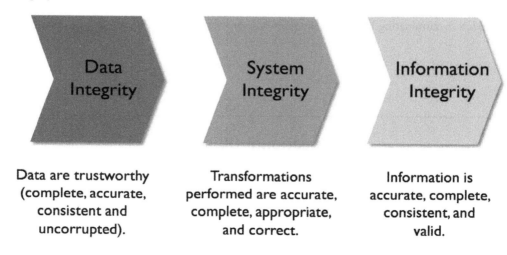

Figure 4.1 Data integrity and information integrity, adapted from *What constitutes information integrity?* S Flowerday and R. von Solms, December 2007 viewed at http://bit.ly/2rG5SAi (accessed February 2, 2015)

Introduction to Relational Databases

Figure 4.2 offers a simple, hypothetical example through which to introduce some fundamental database concepts. It presents collections of data used by the Human Resources (HR), Marketing, and facilities management departments at ABC Insurance Company.

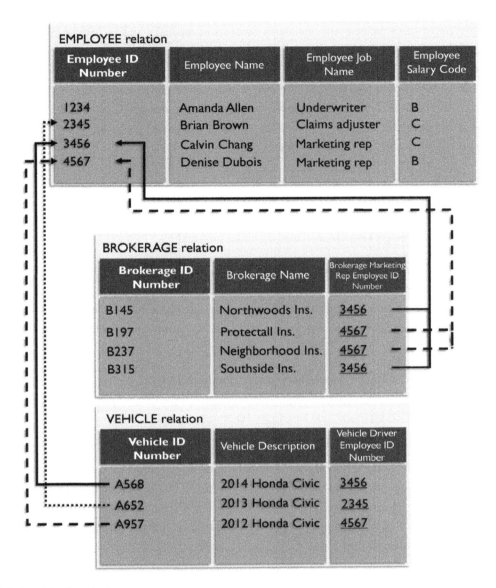

Figure 4.2 Relational database basics

The HR department collects and maintains data about the company's employees. Relational Insurance is a large organization and because it could conceivably have two employees with the same name, each employee is assigned a unique Employee ID Number. In the HR system, information about the company's employees is stored in a file with columns and rows similar to a spreadsheet. The file is referred to formally as a **relation**, or more commonly, a table. A relational database comprises a collection of these tables.

Each row in the EMPLOYEE table contains information about an individual employee. For example, employee number 1234, Amanda Allen, works as an underwriter and has a salary grade of B. This row, this collection of information about Amanda, is a **record**. Amanda herself is an entity; someone or something about which ABC's HR department collects or creates data. A collection of similar entities, in this case, ABC's employees, is an **entity set**, or **data set**. The columns in the table represent specific attributes of the entities, for example, their name, job category, and salary grade. The point at which a row and column intersect is called a **field**. Each field contains a single data element.

ABC's Marketing Department collects and maintains data about the independent insurance brokerages through which the company markets its products and services. These data are stored in the BROKERAGE table and each organization has a unique Brokerage ID Number. This unique identifier, like the Employee ID Number, is referred to as a **primary key**. Sometimes, a combination of two or more of an entity's attributes serves as a primary key. For example, in a CUSTOMER table, the combination of Customer Name and Customer Address might serve as the primary key. The essential feature of a primary key is that it is unique. The primary keys in each of the three tables illustrated in Figure 4.2 are indicated by boldface text.

When a primary key from one table appears in another table, it is referred to as a **foreign key**. For example, the BROKERAGE table includes the Employee ID Number for the marketing representative assigned to each brokerage. In the EMPLOYEE table, Employee ID Number is the primary key; in the BROKERAGE table, it is a foreign key. In Figure 4.2, foreign keys are indicated by underlined text.

Foreign keys point, or refer, to data contained in other tables. The use of primary keys and foreign keys helps define relationships between entities. For example, each brokerage is served by one of ABC's marketing representatives, and each marketing representative services several brokerages. Determining the name of the marketing representative responsible for Brokerage Number B145, Northland Insurance, involves a number of steps:

1. Go to the BROKERAGE table and find Brokerage Number B145.
2. Find the value in the Brokerage Marketing Rep Employee ID Number column for that record (3456).
3. Go to the EMPLOYEE table and find Employee ID Number 3456.
4. Find the Employee Name field for that record (Calvin Chang).

The facilities management department collects and maintains data about entities such as buildings, equipment, and company vehicles. ABC Insurance provides cars for all of its marketing representatives and some of its claims adjusters. Marketing representatives are assigned large territories and are expected to spend most of their time in the field meeting with brokers. Claims adjusters, on the other hand, are tasked with settling claims as promptly as possible and spending only as much time out of the office as is necessary to do so.

The facilities manager needs to know which vehicle is assigned to which employee. In addition, to determine whether vehicle usage is appropriate in terms of annual mileage, he or she also needs to know whether that employee is a marketing representative or a claims adjuster. When designing the VEHICLE table, rather than using the foreign key Vehicle Driver Employee ID Number, the designer could as easily have included one column for Employee Name and a second for Employee Job Category. This would have provided the facilities manager with the information he or she requires. However, designing the table that way would cause data redundancy and a potential loss of data integrity.

The addition of the two columns in the VEHICLE table would cause data redundancy because Employee Name and Employee Job Category would appear in both the EMPLOYEE table and the VEHICLE table. This data redundancy could result in a loss of data integrity. For example, if Brian Brown left the claims department to become a marketing representative, that change in job category would need to be updated in both the VEHICLE table and the EMPLOYEE table. The HR department would be involved in Brian's transfer and so the EMPLOYEE table would be updated appropriately. However, there is no reason, particularly in a large organization, that the facilities manager would be aware of Brian's job change. The most probable result is that Brian's Employee Job Category field would not be updated in the VEHICLE table. ABC's data about Brian Brown would no longer have integrity. By implementing the VEHICLE table using a foreign key, the database designer protects data integrity by reducing data redundancy.

While foreign keys protect against loss of data integrity in some cases, in others they can actually expose a database to integrity issues. For example, if Denise Dubois were to leave ABC Insurance, HR would delete her record from the EMPLOYEE table. But her Employee ID Number could remain as a foreign key in the BROKERAGE table for the entities Protectall Insurance and Neighborhood Insurance, and in the VEHICLE table for vehicle A957. If the system tries to refer to the data in the EMPLOYEE table using the foreign key in either the BROKERAGE table or the VEHICLE table, there is no longer a match. The reference cannot be completed. Deleting Denise's record from the EMPLOYEE table has caused a lack of integrity within the database.

Some data integrity issues can be recognized and resolved relatively easily. For example, assume that the VEHICLE table had been implemented with the two additional columns rather than the foreign key. Brian Brown's transfer from the claims department to the marketing department would result in a significant increase in the mileage on his company car. The facilities manager would most probably contact Brian to ask about the increase and would discover Brian's job change at that point. The Employee Job Category field in the VEHICLE table would be updated and data integrity would be restored. This is a simple example. Data integrity issues are often far more difficult to recognize and resolve.

Data Integrity Issues

As the size, number, and complexity of an organization's systems and systems interfaces grow, the risk of data corruption grows as well. Although some data integrity issues may not be considered critical, others can present serious challenges. In the absence of careful database design, and implementation of tools and techniques to help ensure data integrity, "dirty data" can occur, leading to a variety of problems:

- System crashes
- Cost of system downtime
- Silent data corruption
- Lost credibility
- Inappropriate business decisions
- Lost confidence in data
- Regulatory intervention

System Crashes

When an application accesses a table in which data have become corrupted, unexpected results can occur. Depending on the situation, the outcome may be relatively minor. However, in some cases an unexpected result may actually cause an application to "crash", or stop running. Without appropriate backup resources and immediate corrective action, system crashes can be debilitating.

Cost of System Downtime

Even without a system crash, once data corruption has been discovered it may be necessary to take a system off line to isolate and correct the problem, and restore the data. There are direct and indirect costs associated with these activities. IT expenses are the direct costs. While the system is unavailable, the organization may lose sales or be unable to service existing customers, resulting in indirect costs. For example, if an online retailer's customer interface system is down for a week between Thanksgiving and Christmas, the immediate financial losses could be significant. In addition, during that period customers may gravitate to another site, resulting in lost future sales. For an insurer, system down time could impact customer service in terms of policy issuance or claims adjusting. This could result in customer dissatisfaction and a loss of in-force business.

Silent Data Corruption

One of the challenges in maintaining data integrity is that "dirty data" often go unrecognized because they resemble good data. This undetected damage to data integrity is referred to as **silent data corruption**. When undetected for any length of time, the corruption can infect backups and spread to other systems, significantly increasing the time, effort, and cost involved in restoring data integrity.

Lost Credibility

Data integrity issues, particularly ongoing ones, can result in the loss of an organization's credibility. Customers, suppliers, distributors, shareholders, and others lose confidence when it becomes clear that an organization is unable to protect the quality of its data effectively. For example, brokers may be unwilling to place business with an insurer that routinely has errors or omissions in policy documents.

Inappropriate Business Decisions

A lack of data integrity leads to a lack of information integrity. Particularly in today's fast-paced, complex business environment, high-quality information is essential to strategic and tactical planning, and effective decision making. Executives and managers who are unaware of issues with the quality of their organization's data make strategic and tactical decisions based on poor quality information. The outcomes of these decisions are likely to be less than optimal.

Lost Confidence in Data

When executives, managers, and other stakeholders become aware of data integrity issues, they can often lose confidence in all of the organization's data, even if data corruption is not widespread. Being unable to identify for certain which information is based on good data and which is based on "dirty data", they distrust it all. This can be just as detrimental to planning and decision making as unknowingly relying on data and information that lack integrity.

Regulatory Intervention

Under the terms of the Sarbanes-Oxley Act, executives are responsible for ensuring that the organization's financial data are accurate and are adequately protected to guarantee their ongoing correctness. Various other acts and regulations also deal with the accuracy and completeness of organizations' data. Particularly in highly regulated industries, a demonstrated lack of data integrity can result in increased regulatory scrutiny. For example, insurers are required to report both financial and statistical data to state regulators. Inaccuracies in those data can have significant consequences in terms of regulatory intervention.

Data Integrity Goals

The objective of data management is to prevent these problems from arising as much as possible. Data management activities aimed at enhancing and maintaining data integrity help achieve these goals:

- Ensure the quality and integrity of the information derived from data
- Prevent system crashes resulting from data corruption
- Reduce the direct and indirect costs of system downtime
- Recognize "dirty data" promptly to prevent silent data corruption
- Protect the organization's credibility with stakeholders and others
- Support appropriate business planning and decision making
- Enhance confidence in the trustworthiness of data
- Comply with regulatory requirements

Transaction Management

In an insurance company environment, transactions occur constantly. The insurer issues policies; processes endorsements; accepts payments; opens, adjusts, and closes claims; and completes a variety of other operations. All of these involve reading from, or writing to, the organization's databases. Reading data from a database does not change the data. However, writing to a database—inserting, updating, or deleting records— changes the data. Whenever data are changed, there is a possibility that they might become corrupted.

For example, assume a customer telephones her insurer to advise of an address change from Anytown, California, to Newtown, Georgia. If a problem such as a power failure or system crash occurs part way through updating the four data elements involved (Street Address, City, State, and United States ZIP, or postal code), then the resulting address would be incorrect. Figure 4.3 illustrates how an incomplete transaction could result in a loss of data integrity.

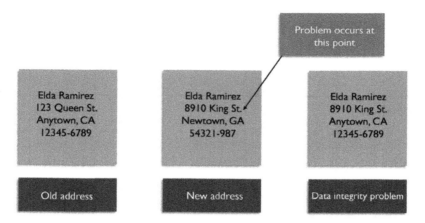

Figure 4.3 The need for transaction management

To prevent this, and to ensure that transactions process reliably, database designers have for years employed a variety of transaction management principles and techniques. One, commonly used in commercially available databases, is an approach that allows systems to automatically manage transactions in a way that helps preserve data integrity. Theoretically, it involves ensuring that all transactions have four specific properties:

- Atomicity
- Consistency
- Isolation
- Durability

These are referred to as **ACID Properties**. The first, **atomicity**, requires that all steps in a transaction must complete successfully; otherwise, none of them is reflected in the database. The database remains as it was prior to the attempted transaction. For example, a customer goes to an ATM to transfer $500 from his or her savings account to a checking account. Conceptually, the process involves these steps:

1. Open the savings account
2. Verify the balance in the savings account is sufficient to allow the transfer
3. Reduce the amount in the savings account by $500
4. Open the checking account
5. Increase the amount in the checking account by $500
6. Update (i.e. analogous to "Save") the new account balances in the database

If the deposit to the checking account cannot be processed for some reason, atomicity ensures that the withdrawal from the savings account is reversed. The customer's $500 remains in the savings account.

Transactions move through a number of states. A transaction is **active** when it is initiated. In this case, the transaction becomes active when the customer enters the transfer instructions at the ATM. As the transaction proceeds successfully through the balance verification and withdrawal from savings account steps, it is **partially committed**. When the deposit to the checking account cannot be completed, the transaction enters a **failed** state. At this point, any change to the data, in this case the withdrawal from the savings account, is reversed. When the data have been restored, when the savings account balance no longer reflects the withdrawal, the transaction is in an **aborted** state. If the transaction completes successfully, with no failure, then it is **committed** and the results of the successful transaction are permanently stored in the database.

The second ACID property, **consistency**, is related to atomicity. It requires that a database be as consistent, or reconcilable, after a transaction as it was before the transaction. In the example, if atomicity did not apply, after the failed transaction the customer would have $500 less than before the transaction; the database would be inconsistent. In addition, the consistency property requires that data are consistent for all users while a transaction is in process. In the example, if a bank employee looks up the customer's savings account balance while the ATM transaction is in process, he or she would see the pre-transaction balance until the ATM transaction was successfully completed.

Often, multiple transactions are processed concurrently using shared system resources. When this is the case, the third ACID property requires that each transaction completes as if it were processed in **isolation**. One transaction cannot inadvertently change another. One method of ensuring isolation is the use of **locks**. When one transaction needs to change a specific data element, it locks that element so that it is unavailable to other transactions until the locking transaction is either committed or aborted. In the example, the transaction would lock both the savings account and checking account balances until both have been updated successfully or until the transfer fails and aborts.

The final ACID Property, **durability**, ensures that once a transaction has completed successfully, when it is in the committed state, it is "etched in stone". Its details persist regardless of power failures or system malfunctions. The changes are logged, written to the database and available for recovery.

To ensure atomicity, consistency, isolation, and durability, ACID transactions typically involve a number of steps:

1. Document the transaction request in a transaction log
2. Obtain write locks on all the data elements involved in the transaction
3. Insert the new values into the appropriate fields
4. Move the changes from temporary to permanent storage (i.e. analogous to "Save")
5. Update the transaction log to flag the transaction as completed

Maintaining Data Integrity

There are a number of techniques data management professionals can use to help ensure data integrity:

- Normalizing data
- Defining business rules
- Validating data
- Using constraints
- Imposing referential integrity
- Using generation data groups

Data Normalization

Figure 4.4 returns to ABC Insurance for a simple illustration of **data normalization**. Data normalization is a method for increasing the quality of database design.

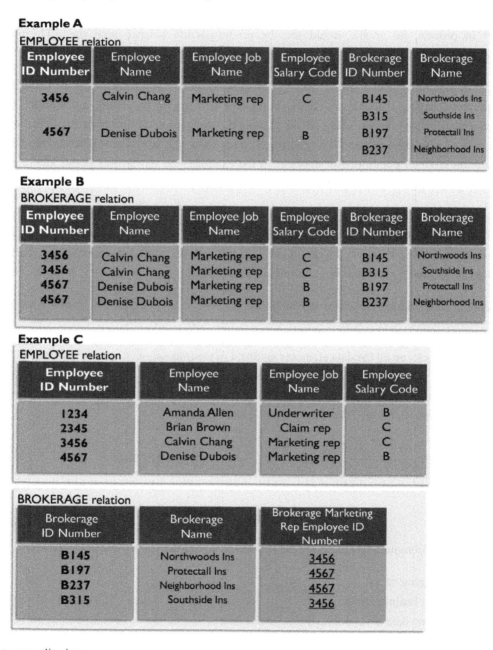

Figure 4.4 Data normalization

The objective is to store "one fact in one place"; to ensure that a specific attribute is assigned to only one entity. It focuses on including only attributes of the primary key in each table. Data normalization enhances the efficiency of a database.

The insurer needs to know which of its marketing representatives services which brokers. The database designer could include information about both employees and brokerages in the EMPLOYEE table or the BROKERAGE table; however, that approach would be less than optimal.

In Example A in Figure 4.4, for each record in the database, two of the attributes (Brokerage ID Number and Brokerage Name) would have multiple values. In the example, there are only two values for each. In reality, each marketing representative could serve a large number of brokerages. Example B introduces data redundancy since each marketing representative's employee data are repeated for each brokerage. Neither Example A nor Example B represents normalized data.

Example C, on the other hand, illustrates normalized data. Data about employees are stored in the EMPLOYEE table and data about brokerages are stored in the BROKERAGE table. The relationships between marketing representatives and brokerages are established by using Employee ID Number as a foreign key in the BROKERAGE table.

Business Rules

A **business rule** is a formal statement that stipulates what an organization will or will not do. It defines or limits some particular aspect of the organization's operations. Business rules are developed by non-technical operational managers to direct and control the various activities of the organization. Operational business rules are often referred to as policies or guidelines. Examples of insurance business rules might include the following:

- All personal lines policies must have a deductible expressed in terms of dollars.
- Vehicles aged 15 years or older are ineligible for physical damage coverage.
- Only homes built within the last 35 years are eligible for Platinum Form coverage.
- Agents have binding authority only for those lines they are authorized to write.
- Only the assigned adjuster is allowed to make changes to an open claim file.
- Policy renewals must be processed 60 days prior to the effective date.

Business policies and guidelines can be ambiguous, inconsistent, or open to misinterpretation. Data management professionals are tasked with translating these policies or guidelines into unambiguous business rules that strictly, consistently, and accurately enforce the intent of the operational policies or guidelines.

For example, an insurer may have an underwriting rule that young drivers operating sports cars are ineligible for personal auto coverage. A sports car operator who is not a young driver and who has an acceptable driving history in terms of traffic violations and accidents would be eligible for coverage.

An underwriter would know what constitutes a young driver, and what qualifies as a sports car. The underwriter would also know that, in certain jurisdictions, age is not considered an acceptable underwriting factor. In those jurisdictions, the insurer's underwriting guidelines specify that any sports car operator with less than ten years' accident-free driving is ineligible for personal auto coverage. The underwriter evaluates a variety of factors and works through a number of steps when underwriting a sports car. These can be expressed as follows:

- Identify the vehicle.
    - Determine whether the vehicle qualifies as a sports car.

- o If it qualifies as a sports car, then determine the appropriate underwriting factor to evaluate (i.e. age or driving experience).
- o If it does not qualify as a sports car, then continue underwriting the risk as usual.

- Identify the jurisdiction in which the applicant lives and/or operates the vehicle.
  - Determine whether age is an acceptable underwriting factor in that jurisdiction.
    - o If age is an acceptable underwriting factor, then determine whether the operator is a young driver.
      - If the operator is a young driver, then decline the insurance application.
      - If the operator is not a young driver, then verify whether the operator's driving record qualifies him or her for coverage.
        - If the operator's driving record is acceptable, then issue the policy.
        - If the operator's driving record is unacceptable, then decline the insurance application.
    - o If age is not an acceptable underwriting factor, then determine whether the operator has at least ten years accident-free driving history.
      - If the operator has had ten years accident-free driving, then issue the policy.
      - If the operator has not had ten years accident-free driving, then decline the insurance application.

Data management professionals translate broadly worded operational policies and guidelines into a set of formally stated, detailed business rules in a vocabulary that operational managers can understand. Often business rules are expressed as "if-then" statements as illustrated above. Alternatively, business rules can be defined by tables or decision trees. Figure 4.5 illustrates a simple decision tree.

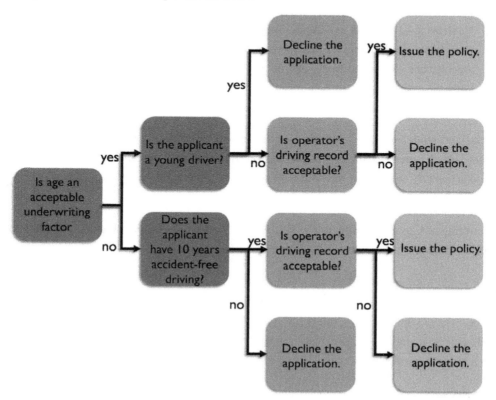

Figure 4.5 Decision tree example

Business rules allow processes to be automated, for example personal lines underwriting. Automating processes helps to ensure consistency and preserve data integrity. A single operational policy or guideline can generate many business rules. Once business managers agree that the formal business rules developed by the data management professionals accurately reflect the intention of the organization's operational guidelines and policies, the business rules can be converted into technical or programming rules for use by the organization's applications. Data managers also define business rules relating to data access including inserting, updating, deleting, and viewing data.

Rather than implementing business rules at the application level, some organizations use **business rule management systems (BRMS)**. A BRMS separates business rules out from the rest of an application. It provides a facility for business managers to modify business rules without the IT department having to make changes to the application itself. This allows organizations to respond more quickly to regulatory or market changes.

Data Validation

Validation is the process of "determining and confirming that something meets requirements, follows rules and conforms to standards."[40] Data validation involves verifying that the data in each field are as expected—it is not necessarily a method for determining whether the data are accurate. For example, data validation can confirm that the data in a Telephone Number column are in the correct format and have the correct number of digits; however, it cannot determine whether each telephone number was entered accurately.

Data validation techniques can be implemented in several different ways. For example, the user interface can prompt users to complete required fields or format their input in a specific way. Data validation can also be accomplished through the application itself or through the use of database constraints. There are several types of data validation methods.

- **Data type validation** checks whether the data in a field are of the type expected, for example if the data in a numeric field are actually numeric. If the data are alphabetic or alphanumeric, they are not valid.

- **Allowed character checks** verify whether the characters entered are among those allowed or required. For example, an email address must include at least one ampersand (@).

- **Range checking** involves determining whether the data in a field are within the expected range. If an insurer only provides homeowners coverage for homes with replacement values between $75,000 and $350,000, the dwelling coverage limit on all homeowner's policies should fall within that range.

- **Code checking** verifies that a code entered in a field is valid. For example, an insurer may have specific codes to indicate a private passenger automobile policy is eligible for a discount (e.g. multi-vehicle, mature driver, driver training). The system would check the discount code entered against a lookup table of acceptable codes.

- **Complex validation** can involve a combination of simple data validation methods with the addition of more complex processing.

---

[40]The DAMA Dictionary of Data Management, First Edition 2008, Mark Mosley Editor, Technics Publications LLC, New Jersey, copyright 2008 DAMA International, p. 121.

Constraints

Constraints help to preserve data integrity by controlling or limiting the values that can be inserted into columns in a table. There are several types of constraints in general use.

- **Check constraints** specify the acceptable format of data in a column. For example, the data in each field in a Telephone Number column must be three digits followed by a hyphen, followed by three digits, followed by a hyphen, followed by four digits (e.g. 123-456-7890).

- **Not null constraints** do not allow a field to be left blank. It is essential that an insurer know the names of its insureds, so a not null constraint would be appropriate for the Insured Given Name and Insured Family Name columns.

- **Unique constraints** ensure that unique values remain so. For example, no two insurance brokerages would have the same telephone number. A unique constraint would ensure that there is no duplication of entries in the Brokerage Telephone Number column. Unique constraints would also be appropriate with vehicle identification numbers (VIN) or Social Security numbers.

- **Primary key constraints** are essentially a combination of not null constraints and unique constraints that apply to the primary key column in a table. They ensure that each record has a primary key and each is unique.

- **Foreign key constraints** ensure that the value in a foreign key column in one table matches a primary key in another table. In the ABC Insurance example, when Denise Dubois leaves the company, she would be deleted from the EMPLOYEE relation. The foreign keys in the BROKERAGE relation would be changed to the Employee ID Number of the marketing representative to which her brokerages are reassigned, or set to null.

Referential Integrity

Foreign key constraints help ensure **referential integrity**. Referential integrity maintains the accuracy of a database. Its application means that every foreign key in a table has an identical primary key in that same table or another table. Referential integrity ensures that relationships between entities remain intact and that records are not inadvertently "orphaned" when associated records are deleted.

Referential integrity relies on a variety of rules. For example:

- A foreign key cannot be added to a table unless it exists as a primary key in another table.
- A row, or record, cannot be deleted from a table if foreign keys in other tables refer to that record.
- A record cannot be added to a table unless the foreign key for that record matches a primary key in the table to which the foreign key refers.

Generation Data Groups

A **generation data group** is essentially a collection of sequential automatic backups of a particular data set. A data set is the contents of a table, for example all of the data for all of the records in the EMPLOYEE table. Each backup, or "snapshot" of the data set, is referred to as a **generation**.

An organization can select the frequency of the backups (e.g. daily, weekly, monthly) as well as the number of backups to be included in the collection. For example, an organization may elect to perform a backup of a particular data set daily to a maximum of 30 backups, which would represent "snapshots" of the data each day for 30 days. Each is given a unique number and is "aged" relative to the current generation. Once a generation data set has reached the specified age, in the example 30 days, it is dropped from the group as the next generation "snapshot" of the data set is taken and added to the collection.

Implementing generation data groups offers a number of benefits:

- Facilitating recovery if data become corrupted
- Allowing validation of new data by comparing them to the previous generation data set
- Providing historical data for summary, analysis, or reporting

Disparate Data

Organizations, particularly large ones, have vast quantities of data. However, the data are usually in different formats, in different systems, implemented in different ways on different platforms. This is particularly the case in organizations with legacy systems, which were designed to operate independently, not sharing data with other systems. An organization's data are often locked in information silos and are not generally accessible across the organization. Typically, organizations do not maintain detailed inventories of their data, even though they are an important asset.

Business managers may be familiar with the data collected, created, and used in their particular operational area, but they are usually unfamiliar with, or unaware of, the enterprise's complete collection of data resources. Alternatively, business managers may be aware of at least some additional data resources, but they may not understand the data, may not trust the data, or may not be able to access the data. As a result, when a need for additional data arises, they create or acquire them rather than use existing data. This results in a high degree of data redundancy, and variability in data structure, format, and quality. The result is referred to as **disparate data**, and the data manager's goal is to consolidate them as much as is possible.

Disparate data are heterogeneous; they are dissimilar in structure, format, or meaning. For example, data architecture differences between two systems could result in a field in both systems having the same name, but actually containing data about different entities. Different systems may use different field names for what is, in fact, the same piece of data. Different areas within an enterprise may define terms differently, or definitions of business terms and data elements may be ambiguous or inaccurate. The problem with disparate data is that they perpetuate a spiraling cycle of increasingly disparate data. The Disparate Data Cycle is illustrated in Figure 4.6.

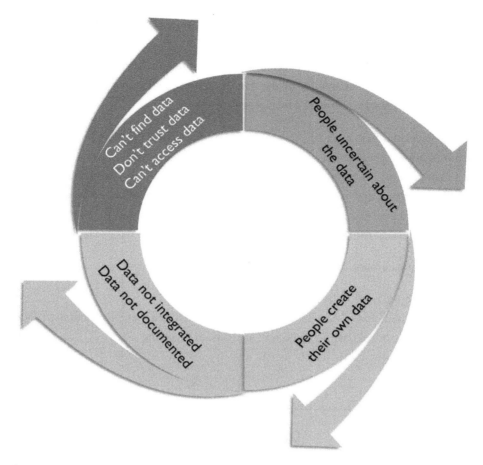

Figure 4.6 The disparate data cycle, adapted from *Disparate Data to an Enterprise-Wide Data Resource*, Michael H. Brackett IRMAC Toronto 2007, viewed at http://bit.ly/2sCHqEP (accessed January 29, 2015)

One effective way of breaking the Disparate Data Cycle is through the development of an integrated data resource with common data architecture.

Integrated Data Resources and Common Data Architecture

The concept of data integration was introduced earlier in this course. It is the process of extracting data from an organization's operational systems, scrubbing the data, transforming them, and storing them for operational or analytical purposes. Physical data warehousing and virtual data federation are two types of data integration. The problem with these types of integration is that, while the data in the warehouse or federation are integrated, the data in the systems from which they originated remain disparate.

Data resource integration differs from data integration. **Data resource integration** is the process of making disparate data across an enterprise homogeneous and ensuring that they remain so and are adequate to meet both present and future business information requirements.

Formal data resource integration involves four steps[41]:

- Cataloging, or taking inventory of, all of an enterprise's current data, and defining and documenting the data to create a shared vocabulary

- Developing a common, enterprise-wide data architecture and overlaying the inventoried data onto the common data architecture to ensure a thorough understanding of the data

- Deciding on a preferred data architecture that defines how data will be represented so that they can be best understood and shared

- Transforming the organization's disparate data into homogeneous data based on the preferred data architecture and following formal data transformation rules

This process transforms an organization's various disparate data resources into a homogeneous data resource that exists at the operational level rather than simply within a data warehouse or federation. A common, enterprise-wide data architecture is an essential element of data resource integration. An **enterprise data architecture** is a formal, comprehensive data architecture that provides a common context within which an integrated data resource is developed across an enterprise. Essentially, it is a blueprint for aligning IT functions with the organization's business strategy.

Summary

Data have integrity when they are trustworthy, that is, when they are complete, accurate, consistent, and uncorrupted. When data have these attributes and when the transformations performed on them are accurate, complete, appropriate, and correct, the resulting information also has integrity. It is accurate, complete, consistent, and valid. A lack of data integrity can result in system crashes, costly downtime, silent data corruption that can spread to other systems, lost credibility for the organization, inappropriate business decisions, a loss of confidence in the data on the part of business managers, and even regulatory intervention. An organization's goals with respect to data integrity involve preventing these problems.

Relational databases are collections of files with rows and columns like a spreadsheet. Each file is formally called a relation, or more commonly, a table. Each record in a table represents an entity and each column is an attribute of that entity. Database designers use primary keys and foreign keys to reduce data redundancy and support data integrity.

Data managers use a variety of techniques to promote data integrity including transaction management, data normalization, definition of business rules, data validation, constraints, imposition of referential integrity, and implementation of generation data groups. Unfortunately, these techniques are not effective in resolving the issue of disparate data. One effective way of resolving disparate data is through data resource integration, which is a

---

[41] Data Integration versus Data Resource Integration, Michael Brackett, May 1, 2012, viewed at http://www.dataversity.net/data-integration-versus-data -resource-integration/ (accessed February 18, 2016).

formal process based on common data architecture. Data resource integration results in high quality, homogeneous data that can be shared and accessed across the enterprise as a whole.

Bibliography

What is Data Integrity? Learn How to Ensure Database Data Integrity via Checks, Tests & Best Practices Veracode, Michael Teeling, May 14, 2012, viewed at http://vera.cd/1nuHcbU (accessed January 28, 2016).

Data Integrity, Microsoft Developer Network, viewed at http://bit.ly/2sbd5Md (accessed January 28, 2016).

Confidentiality, integrity, and availability (CIA triad). This was last updated in November 2014, Contributor(s): Matthew Haughn, Stan Gibilisco. Posted by: Margaret Rouse, viewed at http://bit.ly/2rGf3k5 (accessed January 28, 2015).

Best Practices in Data Resource Management, Takeaway notes from "The Learning Curve" webinar. By Aliza Bornstein, copywriter, Melissa Data, The eLearning Curve data quality series, hosted by Eric Kavanagh and conducted by Mike Brackett, October 2, 2009 (www.elearningcurve.com) viewed at http://bit.ly/2rpwfLp (accessed January 28, 2016).

Data Resource Integration, by Michael H. Brackett, Published: May 1, 2012, The Data Administration Newsletter – TDAN.com, Robert S. Seiner – Publisher, excerpted from *Data Resource Integration: Understanding and Resolving a Disparate Data Resource* viewed at http://bit.ly/2sD29s2 (accessed January 28, 2016).

Disparate Data, Geek Interview, viewed at http://bit.ly/2rB12JC (accessed January 28, 2016).

Database Integrity: Security, Reliability, and Performance Considerations, Susan Gordon, Indiana University South Bend, 1700 Mishawaka Avenue, South Bend, IN 46634, slgordon@iusb.edu viewed at http://bit.ly/2tcO6Xm (accessed January 29, 2016).

Understanding Generation Data Sets, viewed at http://bit.ly/2rpE6ZF (accessed January 29, 2016).

Fundamentals of Database Management Systems, 2nd Edition, Mark L. Gillenson, Fogelman College of Business and Economics, University of Memphis, published by John Wiley & Sons, Inc., printed and bound by RR Donnelley, copyright 2012, 2005 by John Wiley & Sons, ISBN 978-0-470-62470-8.

Primary and Foreign Key Constraints, SQL Server 2014, viewed at http://bit.ly/2sIjU9m (accessed February 3, 2016).

Handling Data Integrity Issues in Analysis Services 2005, T.K. Anand, Microsoft Corporation, March 2005, viewed at http://bit.ly/2txB462 (accessed February 5, 2016).

Dancing With Dirty Data -Methods for Exploring and Cleaning Data, Louise A. Francis, FCAS, MAAA, Casualty Actuarial Society Forum, winter 2005, viewed at http://bit.ly/2rpSp0f (accessed February 8, 2016).

Sabyasachi De, TRANSACTION MANAGEMENT, viewed at http://bit.ly/2txrKiw (accessed February 29, 2016).

DBMS Transaction, viewed at http://bit.ly/2sbdiyZ accessed (accessed February 9, 2016).

Oracle, Database Concepts, Transaction Management, viewed at http://bit.ly/2rpxQkF (accessed February 11, 2016).

The ACID Model, By Mike Chapple, viewed at http://bit.ly/2rpThSx (accessed February 11, 2016).

Metadata and Metadata Management

Metadata are business and technical information about an organization's data. They help put data in context, reveal their meaning and make them accessible. They are often compared to a library's card catalogue. Metadata management can be challenging in part because of the diversity of metadata as well as their scope. A single data element can have a variety of associated metadata. However, there are a number of tools and techniques available to help organize, catalogue, and access metadata.

Metadata can be categorized as business, technical, operational, process, or data stewardship metadata. To best use its data, an organization needs good quality metadata. One of the benefits of quality metadata is that they help information consumers understand where their information came from. This increases confidence in its accuracy and validity. Many individuals throughout an organization rely on quality metadata including senior management, actuaries and analysts, underwriters, claims managers, finance and internal audit staff, marketing staff, and those involved in statistical and regulatory compliance. Insurance regulators and data collection organizations also rely on metadata to bring meaning to insurers' data.

To manage metadata effectively, insurers need a metadata strategy. However, developing and implementing one can be challenging. An essential element of a metadata strategy is determining the structure and capabilities of a metadata repository, a sort of data warehouse for metadata. A repository can be centralized, decentralized, or a hybrid of the two, and an organization can choose to purchase a vendor's product or to develop a repository in-house.

Educational Objectives

Upon completion of this assignment, you should be able to:

1. Define metadata and explain their importance.
2. Discuss the challenges of managing metadata.
3. Define semantics and taxonomy.
4. Identify the major types of metadata classification.
5. List the advantages of having high quality metadata and the disadvantages of having poor quality metadata.
6. Explain data lineage and describe how it is useful to the metadata user.

7. Describe how different types of data users employ metadata.

8. Explain the rationale for implementing a metadata strategy.

9. Describe the challenges in implementing a metadata strategy.

10. Explain the role of metadata repositories.

11. Discuss the value of an enterprise metadata repository.

12. Contrast centralized vs. autonomous metadata.

13. List the characteristics of an enterprise metadata repository.

14. Describe metadata user requirements, architecture, and standards.

15. Discuss the challenges of implementing and managing an enterprise metadata repository.

16. Discuss the considerations for buying versus building a metadata repository.

Defining Metadata

Metadata are commonly defined as "data about data". While this definition is accurate, it is not particularly explanatory. Figure 5.1 helps to clarify the relationship between data and metadata by illustrating a simple data entry screen.

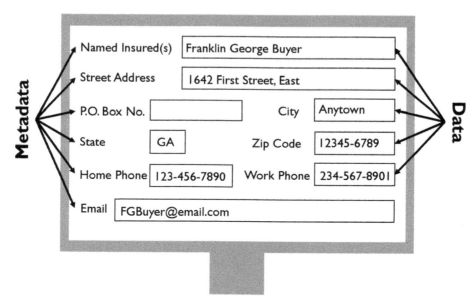

Figure 5.1 Metadata and data

The data that have been entered are details about a particular individual. The metadata describe those data. For example, without the metadata "Named Insured(s)", the data "Franklin George Buyer" might be recognizable as a name. However, that name could represent an insured, a mortgagee, an insurance agent, a claimant, a sales prospect, or a marketing representative. In the absence of the metadata "Home Phone", the numeric string "123-456-7890" could be a telephone number, a product code, an insurance policy number, or an employee identification number.

A single data element can have an assortment of associated metadata. For example, in Figure 5.1, in addition to its name, each field could have metadata to indicate whether it is a text or numeric field, and how many characters long it is. For the State field, metadata could include a list of valid state codes.

Metadata are business and technical information about an organization's data. Metadata can best be defined in terms of what they do, and it is what they do that makes them important. They describe the content, quality, condition and other attributes of the data, and the structure of the database. They include the definition of each data element, its characteristics and data type (i.e. numeric, text, date), the size of each field, a cross-reference to the source system from which the data came, and information about any transformations the data have undergone.

Metadata put data in context, reveal their meaning, and make them accessible and usable. Figure 5.2 demonstrates how metadata transform data into information by illustrating a simple income statement. Without the report title and line items on the left, the data on the right would be meaningless. Clearly and consistently defined metadata ensure that all users of the information contained in the income statement understand exactly what each line item comprises and how they are related and calculated.

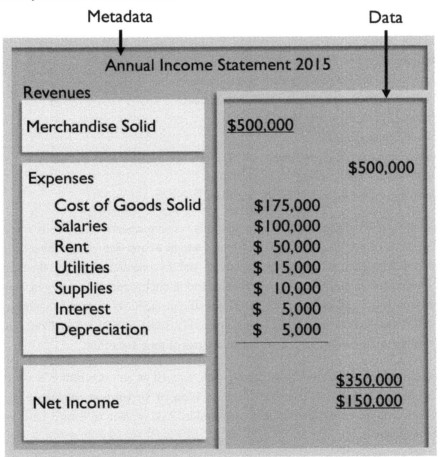

Figure 5.2 Importance of metadata

Sources of insurance metadata include insurers' policy administration systems, billing systems, claims systems, information and reporting systems, and the content management systems used for storing unstructured data. Other sources of insurance metadata include insurance regulators and data collection organizations (i.e. with respect to regulatory reporting requirements), and other third parties. Data architecture activities, such as data modeling and extract, transform and load (ETL), also produce metadata. Tools can capture and store these metadata for future reference.

Metadata serve as the foundation for data quality, data profiling (i.e. the automated analysis of data quality) and data use. They also enable many technical operations, and serve as an essential component of business intelligence (BI) and statistical or other reporting capability.

Metadata Management and Associated Challenges

Just as an organization's data assets require management, so too do its metadata. **Metadata management** is the preparation, definition, organization, managed access, and maintenance of an organization's metadata.

Metadata management includes:

- Understanding metadata requirements;
- Defining metadata architecture;
- Developing and maintaining metadata standards;
- Implementing a managed metadata environment;
- Creating and maintaining metadata;
- Integrating metadata;
- Managing metadata repositories;
- Distributing and delivering metadata; and
- Querying, reporting and analyzing metadata.[42]

Metadata management faces a number of challenges. The first is that metadata are typically found in various forms and locations throughout an enterprise, particularly in organizations of any size, or those that have been involved in mergers or acquisitions. Metadata can be formal, structured, and documented. However, they can also be informal and unstructured, for example in emails or scanned images, and in organizational memory including the knowledge of individual employees. It is essential to identify which specific metadata to manage; attempts to manage all of an organization's metadata are likely to stall. Discovering, collecting, standardizing, rationalizing, and documenting an organization's metadata require a significant investment in terms of time and effort.

Determining and documenting the relationships among data, as well as an organization's assorted business rules and processes, can be challenging. In addition, each division or department may have a common internal vocabulary with which employees are familiar and comfortable. Asking them to learn a new business "language" can meet with some resistance.

Effective governance is an important element of effective metadata management. And while the benefits of metadata management are generally understood by data management professionals, stakeholders on the business side typically do not appreciate the business benefits of a coordinated approach to metadata. Many executives and

---

[42] Adapted from The DAMA Guide to the Data Management Body of Knowledge (DAMA-DMBOK) First Edition, DAMA International, Technics Publications LLC, New Jersey, copyright 2009 DAMA International, p. 260.

managers still think of metadata management as an IT function rather than an enterprise-wide responsibility. Finally, many organizations, including insurers, often obtain data from third parties. They may not have access to the same amount or quality of metadata for third party data as they have for their own, nor are they likely to be able to easily implement, for third party data, the controls required for good metadata.

Semantics and Taxonomy

The English language, in fact many languages, can be ambiguous. The same word or phrase can mean different things to different people in different contexts. For example, the term "policy" can refer to an insurance contract, or to a rule or guideline (e.g. an insurer's underwriting policies). This ambiguity can lead to misunderstanding, which in turn can lead to poor decision making. Semantics and taxonomy are essential elements in developing robust, structured metadata that reduce ambiguity and create a common understanding across an organization.

Semantics is a branch of linguistics that focuses on analyzing, understanding, and documenting the meaning of words. In the context of data management, semantics is the process of clearly defining and documenting the business and technical terms used within an organization. Different terms that are used synonymously by different departments or divisions, for example "customer", "insured", and "client", should be clearly documented so that anyone using these data understands their meaning in context. Different systems within the same department or division may also use different terminology and each should have its own data dictionary when not in conformance with an enterprise data dictionary.

In science, **taxonomy** is the classification of living or extinct organisms based on their characteristics. For example, whales and horses are mammals; humpbacks and belugas are types of whales. In data management, taxonomy is also a classification system. Items can be classified in simple lists, hierarchically, or when an item needs to be categorized in a variety of ways, using a faceted classification method. Figure 5.3 presents a simple illustration of a hierarchical taxonomy using insurance policy types. Each policy type can be further broken down by coverage (e.g. auto liability and auto physical damage) and further still, for example by peril (e.g. collision, fire, theft).

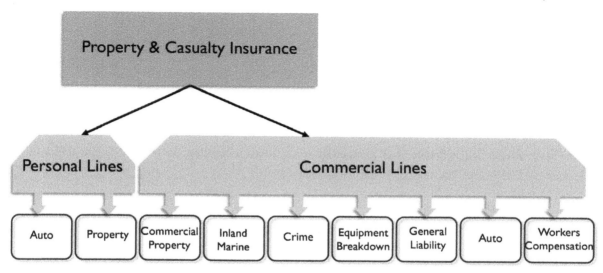

Figure 5.3 Hierarchical taxonomy

Figure 5.4 illustrates a faceted taxonomy in which an insurance brokerage can be classified based on location, the lines of business it is authorized to write, the commission level it receives, its loss ratio, and its written premiums.

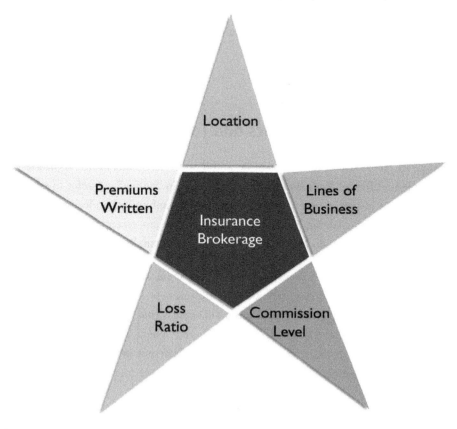

Figure 5.4 Faceted taxonomy

In insurance, an important central question is "What is the best way to categorize metadata for this insurance company's data environment?" The data architect should consider, for example, the types of insurance the organization sells, as well as its operations, reporting requirements, geographic location, organizational structure, and data governance policies. This will help determine the various types of metadata that are required and how they should be organized.

Categories of Metadata

Theorists have categorized metadata in a number of ways, often depending on the environment in which the metadata are used. However, one method classifies metadata as:

- Business metadata;
- Technical metadata;
- Operational metadata;
- Process metadata; or
- Data stewardship metadata.

While theorists may assign a specific metadata element to different categories depending on the theorist's focus, generally speaking **business metadata** are non-technical and have meaning to business users of the data. They define data and their attributes in business terms. Business metadata include such things as field names on data input screens, report names, data definitions, and business rules. The metadata in Figures 5.1 and 5.2 are examples of business metadata.

Debates on data quality often arise because various definitions exist for the same piece of data. For example, the term "loss ratio" may have a textbook definition that differs from the one used to create an agent's year-end bonus report or an underwriting profitability report. Effective business metadata stewards collaborate with other data stewards to develop a consistent view of the organization's data.

Technical metadata are used by an organization's systems to manipulate data resources to meet business needs. Typically, technical metadata are stored in a database or in the flat files used by many insurance companies. A flat file is a method of storing data in a single table rather than in multiple tables linked through foreign keys like a relational database.

Technical metadata can be discovered by examining databases and files, or captured using vendor software packages. It is important to understand what users want to know about where in individual systems data reside and where the data originate. The granularity of metadata are another consideration. Granularity refers to their level of detail. At a high level, technical metadata include identifiers for applications, databases, tables, and columns. Low level metadata (i.e. more granular metadata) include data type and size, file type, domain structures, and their allowed values.

Operational metadata describe the data's availability, movement from source to target systems, timeliness, and usage. Examples of operational metadata include the date and time a file was last updated, and whether the data are active, archived, or purged. Operational metadata also have data security uses, for example indicating who has accessed the data and when.

Process metadata focus on the business value chain. In insurance, the value chain begins when an individual submits a homeowner's application and ends when his or her home is rebuilt after a fire. Process metadata provide information about a business process, for example issuing an insurance policy, or a step in a process. Examples of process metadata include the process name, the start and end time of a process, and the number of records processed.

Data stewardship metadata include information about data stewards and data stewardship processes. Rules about who has the authority or responsibility for creating, reading, updating or deleting data (CRUD) are examples of data stewardship metadata, as is a list of the individuals serving on an organization's data governance council.

Some metadata theorists include additional metadata categories, for example statistical, quality, geospatial, design, runtime, usage, local, or audit trail metadata. One organization defines approximately 160 types of metadata. [43] However, in the insurance industry, metadata can be broadly characterized as being either technically-focused or business-related.

---

[43] Understanding Metadata Types, viewed at http://support.sas.com/documentation/cdl/en/omamod (accessed March 22, 2015).

Business, technical, operational, process, and data stewardship metadata are typically associated with structured data—data in databases. In the case of unstructured data, for example photographs or scanned images of insurance applications, metadata are categorized differently. Metadata about unstructured data are characterized as:

- Descriptive;
- Technical/structural; or
- Administrative.

Descriptive metadata are data about the content of unstructured data. In the case of a scanned auto application, they could include, for example, the insured's name and policy number, and the effective date of the policy. Descriptive metadata help locate required data.

Technical/structural metadata describe the format, internal structure, and organization of data. A table of contents in a book is an example of technical/structural metadata. This category of metadata facilitates navigation through unstructured data.

Administrative metadata relate to the management of unstructured data resources. Administrative metadata could include such things as a document's creation date, copyright information, or retention requirements.

Metadata Examples[44]

Metadata Can Include:	
Access restrictions	Data uses
Code values	Format
Completeness/coverage	Format length
Data model (logical, physical) for the data set	Information creation/discontinued dates
Data quality	Information name
Data retention of the data set	Reporting/update frequency
Data set owner/subject matter experts (SME)	Restrictions as to use
Data set size	Source field definitions (or derivation)
Data source/defining entity	Source field location
Data standards	Source field name
Data type	Taxonomy (classification, data category)

---

[44] Adapted from The Whodunit of Big Data, by Peter Marotta, Risk & Insurance, September 15, 2013, viewed at http://www.riskandinsurance.com/the-whodunit-of-big-data, (accessed May 27, 2015).

Metadata Quality

Metadata are often compared to a library's card catalogue. In a card catalogue, specific information is included for each book such as the author's name, the title, the subject, the publisher, the publication date, a brief description of the contents, and a number indicating where on the library shelves the book can be found. A card catalogue allows readers to find the specific book for which they are looking, to search all of the books written by a particular author, or to discover interesting books of which they had previously been unaware. In the absence of a card catalogue, or the presence of one that does not include all of the usual details, readers find it much more difficult to discover, select, and locate a book.

The same can be said for metadata. In the absence of good quality, consistent metadata, an organization's access to information is limited. When metadata are insufficient, inconsistent, ambiguous, redundant, or disparate, they make it difficult for an organization to:

- Discover all of its data resources;
- Understand its data and have confidence in them;
- Identify appropriate data for specific analysis and decision-making;
- Locate and access required data;
- Share data; and
- Reuse data.

This results in wasted time, and duplicating or reworking information. Poor quality metadata result in poor quality information. For example, assume one division of an organization refers to customers as "clients" and another division uses the term "insureds". The fact that the terms are used synonymously has not been documented. If head office marketing generates an age demographic report on individuals identified as "insureds", the report will probably not include data relating to "clients". The information in the report will not accurately reflect the age demographic of the organization's entire customer base. As another example, an insurer writing business in several different countries would require metadata to indicate the currency in which premiums are calculated and collected, and claims are paid. In the absence of those metadata it would be impossible to generate accurate aggregate financial statements.

Good quality metadata are accurate, complete, current, consistent, and have integrity. They allow an organization to:

- Find, access, categorize, transform, analyze, interpret, use, and reuse data efficiently;
- Understand and have confidence in its data and the information derived from them;
- Create and share information more efficiently; and
- Communicate more effectively through a common vocabulary.

Taken together, these benefits can significantly enhance an organization's ability to compete successfully.

Data Lineage

Data lineage is sometimes referred to as data provenance. In everyday English, the term "lineage" refers to a person's ancestry and "provenance" refers to the origin of an item. **Data lineage** is the history of a particular data element from its original creation or acquisition to its current or future form. It includes all of the processes, transformations, manual interventions and validations the data have undergone, and identifies the various systems through which they have flowed. It is sometimes referred to as a data lifecycle, but it actually describes a subset of the data lifecycle introduced in the first chapter. Figure 5.5 illustrates the high-level phases of data lineage.

As an example, consider a Monthly Call Center Service Levels report. The report might be compiled by an individual in the Marketing department using data collected from several different sources, aggregated in a spreadsheet and reformatted for presentation, perhaps after calculations of percentages or totals. This is one small portion of the lineage of the report data. Upstream, in the various systems from which the compiler obtained the data, they may have been manipulated in a variety of ways and may be quite different from their original form.

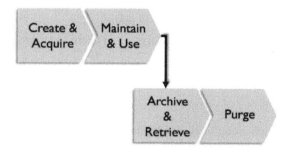

Figure 5.5 Data lineage

Using metadata, it is possible to trace data from the original producer, and determine where they flow and how they are transformed as they travel through the enterprise. For example, in insurance, data lineage might start with data being entered into an agency management system by a producer. The data are then transmitted to an insurer. They might go to a data warehouse, and even further to a data mart. Metadata can be captured at each step in the data's lineage.

Data lineage is useful in a variety of ways. It helps organizations comply with regulatory requirements related to financial and statutory reporting, and to demonstrate the accuracy and integrity of the information contained in its reports. When data accuracy or integrity issues are identified, data lineage can help data management professionals more quickly identify and correct the source of the problem. When changes to business systems or processes are under development, data lineage can help highlight the impact of those changes on downstream systems or processes, and on the users of the information they generate.

Data lineage is also helpful in creating business intelligence (BI), the process of querying an organization's data stores to gain greater insights into its operations and performance. Understanding the lineage of its data can help an organization to better protect sensitive or confidential data. Finally, an organization can reduce data collection, storage, and dispersal costs using metadata. For example, investigating the data lineage for a particular report could highlight redundancies and opportunities for process improvement.

Using Metadata

Good quality, consistent metadata support a variety of organizational objectives including informed strategic planning, regulatory compliance, revenue generation, and operational efficiency. Each of the following relies on robust metadata:

- Senior Management
- Analytics
- Underwriting and Product Management
- Claims
- Finance and Internal Audit
- Information Technology
- Marketing
- Statistical and Regulatory Compliance

Senior Management

Senior management needs to have confidence in the reports they use for decision making. Effective metadata management results in consistent definitions, documented data lineage, active involvement of data stewards, and mapping of business metadata to technical metadata. All of these help ensure the accuracy, validity, and completeness of the data used in analysis and reporting. For example, effective metadata management helps prevent a situation in which an executive receives contradictory reports from two different departments because they are based on different data with the same name.

In addition, insurance executives are held personally liable for inaccurate financial reports or breaches in confidentiality involving the release of a customer's personal information. Metadata management helps alleviate concerns in these areas by providing the data's full lineage, and defining the levels of privacy needed for each piece of data.

Analytics

Metadata help to ensure that the data used in actuarial and statistical analysis and ratemaking are accurate. Data profiling (i.e. automated data quality analysis), data cleansing, and data standardization tools all use metadata to help improve data quality. Better quality data enhance the value of predictive analytics, a type of data analysis used to predict future trends in areas such as customer needs and behaviors, the marketplace, or the regulatory environment.

Actuaries and other analysts not only need accurate data; they need to have the right data for analysis. Metadata provide information about data, their characteristics, where they came from, and the transformations they have undergone. This not only confirms that they are good quality data but also that they are the correct data.

The chief actuary and chief financial officer must approve and sign an insurer's annual statements. Metadata tools and metadata management techniques help to ensure the reports' accuracy and completeness, allowing the executives to sign with confidence.

Underwriting and Product Management

Underwriting includes the evaluation of applicants, determination of appropriate coverage, proper risk classification, and selection of an adequate rate or premium. The process involves gathering a significant amount of data, all of which require good quality metadata in order to be meaningful.

Metadata can facilitate access to customer data that can be critical to underwriting. For example, before denying policyholder coverage for a marginally unacceptable new property, it would be useful for the underwriter to understand the full extent of the policyholder's relationship with the insurer.

Metadata are important for the data used to formulate, enforce, and measure the effectiveness of underwriting policy, and the guidelines applicable to both individual risks and overall insurance programs. At the portfolio level, metadata help define the data used to quantify underwriting results, identify profitable and unprofitable coverages or lines of business, and determine the changes required to improve unacceptable results.

Metadata can also help in the development of rates for current and future products, evaluation of suppliers' and producers' performance, negotiation and evaluation of reinsurance programs, and review and revision of rating plans.

Claims

In claims, metadata help maximize profit potential by speeding the processing of legitimate claims and identifying potentially fraudulent activities. For example, in one case, an insured submitted a claim for the theft of over $20,000 of home electronics and provided digital photos of the items in support of the claim. The claims adjuster was able to determine that the date and time stamp that formed part of the metadata of the photos proved they had been taken after the date of the alleged theft.

Metadata can provide a baseline for industry data comparison and analysis by ensuring that the data used in the analysis have been defined and managed according to accepted data management standards. Metadata provide for efficiency and utility in claims data management by promoting standards for file formats, data definitions, and value lists, and by facilitating communication with external organizations. Metadata also ensure that claim system data management is compliant with state regulatory requirements.

Finance and Internal Audit

Accurate and complete definitions of accounting terms and calculated amounts lead to more accurate financial reports and enhanced understanding of those reports. As well, technical metadata assist in reconciling premium and loss transactions as they pass from system to system, or from job to job during a batch cycle. A batch cycle involves automatically completing a series of processes, or "jobs", often at night when system resources are less busy. Metadata help to promote the recognition of the value of an organization's data. Some companies actually list data on their balance sheet as an asset.

Information Technology

Metadata support the technical capabilities of applications, databases, utilities, and other technologies that facilitate business operations. In addition, they help reduce the cost of data collection, storage, and dispersal by reducing the tendency to create and store redundant data.

Development of new systems is more efficient if developers analyze the existing technical landscape before building a new application or creating new data to be used in existing systems. Analysis of existing metadata can help business systems analysts and project managers create software and systems specifications for application enhancements and new development initiatives. System engineers and developers can simplify their efforts by accessing these metadata during systems development. This is also critical for integration teams.

Marketing

Gaining market share can only be accomplished through proper data analysis. Targeting the right customers gives an insurer a strong competitive advantage. Linking data about prospects and customers across systems internally and externally can support marketing efforts, for example by classifying customers based on demographics.

Metadata can help to reduce insurance marketing costs. For example, metadata can prevent an insurer from targeting existing auto insurance customers as new auto business prospects, or sending multiple mailings to the same household.

Metadata can improve service for traditional customers, online shoppers, and call center users. They can help identify customers, determine the members of a household, or find all of the insurance policies linked to each customer. They facilitate communication about products, services, programs, and technologies. This is especially true for Internet searches, which can be enhanced by the use of HTML (hypertext markup language) meta-tags. **Meta-tags** are words that are tagged to items on the web. If an individual enters those words in an online search engine, the search will discover the items with those words tagged to them. For example, a person can search for "auto insurance quote" and easily obtain the service he or she requires.

Metadata can also facilitate effective communication with trading partners, such as agents, brokers, third party administrators, or managing general agents, based on a shared common vocabulary.

Statistical and Regulatory Compliance

Metadata help identify the best sources for statutory and financial reporting data through data lineage. State examiners, regulators, and auditors typically use metadata to investigate certain attributes of insurers' data. Market conduct auditors generally use underwriting and rating metadata to verify appropriate pricing and regulatory compliance.

Statistical Plans from external bureaus and advisory organizations include metadata specifications such as definitions, field lengths, and submission file layouts. Laws and regulations mandate that each organization provide consistent metadata for insurance data. The National Association of Insurance Commissioners (NAIC) Statistical Handbook makes recommendations to the states as to what forms of metadata to collect. Most Statistical Plans are consistent because the states collaborate on their data and metadata requirements. This consistency allows for cross-organizational industry analysis.

Because metadata support compliance with reporting requirements and other data regulations, they help avoid the costs associated with non-compliance such as fines.

Metadata Strategy

To make best use of its metadata, an organization needs to manage them effectively and that requires a metadata strategy. A metadata strategy is formulated at the same organizational level as other strategic plans and integrated into the enterprise data management strategy. The rationale for devising and implementing a metadata strategy is that, effectively executed, it can result in a number of benefits:

- Increased recognition of the importance of data and metadata quality
- Integration of sound metadata management practices across the organization
- Enhanced ability to derive information from operational data
- Development of a common, shared vocabulary
- Establishment of a framework for meeting future information needs

Perhaps the most important element in a metadata strategy is consensus about the organization's current and future business and information requirements. The organization's business needs should drive a metadata strategy. As with all strategic plans, a metadata strategy looks forward and provides a roadmap for reaching a desired future state. Effective data stewardship is an important factor in successfully implementing a metadata strategy since it is the data stewards who are usually responsible for both data and metadata. Project phases typically include:

- Planning;
- Interviewing key stakeholders;
- Assessing existing metadata sources and architecture;
- Developing future metadata architecture; and
- Developing a phased implementation strategy.[45]

---

[45] Adapted from The DAMA Guide to the Data Management Body of Knowledge (DAMA-DMBOK) First Edition, DAMA International, Technics Publications LLC, New Jersey, copyright 2009 DAMA International, p. 268.

Although a metadata strategy offers significant benefits to an organization, its development and implementation can face a number of challenges. Some organizations do not take the time to formulate a cohesive metadata strategy. Rather, they take a "Let's get a tool." approach, which generally proves ineffective.

As with any strategic plan, a metadata strategy requires support and commitment at the executive level. Without these, it is unlikely to be successful. In many organizations, implementation requires a cultural shift from the traditional view of IT having responsibility for processes involving data, to the much broader view of the organization as a whole exercising stewardship over its data and metadata. It may even necessitate some internal reengineering of both the business and IT functions. This kind of organizational change requires careful planning and management, and adds to the complexity of the metadata strategy implementation.

The sheer volume of an enterprise's metadata can be daunting. To identify, define, integrate, consolidate, and document every piece of business and technical metadata in every process and every system can be very labor intensive and require a significant investment. As a result, scoping is an essential element of a well-crafted metadata strategy. In addition, once an enterprise metadata strategy has been implemented, there are ongoing effort and costs associated with metadata maintenance.

Implementation of a metadata strategy requires a variety of resources including staff with appropriate skills, adequate funding, and suitable tools. As well, although often regarded as technical initiatives, metadata strategy development and implementation are actually business initiatives. The project must engage business users of data as much as possible. For example, they should be involved in the development of definitions and the documentation of business rules and data standards. This requires clear data governance policies that define and establish ownership of, and authority over, the organization's data and metadata, as well as training to familiarize management and staff with data stewardship roles and responsibilities.

Accessing Enterprise Metadata

The rationale for data management is treating data as an asset. Effective metadata management allows an organization to maximize the value of that asset. As insurance systems have become more complex, a simple data dictionary can no longer provide the full range of metadata necessary for efficient analysis, research, integration, and control of an insurer's data.

Metadata Repositories

Metadata are stored in a variety of places, for example in databases, applications, data models, and various business documents. This can result in a lack of cohesive management of metadata across an organization. To remedy this, many insurers have built or purchased a metadata repository.

A **metadata repository** is a database and software used to capture, manage and access metadata. It serves essentially the same purpose as a data warehouse. It is where an organization collects, integrates, standardizes, consolidates, organizes, controls, and stores its metadata, and makes them available for shared general use.

Before building or purchasing a metadata repository, an organization should consider developing a metamodel. For the present purpose, a **metamodel** is a data model for a metadata database. However, the term is also used in a broader context to refer to a high-level, conceptual model of a model. Creating a metamodel helps an organization understand its metadata requirements.

Many vendors use standards as a basis for their software to ensure compliance with accepted industry practices. There are open source providers of metamodels that are compliant with standards. The term "open source" indicates that the software can be modified or enhanced by any user. Many corporations avoid open source software because there is no guarantee of sustainability in terms of quality, versioning, and upgrades; however, these concerns do not typically apply to the use of open source models.

The Value of an Enterprise Metadata Repository

An enterprise metadata repository offers a number of benefits. First, it requires clear definitions for both business and technical metadata. This facilitates a broader understanding of business processes and the IT implementation of those processes. This, in turn, leads to an increased awareness of the cross-functional business and technical implications associated with changes in processes or systems.

A metadata repository also encourages individuals across the organization to think about metadata in a similar way, and to recognize their importance. This helps improve and preserve the consistency and quality of the organization's metadata.

From a technical perspective, system engineers and developers can simplify their research and speed system development by accessing existing metadata. This is also true for integration teams.

Finally, and perhaps most importantly, implementation of an enterprise metadata repository allows an organization to capture the tacit knowledge of its employees and to make that knowledge available for general use. Often, some individuals within an organization have a thorough understanding of its business processes, systems or data. This represents a wealth of metadata that could be lost if those individuals were to retire or leave the organization. An enterprise metadata repository provides a means for ensuring that the metadata in employees' minds is captured, preserved, and accessible.

Taken together, all of these benefits can result in:

- Reduced operating costs;
- Increased productivity;
- Improved utilization of resources; and
- Enhanced delivery of products and services.

Repository Metadata vs. Autonomous Metadata

At first glance, it would appear that centralizing all of an organization's metadata into a single repository would be the preferred approach. This would ensure consistency, integration, and control, and facilitate the sharing of metadata across the organization.

However, some, in fact much, of an organization's metadata do not need to be shared. For example, a business unit institutes a Dress Down Friday program in which employees pay a nominal amount each week for the privilege of coming to work on Fridays casually dressed. At the end of each year, the collected funds are donated to a selected charity. An administrative assistant in the business unit sets up a spreadsheet to keep track of the donations accumulated over the year. Do the business metadata in the spreadsheet need to be included in a centralized repository? Probably they do not. The metadata in the spreadsheet are locally used for a unique purpose and are not of any value to the organization as a whole. They do not need to be standardized or controlled and will not be accessed by anyone other than the administrative assistant who set up the spreadsheet. They can be autonomous or independent from the centralized metadata repository. An example of autonomous technical metadata would be the index in a table. An **index** is an ordered set of pointers to rows in a database table. Indexes are used to accelerate data access and ensure uniqueness. A particular index is used only in its associated table; including it in a centralized metadata repository would provide no benefit.

Considering the volume and complexity of an insurer's metadata, it is important to identify which metadata should remain autonomous and which need to be shared. Including autonomous metadata in the repository would significantly and unnecessarily increase the scope and cost of the repository implementation project with little or no benefit to the organization. However, within an enterprise there is also a significant volume of metadata that needs to be shared across the organization. Those metadata are appropriate for inclusion in the repository. Figure 5.6 provides an example of the information that would be included in a life insurer's metadata repository for two data elements: Conversion Indicator and Owner Age Range Classification.

Business Name	Conversion Indicator	Owner Age Range Classification
Source Table		HDLG_FULL_PROD
Source Field	Derived	HLDG_EFF_DT, BIRTH_DT
Data Field	CONV_FLAG	OWNR_AGE_RNG_CLASS
Data Type	NUM(1)	CHAR(25)
Definition	This indicates if a policy has been converted from Term to Whole Life within the period under analysis	Classification of the owner's age at the effective date of the policy.
Valid Values/ Definition	I - When the Term policy is converted 0 - When the Term policy is not converted	(<30 yrs) (30-45 yrs) (45-65 yrs) (>65 yrs) MISSING
Business Steward	Joe Smith	Joe Smith
Governance Indicator	Y	Y
Last Updated	March 20 2015	January 16 2013

Figure 5.6 Sample metadata

For repository metadata, it is important to identify where in the organization each item of metadata are "owned" and to ensure that only the owner has the authority to change the metadata. Other applications, systems, processes, or individuals must be able to access the shared metadata but cannot be allowed to change them.

Characteristics of an Enterprise Metadata Repository

A well-designed and implemented metadata repository has a number of characteristics. The repository:

- Contains metadata;
- Contains definitions of the metadata;
- Stores information in the database;
- Defines its contents by one or more metamodels;
- Provides extensibility;
- Integrates its contents;
- Enables access to metadata; and
- Facilitates population of the repository.

An essential element of a metadata repository is the quality of its definitions. Good quality definitions make metadata meaningful. For example, consider the term "deductible". "A two-byte code on the coverage screen, representing the deductible" is a poor definition. A better definition might be "The maximum amount an insured would pay in the event of a loss." However, although this is accurate for some coverages and lines of business, for others it would be incorrect. For instance, some property insurance policies include a coinsurance clause. A coinsurance clause reduces the amount of a claim settlement proportionally if the damaged building is underinsured. If a coinsurance clause applies to a loss, the insured would have to pay both the deductible and the amount by which the settlement was reduced. In addition, not all losses are paid; insurers only pay losses that are covered under a policy. Perhaps a better definition might be "The amount above which a covered loss is paid."

Writing descriptive, precise definitions can be challenging and it can be difficult to come to consensus. However, the creation of solid business data definitions is an essential part of any metadata management program. For each data element, a good definition includes:

- Its name and any alternate names;
- A precise description of what it means;
- How it is used;
- If it is derived, how it is derived;
- Where it is located in the organization's various systems; and
- Any variances in the coding structure between systems.

Business rules are also stored in the metadata repository. For example, some limits of insurance may only be available for certain coverages. Some coverage may only be available on certain lines of business. Some lines of business may not be permitted in some states. Like business definitions, business rules are owned by the business. If an organization has implemented a business rules engine, the engine should be connected to the repository. A business rules engine is software that should allow nonprogrammers to add or change business rules.

Extensibility is an essential element of a metadata repository. Its design must take future growth into consideration. Insurers are acquiring, creating, and using increasing amounts of data, all of which have associated metadata. The repository must be able to meet the organization's projected future needs.

A functional metadata repository is fully integrated and allows for tracing a metric or key performance indicator (KPI) from a report back to its original source. This benefits executives, managers, regulators, and auditors since each can see the definition of the KPI or the algorithm that created it.

The presentation layer of the repository—the way in which users access the metadata—is critical. If it is difficult to view or search the metadata, the information in the repository will not be used. Many tools today store metadata, but most do not have a facility to allow technical or business staff to view them. Design of an effective graphical user interface (GUI) is essential.

Finally, the repository needs to be designed in such a way as to facilitate its population. Some automated tools capture and load metadata to a repository. However, some metadata require user input. In either case, it is important to identify all of the elements that need to be included so that data lineages work correctly.

Architecture, Requirements, and Standards

The three most common architectural approaches to shared metadata are:

- Centralizing the metadata;
- Leaving the metadata in distributed systems; or
- A hybrid of the two approaches.

A centralized metadata repository has many advantages. It contains copies of the metadata from source systems, and because it is independent of source systems, the metadata are readily available and can be accessed quickly. The metadata in the repository can also be enhanced by the addition of metadata that exist outside the source systems, for example in organizational memory. However, maintaining a centralized metadata repository and keeping it synchronized with source systems can be challenging. In addition, extracting metadata from the repository may require additional software, and any customization of off-the-shelf products requires additional IT resources.

In a distributed metadata architecture, users access the metadata through a single portal and the retrieval engine brings the metadata directly from the source systems. A retrieval engine is the software that finds and delivers the metadata to the user. In a distributed metadata environment, metadata are always current and valid without the need for the replication and synchronization required in a centralized metadata repository. The disadvantage of a distributed architecture is that, if the source systems are busy, it can negatively impact metadata queries. Also, this architecture does not allow for the inclusion of metadata from outside of source systems because there is no repository in which to place it.

A hybrid metadata architecture offers the benefits of both the centralized and distributed architectures. In a hybrid architecture, much of the metadata comes directly from source systems as is the case with a distributed metadata architecture. However, a hybrid also allows for a limited repository in which to capture and share metadata that does not reside in source systems.

Regardless of the architecture, the scope of a metadata repository implementation is an important consideration. Although an enterprise view would be the ultimate goal, it may not initially be practical. For example, in an insurance conglomerate, property and casualty operations may be separate from life and health operations. If systems and funding for projects are siloed in this way, successfully launching an enterprise-wide initiative would be challenging. Some large insurers have separate metadata repositories for specific lines of business implemented with different architectures and different vendors' systems. This can make consolidation difficult. As with many enterprise level implementations, it may be beneficial to start on a smaller scale and grow the repository gradually. However, even this staged approach should have enterprise architecture oversight and involve the services of data management and metadata management experts.

One approach to building a viewable metadata repository is to use wiki web pages as the viewing mechanism. Wiki software supports a large number of editable, interlinked web pages that can be viewed with any browser. A wiki allows users to easily view, add, and update content. This facilitates contribution by many people. For example, wikis can support the development of business definitions by data stewards. The disadvantage with this approach is that the wiki can become a storage facility for irrelevant or seldom used information. As more people become familiar with wiki capabilities, and as the use of collaborative applications becomes more prevalent, a wiki-based viewing and updating approach can support a fully functional metadata repository.

Another common form of presenting metadata is through spreadsheets. Although spreadsheets were originally developed to mimic a paper accounting ledger, they have become a dominant choice for documentation during a software project lifecycle. Examples of spreadsheet artifacts may include a requirements list, glossary of terms, data mapping spreadsheet, or business rules list. There are two major problems with using spreadsheets, especially at the project level. There is not usually a long-term maintenance strategy for spreadsheets, and they are not collaborative tools.

Paper manuals, for example data dictionaries for legacy systems, are still used for reference. However, there are typically significant gaps in the maintenance of these documents. Reliance on paper manuals or static online manuals should be discouraged.

Business intelligence (BI) tools are not only a good source of metadata; they can also be used as an interface to the metadata repository. Many fully functional metadata repository tools come with access capability for casual users across the enterprise. For those that do not offer a viewer, and for custom built repositories, a BI query tool can be used with the metadata repository just as with any other database.

Extract, transform, and load (ETL) tools incorporate metadata. These metadata should be loaded into the repository using the ETL functions. Some ETL products include a basic metadata management function as part of the product, but this is usually less robust than a fully functional repository. As well, the metadata from an ETL application is usually restricted to the ETL operations.

Since technical metadata can become extremely complex, several organizations publish standards that help control the variability of metadata. These organizations offer recommended models, taxonomies, and data dictionaries that can be used as the foundation for a metadata management program. If an organization chooses to build a custom metadata repository, using these standards can reduce the amount of work associated with the repository's design and architecture. If an organization decides to purchase a metadata repository tool, it is best to find one that is compliant with the latest technical standards, has an open architecture to allow customization, and has been based on common metamodel standards.

Standards and policies in insurance metadata follow many of the non-industry specific standards such as those from Object Management Group (OMG) and Dublin Core. ACORD has collaborated with these groups to offer standards for insurance XML (extensible markup language) tags, and to support the development of an industry standard enterprise data model that includes a related metamodel.

Challenges of Implementing a Metadata Repository

There are several challenges associated with the implementation of a metadata repository. The effective administration of metadata relies on people who are knowledgeable in the areas of data quality management, content management, database management, and other data management functions, and who are familiar with metadata management tools. Individuals with this collection of skills can be difficult to find.

Implementation of metadata management among insurers is not standardized or consistent. And while several off-the-shelf tools exist for metadata repository management, none currently meet all of an insurer's needs. They generally require customization.

Because of the quantity and variety of both structured and unstructured metadata, determining which metadata to include and populating the repository can be significant tasks. As well, defining the access requirements for business users and developing a user interface that presents metadata in a meaningful way can be challenging.

In addition, a repository requires ongoing management and maintenance. Business rules and metadata requirements and definitions change over time. Effective governance is required to ensure that the responsibility for making changes to the repository is clearly assigned, and that administrative functions such as security, versioning, change management, quality audits, and backups are well managed.

Buying or Building a Metadata Repository

Off-the-shelf metadata repository management software is available. Organizations need to consider whether to purchase a vendor's product or to develop their own proprietary system. The principle considerations are:

- Capabilities;
- Cost;
- Customization; and
- Culture.

The essential first step in deciding whether to buy or to build a metadata repository management system is to clearly define the organization's requirements. To properly evaluate off-the-shelf products—or to develop the systems in-house—an organization needs to have a clear understanding of what capabilities their metadata repository system needs in order to meet users' requirements.

Depending on the size of the organization and the complexity of its requirements, the cost of an off-the-shelf system can be significant. However, the cost of developing systems in-house can be as well. IT projects can, at times, run over budget before successful implementation. Typically, an off-the-shelf product will not meet all of an organization's needs. It will require some degree of customization, which can increase the cost of both implementing and maintaining an off-the-shelf solution. Understanding the users' requirements, and mapping them to the capabilities of off-the-shelf products, help IT professionals identify the level of customization that would be required. That can then be factored into the cost of the vendor's product. A cost-benefit analysis can help determine whether to buy or to build would be the better approach for a particular organization.

Finally, some organizations prefer to purchase ready-made solutions while others prefer to develop solutions internally. An organization's culture can sometimes have a significant impact on the decision to buy or build a system.

Summary

Metadata are business and technical information about an organization's data. They describe the content, quality, condition, and other attributes of the data, and the structure of the database. They include the definition of each data element, its characteristics and data type, the size of each field, the source system from which the data came, and any transformations the data have undergone. In fact, it could almost be said that data are data and everything else is metadata.

Managing metadata can be challenging because they are typically found in both structured and unstructured form throughout an organization. Business terms often have ambiguous or conflicting definitions. Insurers use third party data, for which metadata may be limited or unclear. Semantics involves clearly defining the business and technical terms used within an organization and documenting them. Taxonomy is the process of classifying things based on their characteristics or relationships. Semantics and taxonomy are essential elements in developing robust, structured metadata.

Metadata can be categorized as business, technical, operational, process, or data stewardship metadata. Unstructured metadata are characterized as descriptive, technical/structural, or administrative. High quality metadata allow an organization to find, access, categorize, transform, analyze, interpret, use, and reuse data; understand and have confidence in its data; create and share information; and communicate more effectively. Metadata can document data lineage. Data lineage is useful in regulatory compliance; resolving data integrity issues; identifying the impact of system or process changes; protecting sensitive or confidential data; and reducing data collection, storage and dispersal costs.

Metadata are used and relied upon by systems and individuals throughout an organization. A well-crafted metadata strategy can result in increased recognition of the importance of data and metadata quality; integration of sound metadata management practices; an enhanced ability to derive information from operational data; a shared business vocabulary; and a framework for meeting future information needs. However, a metadata strategy requires commitment at the executive level. It may necessitate a cultural shift or internal reengineering, which can meet with resistance. Scoping is essential because of the volume of metadata. Implementation of a metadata strategy requires a variety of resources and the active participation of the business users of data.

One important element of a metadata strategy is the implementation of a metadata repository. One important consideration when implementing a repository is which metadata should be included and which metadata should be autonomous. A good metadata repository contains definitions of metadata and stores them in a database. Its contents are defined by one or more metamodels. It is extensible, integrates its contents, and facilitates access to metadata and population of the repository. Its architecture can be centralized, distributed, or a hybrid of the two. Several organizations publish standards that help control the variability of metadata. These organizations offer models, taxonomies, and data dictionaries that can be used as the foundation for a metadata management program.

Managing a metadata repository requires individuals with a skill set that can be difficult to find. While repository management products are available, they typically require customization. Determining which metadata to include and populating the repository can be significant tasks. User access requirements need to be determined and an appropriate user interface developed. A repository requires ongoing maintenance to be useful. Finally, when determining whether to purchase a repository management system or develop a system in-house, the considerations include the required system capabilities, the cost, any required customization, and the organization's culture.

Bibliography

The DAMA Dictionary of Data Management, First Edition 2008, Mark Mosley Editor, Technics Publications LLC, New Jersey, copyright 2008 DAMA International.

The DAMA Guide to the Data Management Body of Knowledge (DAMA-DMBOK) First Edition, DAMA International, Technics Publications LLC, New Jersey, copyright 2009 DAMA International.

Fundamentals of Database Management Systems, 2nd Edition, Mark L. Gillenson, Fogelman College of Business and Economics, University of Memphis, published by John Wiley & Sons, Inc., printed and bound by RR Donnelley, copyright 2012, 2005 by John Wiley & Sons, ISBN 978-0-470-62470-8.

Business Metadata Capturing Enterprise Knowledge, William Inmon, Bonnie O'Neil, Lowell Fryman, Elseveir, 2008, Morgan Kaufmann Publishers 30 Corporate Drive, Suite 400, Burlington, MA 01803, USA, 2008 by Elsevier Inc. ISBN: 978-0-12-373726-7.

How Important Is Metadata To An Information Management Strategy? By Ian Thomas on Aug 31, 2013, viewed at http://bit.ly/2saZe8I (accessed March 11, 2015).

Why Metadata is Important to the Business, July 16, 2013, Steven MacLauchlan, viewed at http://bit.ly/2txoCmZ (accessed March 11, 2015).

On the Importance of Metadata, September 7, 2010, Craig Mullins, viewed at http://bit.ly/2sJ4DFb (accessed March 11, 2015).

Challenges to Managing Metadata, Jan 12, 2013, Craig Mullins, viewed at http://bit.ly/2sbmxzr (accessed March 11, 2015).

Strategic and Tactical Issues in Metadata Management, by Ian Rowlands viewed at http://bit.ly/2txiqv1 (accessed March 11, 2015).

The benefits of metadata and implementing a metadata management strategy, By: Alex Berson and Larry Dubov, viewed at http://bit.ly/2sD1aIm (accessed March 11, 2015).

Data's Credibility Problem, by Thomas C. Redman Ph.d., From the December 2013 Issue Harard Business Review, viewed at http://bit.ly/2rBlTwf (accessed March 11, 2015).

Data Lineage: An Important First Step for Data Governance, by Saurabh Jain, Binu Thomson, Originally published August 1, 2013, viewed at http://bit.ly/2slg4Qw (accessed March 16, 2015).

Data Lineage, by Cory Jannsen viewed at http://bit.ly/2sIG6Qm (accessed March 16, 2015).

Why data lineage is your secret data quality weapon, by Dylan Jones, March 8, 2013, viewed at http://bit.ly/2rG77Q0 (accessed March 16, 2015).

Turning Data into Knowledge: Creating and Implementing a Meta Data Strategy, Anne Marie Smith, Ph.D. Director of Education, Principal Consultant, EWSolutions, viewed at http://bit.ly/2szNkGe (accessed March 16, 2015).

Meta Data Architecture Fundamentals, by David Marco, Published: October 1, 2001, viewed at http://bit.ly/2sDk3ei (accessed March 8, 2015).

Taxonomies Defined, by Sharee English, Apr 26, 2009 viewed at http://bit.ly/2sbeDWJ (accessed March 23, 2015).

To Buy a Repository Or Not to Buy a Repository? That is the Question...Here is the Answer, by David Marco, April 1, 2002, viewed at http://bit.ly/2sIIDdH (accessed March 24, 2015).

Corporate Information Factory, William H. Inmon Ryan Sousa, The Metadata Component, viewed at http://dssresources.com/dssbookstore/cifexcerpt.html (accessed March 26, 2015).

Enterprise information portal (EIP), by Margaret Rouse, viewed at http://bit.ly/2txvX5Y (accessed March 27, 2015).

What is Open Source? viewed at http://red.ht/1jejJEk (accessed March 27, 2015).

The Whodunit of Big Data, by Peter Marotta, Risk & Insurance, September 15, 2013, viewed athttp://bit.ly/2sA4t2h (accessed January 26, 2016).

Reference Data and Master Data Management

The previous chapter introduced metadata and metadata management. This chapter introduces two additional types of data: reference data and master data. Reference data can be categorized based on the way in which they are structured. Master data can be classified in a variety of ways depending upon an organization's needs. As is the case with any data, effective management is essential to ensure the quality and integrity of reference data and master data.

Reference data management (RDM) focuses on standardizing the codes referred to and used by application systems. This supports data integration. Master data management (MDM) focuses on creating a single, accurate, complete, consistent, and standard set of attributes for each entity. Both RDM and MDM involve a number of activities. Organizations can either purchase or build the set of tools required to complete these activities. An important function of these tools is to help identify, match, and integrate multiple records that, in fact, represent the same entity. These records can come from different sources or from a single source. Duplicate records are identified in a variety of ways based on predetermined matching rules. Both RDM and MDM can be challenging; however, they are both essential, ongoing elements of overall data quality improvement.

Educational Objectives

Upon completion of this assignment, you should be able to:

1. Define reference data.
2. Describe the various types of reference data and value domains. Provide examples of each.
3. Define master data.
4. Describe the various types of master data. Provide an example of each.
5. Describe the differences between reference data and master data.
6. Define the concept of golden records and describe their importance.
7. Describe the most common drivers of reference data and master data management.
8. Describe the activities in implementing reference data and master data management.
9. Define entity resolution.
10. List and define the types of matching rules and their uses.
11. Describe the challenges in implementing reference data and master data management.

12. Explain the principles of implementing reference data and master data management functions into an organization.

13. Explain how reference data and master data contribute to data integrity and quality.

Reference Data and Master Data

Earlier chapters discussed how redundant data, replicated across multiple, non-integrated systems and information silos, can result in significant data quality and integrity problems, particularly for large multi-national organizations. Effective management of two types of data called reference data and master data can help an organization resolve these issues.

Reference Data

Reference data have been described in a variety of ways by data management theorists. For the current purpose, they can be defined as data that are referred to, or read, by business applications but are not updated or altered by those applications. They are commonly stored in look-up or code tables. They define the domain, or set of valid values, for a data element and include a brief description of each. They can be created and defined internally; however, they can also be sourced externally.

Reference data can be categorized based on the way in which they are structured:

- Simple lists of codes and descriptions
- Taxonomies indicating relationships
- Tables revealing multiple attributes of a single entity type
- Code translation or mapping tables

The International Organization for Standardization's (ISO) currency codes provide an example of a simple list of reference data. This ISO standard defines a unique identifier for each official monetary currency. A multinational insurer's systems may use these ISO codes internally. However, on computer screens, reports, or policy documents a more meaningful description would be substituted for the code. The insurer's systems would refer to a look-up table to find the correct description associated with a given currency code. Figure 6.1 illustrates a simple currency code table.[46] In this table, CurrencyCode is the primary key; it is a foreign key in the referring table.

Even this simple approach to reference data allows an organization to:

- Standardize terms for frequently used data ("United States Dollars", "Mexican Pesos");
- Electronically store those terms in a short-hand version (USD, MXN); and
- Interpret data more consistently.

---

[46] Excerpted from ISO 4217 Currency Codes, viewed at http://www.xe.xom/iso4217.php (accessed April 12, 2015).

CurrencyCode	CurrencyDescription
CAD	Canadian Dollars
CHF	Switzerland Francs
GBP	United Kingdom Pounds
MXN	Mexican Pesos
USD	United States Dollars

Figure 6.1 ISO currency code examples

Figure 6.2 illustrates how a simple list of codes might be used to indicate the changing status of insurance claims. In this case, the reference data would have been created internally rather than obtained from an external source, and they would reflect the organization's business rules. The addition of definitions that might, for example, be accessible through an on-screen Help function, facilitates consistent use of the codes and clearer understanding of the status descriptions.

StatusCode	Description	Definition
1	New	The claim has been received but not assigned to an adjuster.
2	Assigned	The claim has been assigned to an adjuster.
3	In Progress	The assigned adjuster is currently investigating the claim.
4	Confirmed	The adjuster has determined that the claim is covered.
5	Denied	The adjuster has denied the claim because it is not covered.
6	Valued	The adjuster has determined the claim settlement amount.
7	Settled	The claimant has received payment and signed a release form.
8	Closed	The claim has been finalized and the claim file is closed.
9	SIU	The file has been sent to the Special Investigation Unit due to suspected fraud.

Figure 6.2 Claim status code examples

In this example, the status codes need not be mutually exclusive. For example, a claim may be assigned, or in progress and referred to the SIU for investigation. If the SIU determines the claim to be fraudulent, it will be denied and the case referred to the authorities. If the SIU determines the claim is not fraudulent, the adjuster could proceed to value and pay the claim.

Reference data can also indicate hierarchical relationships, called taxonomies. The North American Industry Classification System (NAICS) codes are a good example. They classify industries into broad categories using the initial two digits of the code. For example, the initial digits 21 represent Mining industries, Utilities have codes beginning with 22, Construction (23), Manufacturing (31 – 33), Wholesale Trade (42), Retail Trade (44 – 45) and others. The different types of companies that make up the general category are listed and the codes are refined to indicate how they are related. Figure 6.3 illustrates how NAICS codes categorize and clarify relationships among different types of insurance organizations.

CodeValue	Description	ParentCode
52	Finance and Insurance	52
524	Insurance Carriers and Related Activities	52
5241	Insurance Carriers	524
52411	Direct Life, Health, and Medical Insurance Carriers	5241
524113	Direct Life Insurance Carriers	52411
5242	Agencies, Brokerages, and Other Insurance Related Activities	524

Figure 6.3 NAICS code examples, viewed at http://bit.ly/2rpS1yE (accessed May 5, 2015)

Some reference tables include multiple attributes of a single entity type. For example, an organization may have different categories of employees, some of whom are entitled to benefits and a pension and others of whom are not. Figure 6.4 illustrates how a reference table could be used to determine an employee's status and eligibility for benefits or pension based on an Employee Code.

EmployeeCode	FullTimeIndicator	PartTimeIndicator	BenefitsIndicator	PensionIndicator
A	Yes	No	Yes	Yes
B	Yes	No	Yes	No
C	Yes	No	No	No
D	No	Yes	Yes	Yes
E	No	Yes	Yes	No
F	No	Yes	No	No

Figure 6.4 Multiple attributes of an entity

Finally, reference data can map codes used by one system to those used by another. Often the same data element is expressed differently from system to system. State codes are a good example. They have been defined by a number of organizations including the United States Postal Service (USPS), the International Organization for Standardization (ISO), and the United States' Federal Information Processing Standard (FIPS). For example, the USPS code for Iowa is IA, the ISO code is US-IA, and the FIPS code is 19. Some systems use USPS codes or ISO codes; others use FIPS codes. Reference tables allow for translation from one system's code to another's.

The reference data illustrated in Figures 6.1 through 6.4 are all simple, structured data. However, reference data can also be semi-structured, and even unstructured, such as images or audio clips. For example, in an online retailer's customer interface system, reference data could be used to retrieve and display images of products.

Master Data

Master data are data about those things that are essential to an organization's operations or core business processes. They include data about the structure of the enterprise, its assets, its products and services, and the participants in its various transactions. An insurer's master data would include data about insureds, products and services, agents and brokers, employees, competitors, reinsurers, divisions or departments, geographic territories, profit centers, and its chart of accounts (i.e., the data used to create balance sheets and income statements).

Master data differ from **transactional data**, which are data about specific events. Consider the sentence "John Smith purchased a Platinum Protection policy through Anytown Insurance Brokers." Data about "John Smith", "Platinum Protection policy", and "Anytown Insurance Brokers" would be master data. Data about "purchased" would be transactional data.

An example of master data categorizations are the following:

- Party master data;
- Product master data;
- Financial master data; and
- Geographic master data.

Party master data would be data about the people and organizations that are essential to the enterprise's core business. For an insurer, party master data would include data about employees, insureds, agents and brokers, affiliates, competitors, and reinsurers.

Product master data would be data about an organization's products and services. They may also include data about the products and services offered by competitors as well. For insurers, product master data include data about insurance policies and endorsements, loss control services, risk management consulting services, underwriting guidelines, claim settlement practices, line limits, agent and broker training, and ratemaking practices.

Financial master data include such things as data in general ledger accounts, budgets, data about profit centers, financial projections, and projects' calculated return on investment (ROI). Insurers have many of the same types of financial master data as other businesses, but there are some that are specific to the insurance industry. These would include, for example, the various financial ratios used to evaluate insurers' performance, some of which are illustrated in Figure 6.5. NOTE: These ratios are discussed in more detail in a subsequent course, IDMA 202.

Geographic master data include, for example, the addresses and locations of the various parties with whom an organization interacts, or the hierarchical structure of its business units, territories, and regions. Insurers have additional requirements for geographic master data that other industries may not have. For example, insurers need to identify areas prone to windstorm, flood, earthquake, land subsidence, and arson or terrorism. As well, they need to map the locations of buildings they insure, particularly large commercial properties in urban centers to avoid a concentration of risk that could expose them to a catastrophic loss.

Depending on the industry in which it operates, and what specifically it considers essential to its core business, an organization may identify other master data requirements or categorize their master data differently. An insurance company might focus on developing good quality master data in three areas: clients, products, and producers. Other organizations may concentrate on master data about their assets. For example, a large trucking firm would require quality master data about its vehicles including mileage, usage, and maintenance schedules. A large property management firm would need high quality master data about its properties and buildings.

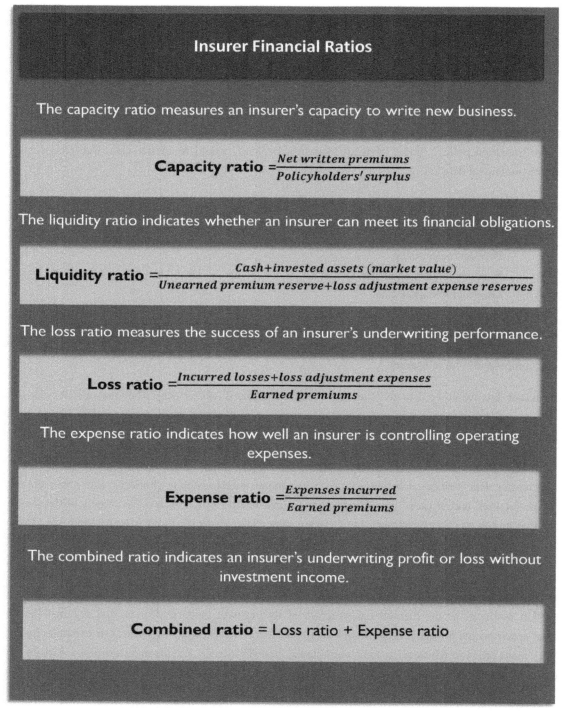

Figure 6.5 Insurer financial ratios

Differences Between Reference and Master Data

Reference data and master data differ in a number of ways. Organizations typically have a lower volume of reference data than master data, and reference data are simpler. Reference data tend not to change, or to change slowly. Master data are more complex and far more changeable. For example, insureds move or change their names.

Reference data are often limited to a relatively small domain. For example, the set of valid values in the Claim Status Codes table in Figure 6.2 is limited to the digits one through nine. In the case of master data, the set of valid values for an attribute can be unlimited (e.g. "Insured Name").

While reference data may be developed internally, they are often obtained from outside sources and are widely used by many different organizations. The International Standards Organization (ISO) currency codes, NAICS industry classification codes, and ZIP codes are all examples of externally sourced reference data that are defined by the organizations that create them. Master data, on the other hand, are generally defined and used internally.

Finally, it can be challenging to reach consensus across an organization as to the definition of master data elements. For example, a claims adjuster might consider an individual to be a "customer" only if that individual were an insured; however, a producer might consider a sales prospect to be a "customer".

The Golden Record

The concept of a "golden record" can be illustrated graphically. Figure 6.6 shows how data can differ among various systems within an organization and how those data can be used to create a "golden record". In this case, it is information about a customer, Joanne Record, but it could be any kind of information.

The data in System A came from a broker's agency management system via electronic data interchange (EDI). The data in System B came from an automobile claim in which Joanne was slightly injured while a passenger in another insured's vehicle. Joanne input the data in System C online, looking for a premium quote on a new automobile. The data in System D were input from a call center when she telephoned for a life insurance quote. The call center employee misunderstood Joanne's name and entered it incorrectly.

A "**golden record**" is a single, complete, accurate, current, and unique set of attributes for an entity, in this case, Joanne Gayle Record. It results when replicated data about that entity are identified and matched, aggregated, corrected, and standardized. These then become the organization's "golden record" of master data. Ideally, they can be shared among all systems across the organization.

There is a variety of tools and techniques for creating "golden records", several of which are discussed later in this chapter. In the case of Joanne Record, a quick call to her broker could help resolve any questions. On a single file this approach would not be onerous, but on an entire book of business it would be highly inefficient. Address correction and verification software is one type of tool used to create "golden records". It helps ensure the accuracy and standardization of address information across an organization.

Figure 6.6 The golden record

Although a "golden record" is the ideal, there are occasions in which the various "non-golden" versions of a record become important. During fraud detection and investigation, the ability to identify the various alternative names and addresses an individual has used, for example in a series of claims, would be essential.

Drivers of Reference Data and Master Data Management

The *DAMA-DMBOK* states that "The two most common drivers of reference and master data management are:

- Improving data quality and integration across data sources, applications, and technologies; and

- Providing a consolidated 360-degree view of information about important business parties, roles, and products, particularly for more effective reporting and analytics."

Reference Data and Master Data Management Activities

Implementing reference and master data management involves a number of activities:

1. Understanding reference and master data integration needs
2. Identifying master and reference data sources and contributors
3. Defining and maintaining the data integration architecture
4. Implementing reference and master data management solutions
5. Defining and maintaining matching rules
6. Establishing "golden" records
7. Defining and maintaining hierarchies and affiliations
8. Planning and implementing integration of new data sources
9. Replicating and distributing reference and master data
10. Managing changes to reference and master data[47]

Reference Data Management

Reference data management (RDM) entails identifying or creating "golden records" of reference data for shared use across an organization. RDM's focus is on the codes for, descriptions and definitions of, and relationships among, the organization's internally developed and externally sourced reference data.

Standardized reference data are an important element in data integration efforts and they facilitate the sharing of information. In RDM, data managers or business data stewards attempt to reduce or eliminate variances and inconsistencies in reference data, and to accurately map those system-specific reference data that cannot be standardized. They maintain lists of valid reference data values or codes, and manage their business meanings as controlled vocabularies. A **controlled vocabulary** is simply a set of agreed upon terms that are clearly defined, consistently used, and formally managed with rules about how terms are added, modified, or deleted. One feature of a controlled vocabulary is its ability to indicate relationships between things. Data managers and business data stewards work to clarify hierarchical relationships and affiliations among terms in the vocabulary.

Integrating reference data within a single system is a relatively simple process. Although the ideal would be to integrate reference data among all applications across an enterprise, that can be challenging. Successful reference data management often involves focusing on one area at a time and working incrementally to integrate reference data system by system. However, it is important to develop an understanding of an organization's reference data needs across the enterprise as a whole in order to plan for, implement, and maintain successful integration initiatives. An important part of this involves tracing the lineage of reference data to determine where they are created and maintained as well as to identify all of the downstream systems that access and use them.

There are several approaches to reference data integration. In some cases, a single high quality source can be identified and selected as the system of record for many reference data sets. A **system of record** is the authoritative

---

[47] Ibid p. 172.

source of trustworthy data; it is the only system authorized to change those data, although other systems may access them. Figure 6.7 illustrates this type of reference data architecture.

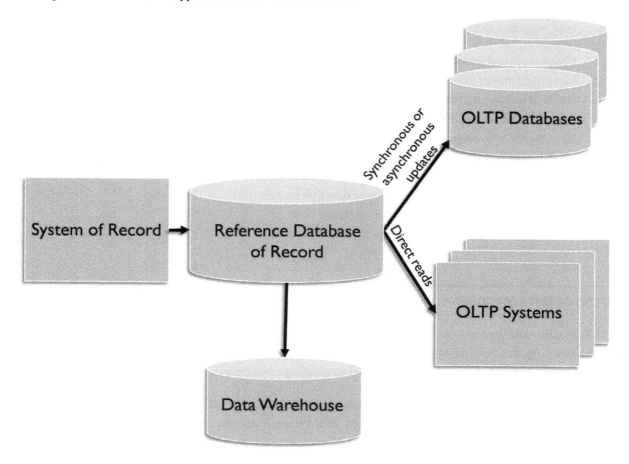

Figure 6.7 Reference data architecture example

In this case, the system of record provides the content for a database of reference data, sometimes referred to as a reference data "hub". This acts as the source of reference data for online transaction processing (OLTP) systems, for example, the underwriting system, policy issuance system, billing system, or claims system, and their associated databases. The database of record is also the source of reference data for the data warehouse and business intelligence (BI) applications.

Applications using these data access them in different ways. They can read reference data directly from the database of record, or they can receive copies of the reference data from it and store them locally. The database of record can update replicated data in real time through synchronous updates, or in near-real time through asynchronous updates.

Although this approach would be ideal, in reality, many organizations have inconsistent reference data among their various application systems. As a result, RDM becomes an ongoing data improvement process. RDM tools are available in the marketplace to assist with that process. Analysis of an enterprise's RDM needs and an evaluation of the capabilities of the various RDM tools will help to identify the most appropriate RDM solution, or solutions, to implement.

Usually, reference data change relatively slowly. However, in the case of a merger or acquisition, for example, it may become necessary to integrate reference data from a new source. In addition, modifications to externally sourced reference data could result in significant changes. Integration of new reference data and changes to existing reference data require careful analysis and planning. Data managers and business data stewards work with IT professionals to manage these changes. In either case, a formal process that involves all stakeholders is critical. Retaining earlier versions and mapping them to the current version of reference data is essential to support analysis of historical data.

Master Data Management

Master data management (MDM) is the process of defining how master data will be created, maintained, and integrated for general use; implementing appropriate governance, technologies and procedures; and maintaining ongoing master data quality. It is a set of processes and technologies that help enterprises better manage their master data flow, integrity, and synchronization.

As is the case with reference data management, master data management is generally more successful when it is implemented incrementally, one area at a time. Any organization initiating a master data management program needs first to determine:

- Which master data should be managed;
- How those master data will be used;
- Who the creators and consumers of the master data are;
- What the most appropriate architecture might be; and
- In which area to begin implementation.

Developing high quality master data involves three steps:

1. Cleansing and standardizing the organization's data
2. Identifying replicated records from multiple sources, or within the same source
3. Resolving replicated records into a "golden record".

After these steps have been completed, the resulting high quality master data can be made available for use in applications across the organization.

The process of cleansing, or "scrubbing", and standardizing data is similar to the extract, transform, and load (ETL) processes used for data in a data warehouse. MDM tools typically support these functions. Cleansing and standardizing facilitate identification of replicated data records.

MDM tools and the data scrubbing tools used for data warehouses often include **inference engines** that can be used to help identify matching records. An inference engine is essentially software that applies rules to existing information to infer, or deduce, new information. For example, an inference engine might include the rule that if the names, birth dates, and Social Security numbers for two different records match, then those records are duplicates and they can be merged.

MDM tools need to be able to capture and illustrate the relationships among the various master data categories. These relationships can be affiliations or hierarchies. Affiliations can be attachments or memberships. For example, data about an employee is party master data. Data about the products that employee is authorized to sell is product master data. There needs to be a link between the employee and the products he or she sells. Data about a brokerage is party master data. Data about the sales territory in which that brokerage is located is geographic master data. Again, there needs to be a link between the brokerage and the territory.

As an example of a hierarchical relationship, Business Unit A is in Territory 8, which is located in the Northwest Region of Country C. Master data about the business unit, the territory, the region, and the country are all geographic master data, but they need to be hierarchically linked. The establishment and maintenance of relationships between master data records is referred to as **affiliation management**.

An organization can either buy or build a set of MDM tools to help manage different types of master data. Customer data integration (CDI) tools manage customer master data. Enterprise resource planning (ERP) tools manage financial master data. Product information management (PIM) tools manage product master data. Human resource management (HRM) tools manage employee master data. Some tools can manage several types of master data. The selection of the appropriate tool set depends on the needs of the organization.

Entity resolution is the identification of records, either from the same source or from different sources, that represent the same entity and the integration of them into a single representation of that entity. In the example in Figure 6.6, it involves recognizing that Joanne G. Record, Joanne Gayle Record, Ms. Jo Record, and Joan Record are in fact the same person and creating a single complete and accurate depiction of her. This then becomes the organization's "golden record" master data about Joanne Record.

Entity resolution is the most important step in creating quality master data and it can be the most challenging, particularly when it involves individuals such as customers. For example, is it safe to assume that Ms. Jo Record and Joanne G. Record are the same person simply because they both live at 123 4th Street? Jo could be Joanne, but she could also be Josephine, Joanne's daughter. Is it safe to assume that Joan Record and Joanne Record are different people living in the same household because their names are different? In this case it would not; the difference in names is simply the result of a misunderstanding.

The precision of matching rules is critical. If actual matches go unidentified, then data redundancy goes unresolved and a single "golden record" is not created for those entities. If records are matched incorrectly, then data integrity is lost. Let's say that an insurer deals with two brokerages that coincidentally have the same name. One is SaveAll Insurance located in Erie, Pennsylvania; the other is SaveAll Insurance located in Savana, Georgia. If the two brokerages are mistakenly matched based solely on the name and are merged, important data would be lost. As a result, it is essential when merging records to retain the previous unmatched versions so that if inappropriate matches are identified they can be reversed.

There are three types of, or approaches to, matching rules:

- Duplicate identification matching rules;
- Match-merge rules; and
- Match-link rules.

All three approaches serve essentially the same purpose. They support entity resolution and the establishment of a "golden record" of master data for each entity. **Duplicate identification matching rules** use a specified set of attributes that uniquely identify an entity, for example, name, birth date, and Social Security number, to discover duplicate records. Records that are determined to be matches are not automatically merged. Rather, data managers or business data stewards review them and decide whether or not they are in fact duplicates and should be merged. While this approach may be time-consuming, it can help avoid matching records incorrectly and the resulting loss of data integrity.

Match-merge rules compare records based on specified criteria and then automatically merge the data from matching records into a single consolidated record. Typically matches are merged when confidence in the match is above a predetermined level. For example, if 95 percent of data elements in two records match, they could be deemed to be duplicates and merged. A 75 percent match could be judged not to be duplicates. Data from the merged master record can supplement or correct data in the source records. For example, in Figure 6.6, data from the "golden record" for Joanne Gayle Record could be used to correct and update her information in Systems A, B, C, and D. Alternatively, Systems A, B, C, and D could access her record from a central source of master data. While the match-merge approach can be efficient, it is highly complex and there is a risk that if records are matched incorrectly, other unrelated records can be changed inappropriately.

Match-link rules compare other records to a selected record to identify possible matches. These are linked to the selected record using a cross-reference table, creating a virtual master record. This approach is simpler than match-merge and does not change the data in the cross-referenced records.

MDM architecture can take a number of forms. In one approach, a system of record is identified for each subject area. For example, customer data integration (CDI) systems manage and maintain accurate and current information about customers. The CDI could be the system of record for customer master data. Other systems would be identified as the system of record for other types, for example, financial, employee, product, or geographic master data. The challenge with this approach is that it becomes quite complex.

Figure 6.8 illustrates an alternative approach. In this case, the various systems of record feed master data for their particular subject area to a master data operational data store (ODS), or "hub", and obtain master data about other subject areas from it. An **operational data store (ODS)** is a vehicle for integrating disparate data from different operational systems. With this approach, an application could use the ODS rather than maintain a database of its own (e.g. System of Record A) and read master data directly from it. Systems that maintain their own database can read master data directly from the ODS or obtain copies of master data from it for local storage.

RDM and MDM present some challenges. With reference data, the principle challenge is mapping different types of externally sourced codes and mapping internal codes from different data sources. For example, the North American Industry Classification System (NAICS) codes differ from the European Industrial Activity Classification (NACE) codes. While the NAICS code for "Finance and Insurance" is 52, the NACE code for "Financial and Insurance Activities" is K. In addition, the NACE codes are more high-level, or less granular, than the NAICS codes. For example, NACE codes categorize "Financial and Insurance" as part of "Maintenance Services, Customer Support Centers, Purchasing Services, and Logistical Services".

A multinational organization needs to be able to accurately map a large volume of interrelated codes and make a determination as to the level of data required. Complicating this further, different applications often use different reference data internally. This adds to the challenge of reference data management because of the time and effort involved in mapping and reconciling codes from various applications. Finally, the definitions or categorization of externally sourced reference data may differ (e.g. NAICS and NACE categorization of "Finance and Insurance"). It is important to identify and document those differences.

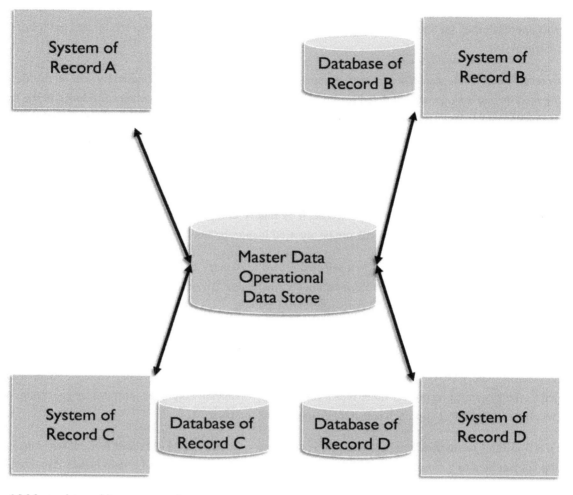

Figure 6.8 Master data architecture example

Challenges in Reference and Master Data Management

In the case of master data management, the principle challenges lie in identifying the one "golden record" from among multiple, often conflicting records, and then using that record rather than other, less accurate ones in all systems across the organization.

Data managers and business data stewards work with IT professionals to enhance the quality of an organization's master data. In some situations, it becomes necessary to change or add to master data. For example, an insurer that had been operating in a centralized environment may restructure to get closer to its customers, and open a number of regional offices across the country. That organization's geographic master data would change. If an insurer that had previously offered only commercial lines products begins offering personal lines products as well, its products master data would change. As is the case with reference data, changes to master data need a formal process and careful management.

Principles in Implementing Reference and Master Data Management

In a December 2011 Tech News World article *"The 5 Pillars of Master Data Management"*, author David Corrigan outlined five principles that can help organizations succeed in their MDM initiatives. These same principles can also be applied to reference data management:

1. Define your business problem
2. Plan beyond phase one to ensure success
3. To succeed, MDM needs a strong governance program in place
4. Recognize that the most important word in MDM is management
5. Partner with an IT vendor who has significant MDM and information governance experience[48]

Rather than concentrating simply on reference data and master data, a successful initiative focuses on applications and business processes. It works to identify the reasons why the organization's reference and master data are not of the required quality and resolve those issues at their source.

Reference data management and master data management are ongoing, iterative processes. An RDM or MDM plan should function in essentially the same way as a strategic plan. It should describe a desired future state and outline the incremental steps to be taken to reach that state. The plan should be reviewed and updated periodically to ensure that the organization continues to improve its RDM and MDM capabilities.

Effective data governance is an essential element of both reference and master data management. It helps to ensure that RDM and MDM are organizational processes rather than IT processes and encourages the participation and involvement of all stakeholders.

RDM and MDM involve systems and technologies, business processes and rules, and the cooperation and collaboration of individuals. All of these need to be effectively managed to ensure the success of RDM and MDM programs.

Each industry can have its own RDM and MDM requirements and the insurance industry is no exception. When purchasing RDM or MDM tools it is important to work with a vendor who understands the particular needs of the insurance industry.

Data Integrity and Quality

Data integrity refers to the accuracy, uniformity, and reliability of the values used to store and manipulate data. Data that have integrity conform to established standards, formats, and business rules. Earlier chapters discussed the costs associated with poor quality data.

---

[48] The 5 Pillars of Master Data Management, by David Corrigan, December 21 2011, viewed at http://www.technewsworld.com/story/74024.html (accessed May 15, 2015).

Effective reference data and master data management can help to ensure that data are accurate, complete, timely, relevant, standardized, and consistent with an organization's business rules. This in turn enhances the quality and value of the information derived from those data, providing strategic advantages and supporting regulatory compliance.

Summary

Reference data are typically held in look-up tables that are read but not altered by various business applications. They can be simple code lists, taxonomies, tables containing multiple attributes of an entity type, or code translation tables. Master data are data about those things that are essential to an organization's core business activities, and they can be categorized in a variety of ways depending on the needs and focus of an organization. The *DAMA DMBOK* categorizes master data as party, product, financial, and geographic master data. However organizations may classify their master data differently. For example, an insurer might have categories such as customer, product, and producer. Although aspects of their management are similar, reference and master data differ in a variety of ways.

A "golden record" is a single, complete, accurate, current, and unique set of attributes for an entity. Reference data management (RDM) and master data management (MDM) work to establish "golden records" for shared use across the various systems within an organization. This is an ongoing, incremental process focused on data quality improvement. RDM and MDM involve a number of steps including understanding the organization's needs, identifying the sources of reference data and master data, selecting and implementing an appropriate data integration architecture, evaluating and selecting appropriate RDM and MDM tools, defining match rules to be used for entity resolution, creating "golden records" and illustrating the relationships among them, and implementing a formal process for dealing with additions, changes or deletions to reference and master data.

There are five important principles in MDM and they apply equally well to RDM:

1. Define your business problem
2. Plan beyond phase one to ensure success
3. To succeed, MDM needs a strong governance program in pace
4. Recognize that the most important word in MDM is management
5. Partner with an IT vendor who has significant MDM and information governance experience[49]

By adhering to these principles, an organization can improve the quality, integrity, and value of its data and information.

---

[49] The 5 Pillars of Master Data Management, by David Corrigan, December 21 2011, viewed at http://bit.ly/2tcAxY8, (accessed May 15, 2015).

Bibliography

Meta Data vs Master/Reference Data, the missing link of data governance?, by Christophe Barriolade, Sep 25th, 2013, viewed at http://bit.ly/2sbdsGu (accessed April 4, 2015).

What is Master Data?, viewed at http://bit.ly/2tcmrps (accessed April 4, 2015).

Reference Data Management and Master Data: Are they Related?, by Mala Narasimharajan on Dec 07, 2012, viewed at http://bit.ly/2txlqYn accessed (accessed April 4, 2015).

The Reference Data Challenge for Data Administration, by Malcolm Chisholm, Published: October 1, 2001, viewed at http://bit.ly/2txJASL (accessed April 10, 2015).

Definitions of Data Categories, Source: Copyright © 2005-2008 Danette McGilvray, Granite Falls Consulting, Inc. and Gwen Thomas, viewed at http://bit.ly/2sbl5wZ (accessed April 12, 2015).

Reference Data Management, IBM Redbooks Solution Guide, viewed at https://ibm.co/2txJD0T (accessed April 20, 2015).

Data Modeling by Example: Volume Three, Barry Williams, Database Answers Ltd., First Kindle Original Edition: London, 2012, viewed at http://bit.ly/2sbmRy9 (accessed April 24, 2015).

Federal Information Processing Standard state code, viewed at http://bit.ly/2rADVPi (accessed April 30, 2015).

The DAMA Dictionary of Data Management, First Edition 2008, Mark Mosley Editor, Technics Publications LLC, New Jersey, copyright 2008 DAMA International.

The DAMA Guide to the Data Management Body of Knowledge (DAMA-DMBOK) First Edition, DAMA International, Technics Publications LLC, New Jersey, copyright 2009 DAMA International.

Mastering Reference Data, Robert Rowe, Dec 4, 2012, viewed at http://bit.ly/2rFSRqC (accessed April 20, 2015).

NAICS Association viewed at http://bit.ly/1RQV0HP accessed (accessed May 5, 2015).

What is Master Data?, by Malcolm Chisholm, Originally published February 6, 2008, viewed at http://bit.ly/22q7vzi, (accessed May 5, 2015).

Master Data Management Drivers: Fantasy, Reality and Quality, A Review and Classification of Potential Benefits of Implementing Master Data Management, David Loshin, viewed at http://bit.ly/2rG1ul1 (accessed May 5, 2015).

Master Data Management (MDM) Hub Architecture, Roger Wolter and Kirk Haselden, Microsoft Corporation, April 2007, viewed at http://bit.ly/2tcqsKI (accessed May 7, 2015).

The What, Why, and How of Master Data Management, Roger Wolter and Kirk Haselden, Microsoft Corporation, November 2006, viewed at http://bit.ly/1zxA50t (accessed May 7, 2015).

What is a Controlled Vocabulary?, viewed at http://bit.ly/2sbahi8 (accessed May 7, 2015).

The 5 Pillars of Master Data Management, By David Corrigan, Dec 21, 2011, Tech News World, Data Management, viewed at http://bit.ly/2tcAxY8 (accessed May 15, 2015).

Part 2: Reference Data Management Challenges, by Prashant Chandramohan viewed at http://bit.ly/2rGpiVA (accessed May 15, 2015).

Data and Information Governance

The concept of data governance was introduced in an earlier chapter. Data governance relates to an organization's high-level data strategy and defines how authority and control will be exercised with respect to the organization's data. Although the terms "data governance", "information governance", and "data and information governance" are often used synonymously, some theorists contend that information governance differs from data governance. However, the two disciplines overlap in a number of areas and practitioners need to coordinate their efforts.

Data governance forms the foundation for all other data management activities. Data and information governance establish principles and policies to ensure effective data and information management, and they are both essential elements of corporate governance. A third governance discipline, information technology (IT) governance, focuses on maximizing the value of investment in IT resources.

The *DAMA-DMBOK* outlines the steps involved in implementing a data governance program. Establishing an information governance program would involve similar steps. Various groups and individuals have a role in data and information governance including executives, the governance council or committee, data managers, IT, business and technical data stewards, coordinating data stewards, and information stewards. There are a number of challenges associated with establishing data and information governance programs, perhaps the most important of which is managing the organizational changes that these programs may necessitate.

Educational Objectives

Upon completion of this assignment, you should be able to:

1. Define data governance and information governance.
2. Contrast data and information governance.
3. Describe the importance of data and information governance to an organization.
4. Discuss the role of data and information governance within corporate governance.
5. Describe how the data governance function differs from the IT governance function.
6. Describe the activities necessary to achieve effective data governance.
7. Identify the roles in the data governance function.
8. Define and differentiate data stewardship and information stewardship.

9. Describe how data stewardship functions within the data governance roles.

10. Describe how information stewardship functions within the information governance roles.

11. Describe the importance of data and information stewardship.

12. Describe the challenges of implementing a governance program.

13. Differentiate between the responsibilities of business management and IT management related to data governance decisions.

"Lumpers" and "Splitters"

An earlier chapter introduced the concept of taxonomy. In sciences like biology, paleontology, and botany, taxonomy involves classifying living or extinct organisms based on their characteristics. One might think this is a precise science, but in fact different researchers classify organisms differently, and there can be heated taxonomic debate.

For example, consider an extinct bird, fossils of which are found over a wide geographic area. Although the fossil remains are quite similar, there is a 30 percent difference in average size between samples found in the eastern half of the range and those found in the western half. Some paleontologists might consider all of the fossils to be the same type of bird based on their similarities. These scientists are informally referred to as "lumpers". Others might classify the fossils as two different types of birds based on the difference in average size. These people are commonly referred to as "splitters".

This tendency to either lump or split is not confined to the classification of organisms. Many areas of study categorize things based either on similarities or differences. This is the case with discussions about data and information governance—there are lumpers and splitters.

For example, in his book *Data Governance, How to Design, Deploy, and Sustain an Effective Data Governance Program*, author John Ladley writes: "This book does not distinguish between *data governance* and *information governance*, although some authors do. From a practical viewpoint, there is no real difference. We could conjure up some philosophical argument that there is a difference, but experience has shown these discussions only serve to confuse and reduce the effectiveness of the program."[50] The first edition of the *DAMA-DMBOK* discusses data governance, but not information governance, and the first edition of the *DAMA Dictionary of Data Management* provides no definition for the term "information governance".

On the other hand, many data management writers and theorists insist that data governance and information governance are, in fact, different. Others add a third element: IT governance. This chapter discusses data governance, information governance, and IT governance separately.

---

[50] John Ladley, Data Governance, How to Design, Deploy, and Sustain an effective Data Governance Program, Morgan Kaufman, 2012, Elsevier Inc., p. 2.

Governance

Governance is the process of governing. An individual or a group that exercises governance has the authority and responsibility to establish principles and policies, and to monitor and enforce compliance with them. Principles are general rules or codes of conduct. Policies describe the activities an organization will undertake in support of its guiding principles.

As an example of governance, consider insurance regulation. The primary reason for insurance regulation is to protect consumers; to ensure that coverage is available at a reasonable price, and that claims are fairly and promptly paid. Monitoring insurers' financial strength is an essential element of consumer protection. Insurers are required to complete and submit the NAIC (National Association of Insurance Commissioners) Annual Statement which provides regulators with detailed financial information. The statutory accounting principles (SAP) used in its completion differ from generally accepted accounting principles (GAAP) and are prescribed by state insurance regulators. Insurers manage their accounting and financial information under the governance of the regulators.

Data and Information

To understand data governance and information governance and the differences between them, it may be useful to revisit some concepts discussed in previous chapters.

- Data are attributes of entities. They can be expressed in a structured way as numbers, characters, or symbols, or in unstructured forms such as images or audio recordings. Data are meaningless without context.
- Effective data management helps ensure that data are fit for their intended use. They are accurate, complete, timely, consistent with business rules, relevant, and have integrity.
- Data stewardship is an important element of effective data management.
- Information is data that have been analyzed, processed, or organized for a particular purpose, and presented in a form and context that are relevant and meaningful, for example, a report or a policy declarations page.
- Effective information management helps ensure that the transformations data undergo to create information are accurate, complete, appropriate, and correct and that the resulting information is valid and has integrity.
- Information stewardship is an important element of effective information management.
- High quality information is essential to strategic, tactical, and operational planning; organizing; leading; and controlling.
- Both data and information have a lifecycle: planning, specifying, enabling, creating and acquiring, maintaining and using, archiving and retrieving, and ultimately purging.

Data Governance and Information Governance

Data and information are different; they are used differently and can be managed differently. Data governance and information governance also differ, as is illustrated in Figure 7.1.

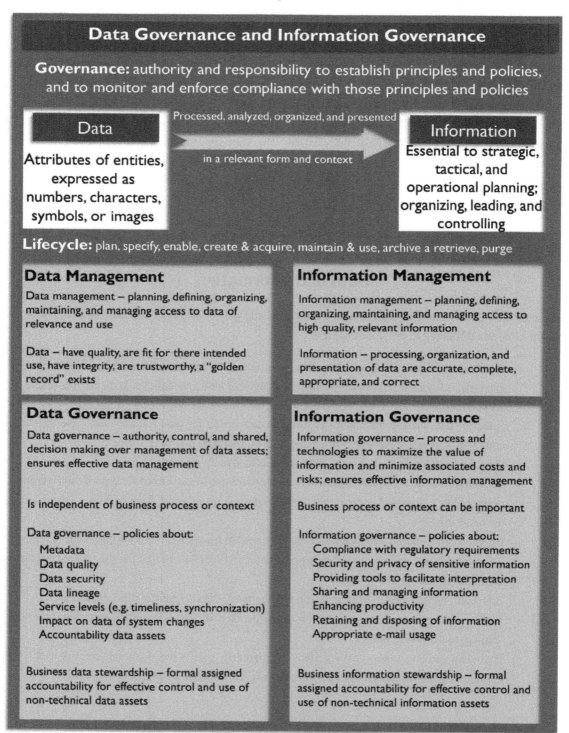

Figure 7.1 Data governance and information governance

Data governance is "the exercise of authority, control, and shared decision making (planning, monitoring, and enforcement) over the management of data assets."[51]

To understand data governance, it is useful to return to the definition of data management introduced in an earlier chapter. Data management is the process of planning, defining, organizing, maintaining, and managing access to digitally created, stored, and transmitted data that are of relevance and use to an organization. Data governance establishes, and monitors and enforces compliance with, the principles and policies that ensure appropriate data management.

Data governance focuses on areas such as metadata; data quality; data security; data lineage; the timeliness of data; the synchronization of data, for example between an operational data store (ODS) and an online transaction processing (OLTP) system; determining the impact of system changes on data; and establishing who is accountable for the maintenance of data stores. Data governance is independent of business processes in that it focuses on the data themselves rather than on transactions, reports, or analysis.

Information management involves identifying an organization's information requirements and then planning, defining, organizing, maintaining, and managing access to high quality, relevant information that meets those requirements. Effective information governance helps to ensure effective information management.

Information governance has been defined by a variety of writers and theorists in a variety of ways. For the present purpose, **information governance** encompasses "the activities and technologies that organizations employ to maximize the value of their information while minimizing associated risks and costs."[52] Information governance is concerned with such things as ensuring that the information needed to manage the business is of high quality and readily available; providing tools to allow business consumers of information to interpret and use it appropriately; complying with regulatory requirements; protecting the security and privacy of sensitive information; sharing and reusing information effectively; enhancing worker productivity; and managing the lifecycle of information (e.g. determining when information must be retained and when it can be discarded). For information governance, the business process or context is relevant. For example, e-mail may be considered an inappropriate vehicle for some types of transactions, particularly those involving sensitive or private information.

The Importance of Data Governance and Information Governance

Data governance and information governance both have a strategic focus and involve senior executives who should articulate a goal and guiding principles. They are ongoing activities that can be managed in a variety of ways; their implementation will vary based on the size, complexity, and culture of the organization. In a small company, they might be the responsibility of a single person; in a larger organization, a committee. Some organizations have separate data governance and information governance groups that focus on different areas but coordinate their efforts, particularly in areas of overlap, such as privacy and security.

---

[51] The DAMA Guide to the Data Management Body of Knowledge (DAMA-DMBOK) First Edition, DAMA International, Technics Publications LLC, New Jersey, copyright 2009 DAMA International, p., p. 37.

[52] The Information Governance Initiative, viewed at http://itginitiative.com, (accessed June 10, 2015).

A concept commonly referred to in discussions of data and information quality is "one version of the truth". Previous chapters discussed data quality, data integrity, reference and master data management, and the importance of having a "golden record" for critical data. Effective data governance helps to ensure "one version of the truth" by providing a foundation on which to base all of the other data management activities:

- Data architecture management
- Data development
- Data operations management
- Data security management
- Data quality management
- Reference and master data management
- Data warehousing and business intelligence management
- Document and content management
- Metadata management

High quality information is essential to an organization's ability to plan, compete, and succeed. Information can only be as good as the data from which it is derived, so data governance plays a vital role in helping to ensure an organization's ongoing viability.

Effective information governance is also important in establishing "one version of the truth". It helps to ensure that internal reports are accurate and consistent, and allows users of those reports to be confident in the information they contain. It enables accurate and timely financial and statistical reporting. In addition, information governance can ensure compliance with legal and regulatory recordkeeping requirements, and privacy and security regulations. It can enhance productivity by facilitating the sharing, interpretation, use and reuse of information. It can also assist in the discovery of, and access to, information necessary, for example, in support of a lawsuit or regulatory investigation.

Data and Information Governance within Corporate Governance

The term **corporate governance** has been defined in a variety of ways, but essentially it is the set of principles and policies an organization develops and implements in an attempt to balance the various interests of its many stakeholders including, for example, the board of directors, shareholders, management, employees, customers, suppliers, government, and the community.

The Sarbanes-Oxley Act was passed in 2002 after several high-profile bankruptcies of large organizations revealed accounting fraud. The Act stipulates that adequate controls must be in place to ensure the accuracy and integrity of an organization's financial information and executives are held personally liable for any inaccuracies or misstatements in the organization's financial statements. Good corporate governance allows an organization to ensure and demonstrate its financial strength. Data and information governance are two essential elements of corporate governance.

Information Technology (IT) Governance

Data and information governance differ from information technology (IT) governance. The objective of **IT governance** is to maximize the value of investment in IT by aligning IT strategy with business strategy and optimizing the use of an organization's IT resources. In a paper entitled *How IT Governance Drives Improved Performance*, authors Kurt Milne and Adrian Bowles identify five elements of IT governance:[53]

- Strategic alignment
- Value delivery
- Resource management
- Risk management
- Performance measures

Effective IT governance establishes principles and policies regarding the investment in, and management of, IT resources. The goal is to help an organization meet strategic, operational, administrative, and regulatory objectives, while minimizing IT risk, for example the risk of system crashes or security breaches. IT governance also involves establishing metrics for measuring IT performance to ensure that it adds value to the organization. IT governance can be an important element of corporate governance.

The International Standard for Corporate Governance of Information Technology ISO/IEC 38500 was developed in 2008. In a 2015 article entitled To Govern IT, or Not to Govern IT? published in the Communications of the ACM, authors Carlos Juiz and Mark Toomey write about ISO/IEC 38500: "While it does not say so explicitly, the standard leads to one inescapable three-part conclusion for which business leaders must assume responsibility:

- *Agenda.* Setting the agenda for IT use as an integral aspect of business strategy;
- *Investment.* Delivery of investments in IT-enabled business capability; and
- *Operations.* Ongoing successful operational use of IT in routine business activity."[54]

Implementing a Governance Program

While implementing data and information governance at the enterprise level is seen as the ideal, it is not always possible for a variety of reasons. An enterprise-wide governance program takes time to establish, and an incremental approach is sometimes useful. It is possible to create segmented data governance processes for individual areas within an enterprise, and some organizations have had some degree of success doing so, especially if the particular area is in a different industry segment than the rest of the enterprise. For example, a property and casualty insurer might implement a separate governance program for a life insurance subsidiary. The reason is that

---

[53] Kurt Milne and Adrian Bowles, How IT Governance Drives Improved Performance, 2990 IT Process Institute, viewed at http://www.isaca.ord/Groups/Professional-English/governance-of-enterprise-it/GroupDocuments/ITPI_IT_Governance-summary-paper.pdf accessed June 17 2015.

[54] Carlos Juiz and mark Toomey, To Govern IT, or Not to Govern IT?, publication Communications of the ACM, 02/2015 Vol. 58 No. 02, Association of Computing Machinery, p. 58.

each of these segments has different statutory reporting models and different rate development and reserving methodologies. Generally, however, there are benefits in having a common standardized data structure supported by enterprise data governance. There have been instances where data or information governance processes have been set up at a functional level (e.g. claims, underwriting, policy processing). This enables resources within a function to speak a common language and develop a common set of reports. However, this approach does not maximize the governance model because it does not result in data and information uniformity and consistency across the enterprise. As a result, disconnects and misunderstandings can occur during cross-function communication.

The *DAMA-DMBOK* outlines the activities involved in implementing a data governance program. Establishing an information governance program would entail similar activities:

- Develop a data strategy to align data management with business needs, and improve and maintain data quality, integrity, security, and access.
- Create data policies that broadly outline what the organization will do in support of the data strategy.
- Define and approve an enterprise data model and enterprise data architecture.
- Create data standards, guidelines, and procedures that specify how the organization will implement its data policies.
- Develop procedures and controls to ensure, monitor, and document compliance with legal and regulatory obligations.
- Establish channels and procedures for identifying and resolving issues related to data.
- Identify, plan, introduce, and manage the organizational and cultural changes necessary to effectively implement the data strategy.
- Consult with IT management to determine the full range of data management and related services the organization requires and plan for required staffing and funding.
- Determine an appropriate method to estimate the tangible and intangible value of the organization's data assets.
- Communicate and promote the value of data assets and the importance of effective data governance.

Even though the activities involved in implementing a governance program are typically similar from organization to organization, the governance programs that result from these activities can vary significantly. This is due to various factors including differences among industries, varying organizational structures, and differences in corporate cultures. Effective governance programs are tailored to meet the specific needs of the organizations implementing them.

Data Governance Roles

Although data governance programs can vary widely, there are certain activities that need to be performed and certain responsibilities that need to be assigned. In an insurance organization, different groups typically have different responsibilities related to data governance.

The Role of the Data Governance Council or Committee

A data governance council or committee (DGC) is a cross-functional group with members from both IT and the organization's operational side. Members of the DGC generally include the chief information officer (CIO), chief data officer (CDO), the data management (DM) leader, and a business executive who acts as chief data steward. It is not uncommon for this group to include executives representing other areas, such as actuarial, underwriting, and claims. The DGC makes high level, strategic decisions about data governance as an integrated function within the organization. Generally, the data governance council or committee is responsible for the following:

- Approving master data definitions
- Approving proposed master data additions or changes
- Approving data standards
- Acting as mediator in cross-functional disputes involving enterprise data
- Identifying compliance requirements for existing and new data, systems, or processes
- Communicating compliance requirements
- Identifying ways of minimizing any burdens related to compliance
- Embedding compliance controls into operational and data management processes
- Defining data quality standards
- Assuring that data-related controls do not conflict or negate each other
- Ensuring that control efforts are effective
- Advising on data security issues
- Monitoring data quality and data lineage
- Delegating tactical development to teams and functional departments

The Role of the Chief Data Officer

The position of chief data officer (CDO) is comparatively new. For decades, organizations have had a chief information officer (CIO) who has been responsible for the computer systems and other technology through which data flow in support of business operations. However, CIOs traditionally have not been assigned formal responsibility for the actual data. As the value of data as an asset has come to be recognized, so too has the need for a data-dedicated role at the executive level: a chief data officer (CDO). While the position does require some technical expertise and skills, it has a business focus with the goal of separating data from technology and IT, and continually improving data quality and integration across the enterprise. The CDO often reports to the Chief Executive Officer (CEO) or Chief Operations Officer (COO).

Because it is a relatively new position, the role of the CDO is still evolving and maturing, and it will differ from organization to organization. In 2014, DATAVERSITY™ conducted a survey entitled "*The Role of the Chief Data Officer*." The results of that survey, supplemented by additional interviews, were published in *Status of the Chief Data Officer: An Update on the CDO Role in Organizations Today*. The authors indicate that:

- "The most common functional responsibility of CDOs across industries is maintaining and/or advising Data Governance procedures and practices. They are also likely to maintain processes and standards to ensure that systems use high quality data.

- Many CDOs provide advice and/ or support for data analytics. Correspondingly, we did not see as many CDOs as the head of analytics; we expected more CDOs to head up analytics.

Some have responsibility for data operations (or aspects of data operations) and/or application development. In cases where the CDO is involved in application development, it is usually for analytical purposes."[55] **Analytics** refers to "business intelligence procedures and techniques for exploration and analysis of data to discover and identify new and meaningful information and trends."[56]

The Role of Data Management

Data management professionals are typically assigned responsibility for the following:

- Ensuring that master data are appropriately documented
- Leading efforts to establish data standards
- Confirming data quality and data lineage
- Supporting data development and associated testing and user acceptance activities
- Identifying and resolving redundant and inconsistent terminology
- Supporting and encouraging the correction of data quality problems

The Role of Information Technology (IT)

IT is accountable for designing and developing, or evaluating and installing, solutions that satisfy data requirements and aligning the enterprise architecture and internal technical standards to the organization's business focus. Operational business leaders determine data requirements; this is not the responsibility of data governance, data management, or IT. Data management assists IT in the following areas:

- Translating business rules into data models
- Maintaining data models
- Resolving data integration issues
- Maintaining the metadata repository

Data Stewardship and Information Stewardship

Data and information stewardship are important elements of data governance and data stewards have a significant role to play. The concept of data stewardship was introduced in an earlier chapter. The *DAMA Dictionary of Data*

---

[55] Tony Shaw, John Ladley and Charles Roe, Status of the Chief Data Officer: An Update on the CDO Role in Organizations Today, DATAVERSITY, 2014.

[56] The DAMA Dictionary of Data Management, First Edition 2008, Mark Mosley Editor, Technics Publications LLC, New Jersey, copyright 2008 DAMA International, p. 10.

Management defines data stewardship as "the formal, specifically assigned and entrusted accountability for business (non-technical) responsibilities ensuring effective control and use of data and information assets."[57]

This text recognizes that data governance differs from information governance, although the two disciplines overlap in some areas and many of the activities and processes involved are similar. Therefore, it follows that data stewardship and information stewardship also differ to some extent. **Business data stewardship** is the formal, specifically assigned accountability for ensuring effective control and use of non-technical data assets. **Business information stewardship** is the formal, specifically assigned accountability for ensuring effective control and use of non-technical information assets.

Data Stewardship within Data Governance

The individuals and groups involved in data governance include the following:

- A data stewardship committee with members from both IT and operational or business functions with responsibility for overseeing data management initiatives identified by the data governance council or committee (DGC).

- Business data stewards, subject matter experts responsible for identifying and defining data and metadata requirements; drafting data model specifications; defining business rules and data quality requirements; identifying and helping to resolve data issues; and assisting in evaluating and improving the quality of the organization's data.

- Data stewardship teams responsible for collaborating on data modeling, specification and data quality improvement in particular business or operational areas.

- Coordinating data stewards who lead data stewardship teams; recruit business data stewards; serve on data stewardship steering committees; work to ensure that the organization's requirements for quality data are met; and review data quality audits.

- Technical data stewards who focus on the organization's technical data requirements.

- Executive data stewards who sit on the DGC and are accountable for planning and oversight of data management and governance programs.

Data stewards and stewardship groups typically represent specific organizations or functional areas; however, to fulfill their data governance responsibilities they need to consider the interests of the enterprise as a whole. They communicate data governance principles and policies within their assigned area and resolve any issues relating to data. If issues arise that they cannot resolve or do not have the authority to resolve, they can forward those issues to data management or to the data governance council or committee for review and resolution.

Data stewards attend data governance meetings, review proposals regarding such things as new code values for data elements or changes to the enterprise's master data, and consult with appropriate stakeholders. Data stewards perform a variety of activities including the following:

---

[57] Ibid, p. 45

- Identifying any necessary security requirements
- Defining data quality thresholds
- Establishing business rules for the data
- Identifying and leveraging existing data prior to creating new data
- Defining and/or documenting metadata
- Verifying data complies with standards
- Ensuring data are used for their intended purpose

Information Stewardship within Information Governance

Like data stewards, information stewards are subject matter experts in particular fields and are assigned specific areas of responsibility. Depending on the size, structure, and culture of an organization, the information stewardship function can be implemented in a variety of ways. In some organizations, a single group performs both data and information governance functions.

Some organizations implement an information governance function without creating a centralized organization to do so. Rather, they set up a committee or council composed of the individuals that have responsibility for managing information in each of the enterprise's organizations or functional areas. This helps to ensure a common understanding and use of data for conversion into information. Ideally, selected members of this committee or council also sit on the data governance council or committee to participate in discussions on data issues. This allows them to keep informed on such things as the collection of new data, the discontinuation of existing data, or changes to the meaning of existing data.

Another option exists in cases where a single organization or functional area within the enterprise is responsible for creating all standardized reports, and setting up and managing the facilities for developing information. Members of this organization or functional area should sit on the data governance council or committee to add their insights and keep informed.

In particularly large enterprises, an information governance council or committee may be established along with the data governance council or committee. However, the two entities should work closely together and selected members of each committee should sit on both.

Regardless of the way in which the information stewardship function is structured, information stewards are responsible for a variety of activities including the following:

- Preparing standard reports for the enterprise
- Supporting the preparation of external reports
- Identifying appropriate data sources for reports
- Translating data into concise, meaningful, readily understandable information
- Training report developers in available data and appropriate data sources
- Identifying situations where additional data are required
- Identifying and communicating data quality issues

The Importance of Data and Information Stewardship

Because data and information are among the most valuable assets in many organizations, they need to be carefully and effectively managed. Data and information stewards understand the company's strategy and the role that data and information play in realizing that strategy. They speak the language of business and can clearly articulate why the enterprise requires detailed, complete, and integrated data. Because of their contextual understanding of how data are used, business data stewards are well equipped to participate in the often politically sensitive activities of data governance. They can contribute to discussions on ownership, access, privacy, and regulatory policy; armed with real-world knowledge of what is important to the enterprise. They can also develop practical approaches to monitoring the usability and value of key data elements. They recognize the strategic value of data and information to the organization and can articulate that value to executives. Gaining the support and participation of senior executives is essential to the success of ongoing data and information governance.

Challenges in Implementing a Governance Program

In an article entitled *Common Challenges in Creating a Data Governance Model and Program*, author Gwen Thomas, founder of the Data Governance Institute, discusses common hurdles that must be overcome when implementing a data governance program. In the article, she differentiates between "'little g governance'—policies and controls that are embedded in processes, systems, data stores, and data flows to ensure that data meets [sic] user expectations—and 'Big G Governance'—the highly political negotiations, decision making and policy setting that informs and supports 'little g governance'."[58]

The key to a successful data governance implementation is executive sponsorship, because all functional areas within the enterprise must consent to place ultimate control of their data in the hands of a data governance council or committee. Without top-level executive participation and support, the initiative is likely to fail. Executives are typically disinclined to support "Big G Governance" unless they have a very clear understanding of its implications and the benefits it can bring the organization.

Many individuals and organizations are naturally resistant to change. This can present a hurdle, particularly when an organization's current data and information management practices appear to be working. If board members and executives have a level of confidence in the organization's legal and regulatory compliance, and the accuracy and completeness of financial and other reports, they may be hesitant to support changes that could potentially introduce a degree of risk into a data and information management environment perceived to be stable.

Another challenge is maintaining the initial momentum of the program. When a governance initiative is launched, participants may be enthusiastic about making a positive change for the organization, and adding value. The new challenges they face are interesting and they see the decisions they are asked to make as significant. Over time, as

---

[58] Gwen Thomas, Common challenges in creating a data governance model and program, viewed at http://searchdatamanagement.techtarget.com/news/2240024273/Common-challenges-in-creating-a-data-governance-model-and-program (accessed June 18, 2015).

the organization's governance program matures, participants may come to perceive their activities as routine and delegate them to others who may not have the necessary skills, experience, or knowledge.

To succeed in the long term, governance programs require adequate staffing and funding. Larger organizations often establish a data governance office (DGO). Facilitators in the DGO act as coordinators, scheduling data governance and stewardship meetings; preparing agendas and minutes; ensuring that data modeling and data architecture activities include representatives from the operational side of the organization; and assisting in other data stewardship initiatives. Some boards and executive groups may be hesitant to fund a DGO.

Finally, implementation of a data or information governance program can necessitate changes to an organization's culture, organizational structure, or leadership roles. Significant organizational change requires skillful people-management, in addition to the technical and business management skills required to implement the governance program. Lack of appropriate attention to the impact of organizational change on the stakeholders involved can cause an otherwise well-designed and implemented governance program to fail.

Responsibilities for Data Governance Decisions

In the context of data governance, business leaders make decisions about those things that fall within their areas of expertise, and directly impact the organization's operations, including such things as crafting and modifying the organization's business model, identifying and recruiting IT leadership, approving any capital investments, determining the amount of funding to provide for research and development activities, and developing the organization's data governance model.

Information technology (IT) management makes decisions about technical issues, such as database architecture, data integration architecture, data warehouse and business intelligence (BI) architecture, and metadata architecture.

Other decisions are made collaboratively by business management, data management, and IT management. For example, specifying information needs or data quality requirements is a business-related function; however, the ability to meet those requirements relies, to a great extent, on IT. Consultation with IT management and data management will allow business leaders to make better decisions in these areas. Conversely, determining enterprise information management policies may be a more IT-focused activity; however, IT will make better decisions for the enterprise after consultation with business management and data management.

The *DAMA-DMBOK* presents an effective illustration of the data governance decision spectrum, an adaptation of which is presented in Figure 7.2.[59]

---

[59] The DAMA Guide to the Data Management Body of Knowledge (DAMA-DMBOK) First Edition, DAMA International, Technics Publications LLC, New Jersey, copyright 2009 DAMA International, p. 38.

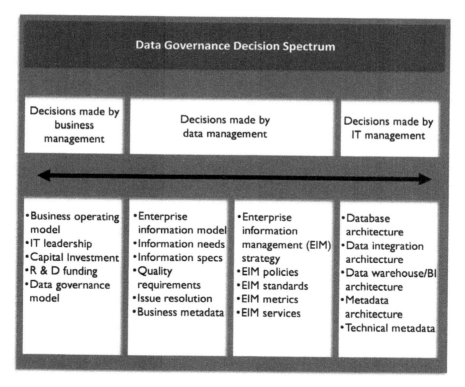

Figure 7.2 Data governance decision spectrum

Summary

Governance involves establishing and monitoring and enforcing compliance with principles and policies. Data governance focuses on governing data assets. Information governance deals maximizing the value in an organization's information assets and reducing the associated costs and risks. IT governance aligns IT strategy to business strategy and maximizes the value of IT investments. All three are important elements of corporate governance.

There are a number of steps involved in implementing a data or information governance program:

- Develop a data strategy
- Create data policies
- Define an enterprise data model and architecture
- Create data standards, guidelines, and procedures
- Develop procedures and controls
- Establish channels for identifying and resolving issues
- Manage the necessary organizational and cultural changes
- Determine the range of data management and related services required
- Determine a method to estimate the value of data assets
- Communicate and promote

Effective data governance involves individuals from across the organization including executives, the data governance council or committee, data managers, IT, business and technical data stewards, coordinating data stewards, and information stewards.

There are a number of challenges associated with implementing a governance program. These include obtaining executive support, maintaining momentum, ensuring adequate staffing and funding, and managing the organizational changes that may be required.

Within the context of data governance, business-related decisions are made by business leaders and technically focused decisions are made by IT leaders. Decisions with both business and technical implications are made collaboratively.

Bibliography

Data Governance - How to Design, Deploy, and Sustain an Effective Data Governance Program, by John Ladley, Acquiring Editor: Andrea Dierna, Development Editor: Robin Day, Project Manager: Andre´ A. Cuello, Designer: Kristen Davis, Morgan Kaufmann is an imprint of Elsevier, 225 Wyman Street, Waltham, MA 02451, USA, 2012 Elsevier Inc. All rights reserved.

The DAMA Dictionary of Data Management, First Edition 2008, Mark Mosley Editor, Technics Publications LLC, New Jersey, copyright 2008 DAMA International.

The DAMA Guide to the Data Management Body of Knowledge (DAMA-DMBOK) First Edition, DAMA International, Technics Publications LLC, New Jersey, copyright 2009 DAMA International.

Defining the Differences between Information Governance, IT Governance, & Data Governance, By Robert Smallwood posted Aug 18, 2014, viewed athttp://bit.ly/2sbbYfI (accessed June 5, 2015).

Information Governance vs. Data Governance – Who Cares? Posted on September 3, 2014 by John Schmidt, viewed at http://infa.media/2txA4Pm (accessed June 7, 2015).

Gartner IT Glossary, viewed at http://gtnr.it/1fnnnLZ (accessed June 7, 2015).

What is Information Governance? And Why is it So Hard?, by Debra Logan, January 11, 2010, viewed at http://gtnr.it/2bLNiP7 (accessed June 7, 2015).

What is Information Management? Viewed at http://bit.ly/2txwiWm (accessed June 15, 2015).

Information management viewed at http://bit.ly/2slpnA3 (accessed June 15, 2015).

The Sedona Conference® Commentary on Information Governance, webinar overview, viewed at http://bit.ly/2rG6OVf (accessed June 15, 2015).

IT Governance Definition and Solutions, By Karen D. Schwartz, CIO, May 22, 2007, viewed at http://bit.ly/1ztV7Sw (accessed June 16, 2015).

Mark Diamond, What's the Difference between Information Governance and Data Governance? Designing Complimentary Initiatives, Contoural Information Governance Webinar June 26 2015, viewed at http://bit.ly/2sIH7YF (accessed June 16, 2015).

Carlos Juiz and Mark Toomey, To Govern IT or Not to Govern IT?, publication Communications of the ACM, 02/2015 Vol. 58 N0. 02, Association for Computing Machinery, p. 58.

ISO/IEC standard for corporate governance of information technology, 5 June 2008, viewed at http://bit.ly/2szLntb (accessed June 17, 2015).

How IT Governance Drives Improved Performance, By Kurt Milne and Adrian Bowles, viewed at http://bit.ly/2sD4i7m (accessed June 17, 2015).

Common challenges in creating a data governance model and program, by Gwen Thomas of the Data Governance Institute, viewed at http://bit.ly/2txOXRE (accessed June 17, 2015).

Corporate Governance, viewed at http://bit.ly/18eScBE (accessed June 20, 2015).

Peter Aiken and Michael Gorman, The Case for the Chief Data Officer, Morgan Kaufman, imprint of Elsevier, 2013.

Tony Shaw, John Ladley and Charles Roe, Status of the Chief Data Officer: An Update on the CDO Role in Organizations Today, DATAVERSITY (accessed June 20, 2015).

Information Security

Insurers, and their various service providers and data collection organizations, collect a large volume of private, potentially sensitive data and information about insureds, agents and brokers, employees, claimants, prospects, and others. It is essential that insurers protect the confidentiality of the information they collect; the consequences of not doing so can be significant. Data and information can be unintentionally lost in a variety of ways. Designing and implementing an effective data and information security program, instituting appropriate controls, and developing a strong backup and recovery plan are all activities that help an organization protect its data and information resources. The individuals and roles involved in data and information security management may vary based on the size, complexity, and culture of an organization; however, there are specific responsibilities that need to be assigned to help ensure the effective implementation of a data security program and appropriate controls. In addition, federal antitrust laws restrict the sharing of specific types of information by insurers.

Educational Objectives

Upon completion of this assignment, you should be able to:

1. Describe different classifications of information.
2. Explain the concept of Personally Identifiable Information (PII).
3. Describe the regulatory requirements for handling PII.
4. Define de-identification and explain its role in information security.
5. Describe the implications of poor data and information security for the organization.
6. Describe the various ways in which data and information can be lost and what can be done to prevent their loss.
7. Explain the activities involved in securing organizational data and information.
8. Identify and describe various data and information security controls: administrative, technical, internal, and external.
9. Explain how backup and recovery procedures contribute to data and information security.
10. Define the role and responsibilities of a security governance committee.
11. Describe different roles and responsibilities for ensuring information security.
12. Define the role and responsibilities of data users to ensure information security.
13. Describe how United States federal antitrust laws and regulations apply to the insurance industry.

Classifying Information

Information can be classified in a number of ways. One approach identifies five categories:

- External public
- Internal public
- Confidential
- Regulated confidential
- Restricted

Press releases and advertisements are examples of **external public information**. The information is made available outside the organization with no restrictions as to its access. Its publication or circulation represents no risk to the organization, provided that the information is correct. **Internal public information** is made readily available for use within an organization. Examples of internal public information include underwriting guidelines and human resources policies. While it is generally used by managers and employees, it may be shared with other stakeholders. For example, agents and brokers need to understand an insurer's underwriting guidelines.

Any information not specifically identified as public should be considered confidential. **Confidential information** should be kept private. It includes such things as personnel records, policyholder information, customer account information, and claimant health records. This is information that could damage the organization or others if made public. For example, if a hacker accessed an insurer's customer records and published them on the Internet, both the insurer and the customers whose records were made public could suffer harm. Within an organization, a variety of individuals may have access to confidential information. For example, doctors, nurses, administrators, and accounting staff may all have access to a hospital's patient records.

Third party confidential information is a subset of confidential information. It belongs or pertains to another organization that has entrusted it to an insurer under a non-disclosure agreement or other contract. Confidential information about agencies and brokerages would be an example.

Insurance company personnel with access to confidential data should have strict guidelines to follow. If an individual is uncertain as to the sensitivity of a particular piece of information, it is important that he or she check with an appropriate resource.

Regulated information is confidential information for which an authorized regulatory or governmental body has stipulated controls. Requirements for managing this information are defined in regulations and in the corporate policies that organizations develop to ensure regulatory compliance. Using individual discretion is not appropriate when dealing with regulated information as noncompliance with regulations can have serious consequences. Most regulations require audits for proof of compliance.

The most confidential information is often referred to as restricted. Access to **restricted information** is highly controlled. For example, only a few bank employees know the combinations to the vault. In an organization negotiating a merger or acquisition, access to details of the negotiations would be limited to those directly involved.

Personally Identifiable Information (PII)

In an article entitled *Privacy and Security Myths and Fallacies of "Personally Identifiable Information"*, authors Arvind Narayanan and Vitaly Shmatikov write "The digital economy relies on the collection of personal data on an ever-increasing scale. Information about our searches, browsing history, social relationships, medical history, and so forth is collected and shared with advertisers, researchers, and government agencies. This raises a number of interesting privacy issues."[60]

Personal information, or personally identifiable information (PII), has been defined in a variety of ways depending on the context in which the term is used. For example, in response to an increase in identify theft; many states have passed **breach notification laws**. These laws require private and government organizations in possession of individuals' personal information to notify them when that information has been accessed through a security breach.

Breach notification laws typically define personally identifiable information in such a way as to prevent identity theft; they do not necessarily focus on protecting an individual's privacy. For example, the state of Maine's breach notification law defines personal information as "an individual's first name, or first initial, and last name in combination with one or more of the following data elements, when either the name or the data elements are not encrypted or redacted:[61]

A. Social Security number;

B. Driver's license number or state identification card number;

C. Account number, credit card number or debit card number, if circumstances exist wherein such a number could be used without additional identifying information, access codes or passwords;

D. Account passwords or personal identification numbers or other access codes; or

E. Any of the data elements contained in paragraphs A to D when not in connection with the individual's first name, or first initial, and last name, if the information is compromised, would be sufficient to permit a person to fraudulently assume or attempt to assume the identity of the person whose information was compromised."[62]

Privacy laws go further to protect individual privacy than breach notification laws. Both the federal government and individual states have passed a variety of laws relating to the privacy of personal information. For example, California's Online Privacy Protection Act requires business operators that collect personally identifiable information online to post a privacy policy on their website that clearly outlines the categories of PII they collect and the types of third parties with whom it will be shared.

---

[60] Arvind Narayanan and Vitaly Shmatikov, Privacy and Security Myths and Fallacies of "Personally Identifiable Information", Communications of the ACM, 06/2010 Vol. 53 No. 06, Association of Computing Machinery, p. 24.

[61] Encryption and redaction are techniques for protecting information by making it unintelligible.

[62] Maine Revised Statutes, Title 10: Commerce and Trade, Part 3: Regulation of Trade, Chapter 210-B: Notice of Risk to Personal Data.

The California Online Privacy Protection Act defines personally identifiable information as "individually identifiable information about an individual consumer collected online by the operator from that individual and maintained by the operator in an accessible form, including any of the following:

1. A first and last name.
2. A home or other physical address, including street name and name of a city or town.
3. An e-mail address.
4. A Social Security number.
5. Any other identifier that permits the physical or online contacting of a specific individual.
6. Information concerning a user that the website or online service collects online from the user and maintains in personally identifiable form in combination with an identifier described in this subdivision."[63]

The International Risk Management Institute (IRMI) defines **personally identifiable information (PII)** as "any information that can be used to uniquely identify, contact, or locate an individual, either alone or in conjunction with other sources, such as their name, Social Security number, driver's license number, date of birth, place of birth, mother's maiden name, and genetic information."[64]

One important type of PII is individually identifiable health information, also referred to as personal health information (PHI). The United States Health Insurance Portability and Accountability Act (HIPAA) establish standards to ensure the confidentiality of individually identifiable health information. HIPAA defines **individually identifiable health information** as "information, including demographic data that relates to:

- the individual's past, present, or future physical or mental health or condition,
- the provision of health care to the individual, or
- the past, present, or future payment for the provision of health care to the individual,

and that identifies the individual or for which there is a reasonable basis to believe it can be used to identify the individual. Individually identifiable health information includes many common identifiers (e.g., name, address, birth date, Social Security number)."[65]

Laws and Regulations Regarding Personally Identifiable Information (PII)

There are various laws and regulations at both the federal and state levels regarding the handling of personally identifiable information. Some are quite specific, for example relating to information minors post on the internet. Others are more general, and some are of particular importance to insurers. Being aware of, and in compliance

[63] California Business and Professions Code Section 22575 – 22579, viewed at http://www.leginfo.ca.gov/cgi-bin/displaycode?section=civ&group=01001-02000&file=1798.80-1798.84 (accessed July 1, 2015).

[64] Insurance and Risk Management Glossary, viewed at http://www.irmi.com/online/insurance-glosary/terms/p/personally-identifiable-information-pii.aspx, (accessed July 3, 2015).

[65] Summary of the HIPAA Privacy Rule, viewed at http://www.hhs.gov/ocr/privacy/hipaa/understanding/summary/ (accessed July 1, 2015).

with, all of the applicable laws and regulations related to the privacy of personally identifiable information can be challenging, but awareness and compliance are essential.

The Financial Services Modernization Act (Gramm-Leach-Bliley Act)

The Financial Services Modernization Act, also known as the Gramm-Leach-Bliley Act, includes provisions to protect consumers' personal information. There are three principle parts to the privacy requirements: the Financial Privacy Rule, the Safeguards Rule, and Pretexting Provisions. The Financial Privacy Rule and the Safeguards Rule apply to "financial institutions", which include not only banks, securities firms, and insurance companies, but also other companies that provide different types of financial products and services to consumers.

The Financial Privacy Rule governs the collection and disclosure of customers' personal financial information. Under the Financial Privacy Rule, a financial institution is required to inform customers of the types of information it obtains about them, and with whom it intends to share that information. The institution must also explain the customers' right to refuse to allow their information to be shared with certain third parties.

The Safeguards Rule requires all financial institutions to develop, implement, and maintain safeguards to protect customer information. The Safeguards Rule applies not only to financial institutions that collect information from their own customers, but also to financial institutions, such as credit reporting agencies, that receive customer information from other financial institutions. Companies are required to develop a written information security plan and complete a number of activities:

- Designate an information security coordinator
- Identify and assess risks to customer information
- Evaluate current safeguards' effectiveness in controlling risks to customer information
- Develop and implement an effective safeguards program
- Monitor and test the effectiveness of the program regularly
- Require service providers to implement adequate safeguards
- Monitor service providers' use of customer information
- Evaluate and adjust the security program as required

The intent of the Pretexting Provisions is to protect consumers from individuals or organizations obtaining their personal financial information under false pretenses, a practice known as **pretexting** or **phishing**. For example, a person might telephone an individual under the pretext of taking a survey and obtain personal information in that way. Alternatively, a person might use forged or stolen documents to obtain a customer's information from a financial institution. It is important that financial institutions verify a customer's identity before releasing any personal information to him or her.

Health Insurance Portability and Accountability Act (HIPAA)

The Administrative Simplification provisions of the Health Insurance Portability and Accountability Act (HIPAA) apply to "Covered Entities". Covered entities fall into three categories:

- Health plans (e.g., group health insurance, health maintenance organizations (HMO))
- Health care clearinghouses (e.g., billing services, re-pricing companies)
- Health care providers (e.g., doctors, nurses, dentists)

The Administrative Simplification provisions of HIPAA include the Privacy Rule and the Security Rule. The Privacy Rule protects all "individually identifiable health information held or transmitted by a covered entity or its business associate, in any form or media, whether electronic, paper, or oral. The Privacy Rule calls this information 'protected health information (PHI)'."[66] The Privacy Rule outlines the circumstances in which a covered entity (CE) can disclose PHI and the permitted uses of PHI. In addition, the Privacy Rule outlines administrative requirements for covered entities in a number of areas including the following:

- Development and implementation of privacy policies
- Appointment of a privacy officer
- Training for employees in privacy policies, and management to ensure compliance
- Implementation of administrative, technical, and physical safeguards for PHI
- A process whereby individuals can make a complaint about the CE's use of PHI
- Documentation and retention of a CE's privacy policies

The HIPAA Security Rule establishes standards for the safeguarding of protected health information that is created, stored, used, or transmitted in electronic form (e-PHI). Safeguards are categorized as administrative, physical, and technical. Administrative safeguards include such things as assigning responsibility for e-PHI security to an individual and providing employees with appropriate training. Physical safeguards control access to computers and other equipment and the data they contain. Technical safeguards include such things as passwords or other unique user identification, for example retina scans.

A number of states have enacted legislation similar to HIPAA, and in some cases, the legislation is more stringent than HIPAA. In addition, some states have passed laws specifically related to personally identifiable information (PII) in the context of insurance. For example, California's Insurance Information and Privacy Protection Act (IIPPA) focuses on personally identifiable information individuals provide to an agent, broker, or insurance company in order to apply for coverage or submit a claim. Agents, brokers, and insurers are required to provide a Privacy Notice describing their policies and procedures to ensure the security and confidentiality of PII. The Privacy Notice must also describe the kinds of information that the agent, broker, or insurer will collect, with whom that information will be shared, and the individual's right to restrict the sharing of that information.[67]

National Association of Insurance Commissioners (NAIC)

The National Association of Insurance Commissioners (NAIC) is an organization made up of insurance regulators from 50 states, the District of Columbia, the Commonwealth of Puerto Rico, and four United States' territories. The NAIC develops standards and provides regulatory support for its members. In response to a number of security

---

[66] United States Department of Health and Human Services Summary of the HIPAA Privacy Rule, viewed at http://www.hhs.gov/ocr/privacy/hipaa/understanding/summary/privacysummary.pdf (accessed July 2, 2015).

[67] California Department of Insurance, Privacy of Nonpublic Personal Information, viewed at http://www.insurance.ca.gov0250-0insurers/0500-gen-legal-info/privacy-of-nonpublic-personal-info.cfm (accessed July 15, 2015).

breaches involving consumer health and financial data, in April of 2015 the NAIC adopted the *Principles for Effective Cybersecurity: Insurance Regulatory Guidance*. The document includes twelve guiding principles that can be summarized as follows:

1. State regulators are responsible for ensuring that personally identifiable information (PII) is protected and that insurers and producers have systems in place to notify affected parties promptly if a security breach occurs.

2. Insurers and producers that collect, store, and transmit confidential or personally identifiable information should safeguard it appropriately.

3. State regulators that collect, store, and transmit PII or confidential information about insurers or producers are responsible for safeguarding that information and notifying affected parties promptly in the event of a security breach.

4. Cybersecurity regulations for insurers and producers should be flexible and consistent with the National Institute of Standards and Technology (NIST) security standards.[68]

5. All insurers and producers that are connected to the Internet must meet a minimum cybersecurity standard.

6. Regulators should conduct insurer examinations to evaluate cybersecurity vulnerability.

7. An effective cybersecurity program includes a plan for insurers, producers, and regulators to respond to a cybersecurity breach.

8. Insurers, producers, and regulators should ensure that third parties and service providers have safeguards in place to protect PII.

9. Management of cybersecurity should be part of an insurer's or producer's enterprise risk management (ERM) program.

10. Information Technology audits that identify a cybersecurity risk should be reviewed with the organization's board of directors.

11. Insurers and producers must keep informed about current and emerging cybersecurity risks.

12. Employee training about cybersecurity is essential for insurers and producers.

International Legislation

Organizations that do business internationally face additional challenges. For example, privacy laws in the United States generally attempt to balance the need for individual privacy with the need for efficiency in commercial transactions. In the European Union, on the other hand, privacy is considered a fundamental right and personal information protection laws and regulations are more restrictive than they are in the United States.

---

[68] The National Institute of Standards and Technology publishes a wide variety of documents on computer security.

The European Parliament and Council Directive 95/46/EC deals with the protection of personal data in both electronic and non-electronic form. It "seeks to strike a balance between a high level of protection for the privacy of individuals and the free movement of personal data within the European Union (EU)."[69] The Directive covers a number of areas:

- The conditions that must be met for data processing to be lawful
- The principles of data quality necessary for lawful data processing
- The rights of individuals whose personal data are being processed
- The exemptions or restrictions on individual's rights with respect to personal data
- The confidentiality and security of data processing
- The legal recourse available to individuals whose rights have been breached
- The transfer of personal data from an EU member to a non-EU member

The Directive was developed in 1995 before the use of the Internet became widespread. In 2012 the European Commission proposed changes to the 1995 Directive intended to enhance individuals' online privacy rights while at the same time supporting Europe's digital economy. Included among the proposed reforms is an individual's "right to be forgotten". If an individual no longer wants an organization to have his or her personal data, and there is no requirement for the organization to retain them, the data must be deleted. Additional reforms include making it easier for individuals to discover what information companies retain about them; and notification requirements if personal data are, for example, lost, altered, or accessed by unauthorized individuals. In June of 2015, the European Council, Parliament, and Commission began deliberations with respect to these and other privacy protection reforms.

Many other countries have laws intended to control and protect the use of personal information. For example, Canada's Personal Information Protection and Electronic Documents Act (PIPEDA) sets out requirements for the collection, use, and disclosure of personal information by private sector organizations engaged in commercial activities. In England, the Data Protection Act specifies how organizations, businesses, and the government are to use and protect individuals' personal information. In Argentina, the Personal Data Protection Act (Act 25.326) provides for the protection of personal information "in order to guarantee the right of individuals to their honor and privacy".[70] In a 2013 article entitled *Data protection regulation in the Asia Pacific: trends and recent developments*, author Wiley Rein LLP writes, "The Asia-Pacific region has seen the most rapid development in privacy laws in recent times. Companies that operate in the region and that collect, store, and use personal information can expect increasing compliance challenges in the face of new and evolving data protection regimes."[71] It is essential that data management professionals familiarize themselves with the information protection legislation in each jurisdiction in which an organization does business, and keep current on any changes to those laws and regulations.

The International Association of Insurance Supervisors (IAIS) is membership organization of insurance supervisors and regulators. The goal of the IAIS is to promote consistent supervision of the insurance industry globally in order

---

[69] Protection of personal data, EUF-Lex, Access to European Union law, viewed at http://eur-lex.europa.eu/legal-content/EN/TXT/?uri=URISERV:|14012 (accessed August 11, 2015).

[70] Personal Data Protection Act viewed at http://protecciondedatos.com.ar/law25326 (accessed August 12, 2015).

[71] Wiley Rein, Data Protection regulation in the Asia Pacific: trends and recent developments, viewed at http://www.lexology.com/library/detail.aspx?=2c6914fe-8faa-4f48-93fc-0d0f3dfc0e12 (accessed AugustT 12, 2015).

to protect policyholders, help ensure stable insurance markets, and contribute to global financial stability. IAIS publishes a document entitled *Insurance Core Principles, Standards, Guidance and Assessment Methodology*, that provides a framework for the global supervision of the insurance industry. One section of the document, *Information Exchange and Confidentiality Requirements*, outlines how insurance supervisors are to exchange information with each other, or with other authorities, as well as confidentiality requirements for information exchange.

De-Identification

While it is important to protect individuals' personal privacy, there are legitimate reasons for sharing information that would be considered private. For example, medical researchers need access to information about individuals with particular conditions in order to develop new treatment protocols.

The United States Department of Health and Human Sciences (HHS) has published a *Guidance Regarding Methods for De-identification of Protected Health Information in Accordance with the Health Insurance Portability and Accountability Act (HIPAA) Privacy Rule*. In the guidance, HHS writes "The process of de-identification, by which identifiers are removed from the health information, mitigates privacy risks to individuals and thereby supports the secondary use of data for comparative effectiveness studies, policy assessment, life sciences research, and other endeavors."[72]

De-identification essentially removes any information that might make the remaining information identifiable as relating to a specific individual. The HIPAA Privacy Rule defines de-identified information as "health information that does not identify an individual and with respect to which there is no reasonable basis to believe that the information can be used to identify an individual."[73]

Other methods of protecting sensitive data and information include encryption, data masking, and tokenizing. These techniques transform data in a way that makes it difficult to extract meaning from them. **Encryption** uses algorithms, mathematical operations, to convert data into ciphertext, which is not readily comprehensible. **Data masking** replaces certain data elements with similarly structured but artificial data to protect sensitive information. Data masking is often used in training or in system development and testing. For example, an insurer would not want to provide personal customer data to a vendor for use in development and testing of a new system. **Tokenizing** replaces sensitive data, for example a credit card number, with a randomly generated "token". The tokens are used in a system in place of the actual data, which are securely stored in a lookup table that links them to the tokens.

---

[72] United States Department of Health and Human Sciences (HHS), Guidance Regarding Methods for De-identification of Protected Health Information in Accordance with the Health Insurance Portability and Accountability Act (HIPAA) Privacy Rule, viewed at http://www.hhs.gov/ocr/privacy/hipaa/understanding/coveredentities/De-identification/guidance.html#rationale (accessed July 6, 2015).

[73] Ibid.

Implications of Poor Data and Information Security

Data and information security comprise policies and practices that protect data and information against misfortune, attacks, casual accidents, and other potential threats. Data and information need to be secure no matter where they are found, for example in databases, applications, networks, printed reports and other documents, or on portable computers and other mobile devices. When data and information are not properly secured, the implications for an organization can be significant:

- Sanctions or penalties due to noncompliance with regulations
- Disclosure of personally identifiable information about customers, employees, and others
- Lawsuits by individuals or organizations whose information has been disclosed
- Damage to the organization's reputation
- Loss of present and future customers
- Leakage of information that is sensitive or proprietary to the organization itself
- Loss of data integrity due to unauthorized or malicious changes to the data
- Destruction of essential data and information

In a 2014 article entitled *Underwriting Insurance Data Security*, author Stephen Treglia writes "While the average cost of a data breach is $5.9 million, the average loss in the value of a brand is $330 million. Arguably, this figure would be significantly higher for insurance companies, whose entire business is built on reputation and trust. And since insurance companies operate in the most complex regulatory environment, the consequences of such data breaches are many and varied."[74]

Loss of Data and Information

Data and information can be lost in a variety of ways that can be broadly categorized as either intentional or unintentional from the perspective of the organization experiencing the loss. Intentional destruction may occur after data and information are no longer needed. Outdated information not subject to regulatory retention requirements can be disposed of, although organizations need to have records management policies and procedures in place to ensure that information is retained, archived, and purged appropriately. When the decision is made to purge data, it is important that sensitive information, such as customer or employee records, be destroyed in an appropriate manner. Documents, CDs, and DVDs should be shredded and disposed of securely; it is technically possible to reconstruct shredded documents and recover data from shredded CDs and DVDs. Before disposing of outdated computers, hard drives should be securely erased or removed and destroyed. The memory in portable devices can be erased or overwritten before disposing of them. The process for doing so differs depending on the make and model of the device. Memory (SD) cards and SIM (Subscriber Identity Module) cards can be removed and securely destroyed.

---

[74] Stephen Treglia, Understanding Insurance Data Security, viewed at http://www.insurancetech.com/compliance/underwriting-insurance-data-security-/a/d-id/1318252 (accessed July 6 2015).

Intentionally removing data from the cloud can be more problematic. To enhance service and ensure that data are always available, cloud services typically have multiple copies of customer data in various locations, often internationally. When a user of a cloud service deletes data, it may only be access to the data that is removed rather than the data themselves. Even when a cloud service removes data, backup copies may remain. The data may continue to exist in multiple locations in the cloud, available to hackers and other unauthorized users. This is an important consideration when sensitive, or personal information is stored in, or accessed from, the cloud.

Unintentional destruction of data and information can occur in a number of ways:

- Employees may delete data, information or files accidentally.
- Notebook computers, USB drives, and mobile devices can be lost or stolen.
- System crashes and hard drive failures can occur.
- Viruses and malware can destroy data.
- Power failures and disasters, such as building fires, can result in losses.
- Coffee or other liquids spilled on notebooks or other devices can cause data loss.
- Employees may intentionally steal data or information.
- Hackers may breach an organization's security to obtain data and information.

An organization needs to have policies and procedures in place to prevent these losses from happening and to respond effectively in the event that a loss does occur. Instituting a data and information security program; implementing appropriate administrative, technical, internal, and external controls; and implementing a robust backup and recovery program can significantly reduce the risk of these sorts of unintentional losses.

Instituting a Data and Information Security Program

Instituting an effective data and information security program is essential for the ongoing viability of almost any organization. The *DAMA-DMBOK* outlines the activities involved in securing an organization's data. These activities also help ensure the security of an organization's information:

1. Understand Data Security Needs and Regulatory Requirements
2. Define Data Security Policy
3. Define Data Security Standards
4. Define Data Security Controls and Procedures
5. Manage Users, Passwords, and Group Membership
6. Manage Data Access Views and Permissions
7. Monitor User Authentication and Access Behavior
8. Classify Information Confidentiality
9. Audit Data Security[75]

---

[75] The DAMA Guide to the Data Management Body of Knowledge (DAMA-DMBOK) First Edition, DAMA International, Technics Publications LLC, New Jersey, copyright 2009 DAMA International, p. 152.

The information collected and created in support of insurance processes needs to be kept safe and confidential while, at the same time, being readily accessible to those who require it. In addition, the financial services industry is strictly regulated, as is the security of its data and information. It is essential to clearly understand an organization's business, ethical, and regulatory requirements regarding data and information security. This understanding forms the basis for what should be the collaborative development of data security policies to help ensure the confidentiality, integrity, and availability of the organization's data and information.

Ideally, data and information security policies are reviewed and approved by a data or information governance council or committee. Some organizations may have a separate data or information security governance committee in which case this would be the group that reviews and approves data security policies.

An organization needs to develop or adopt data security standards and implement controls and procedures to meet those standards. A number of data security standards exist. For example, the Payment Card Industry Security Standards Council has issued data security standards for organizations that process, store, or transmit credit or debit card information. The International Organization for Standardization (ISO) has published information security guidelines and techniques for the financial services industry. The North American Electric Reliability Corporation (NERC) has published a collection of cyber security standards. The security controls and procedures an organization implements in support of its security standards should be clearly documented and readily accessible by all users of data and information.

Access to data and information can be controlled through the use of passwords, and different information access privileges can be given to different groups. For example, underwriters can be given access to underwriting information but not accounting information; accountants can access and update accounting records but not claims files. It is important that individuals be included in the correct group to ensure that information access privileges associated with their password are appropriate.

Another way of controlling access to specific data is through the use of relational database views. A **view** is a "presentation of a set of data from one or more physical tables as one logical table. A view can include some or all of the rows and columns from each contributing table."[76] The use of views can restrict access to data in some rows or columns in a table while allowing access to the data in others.

Monitoring user authentication and access behavior can be done automatically with alerts to a security administrator or data steward when unusual or suspicious activities are detected. Monitoring provides information about who is accessing what information and helps identify security weaknesses that need to be addressed.

Data and information need to be classified based on their level of confidentiality. One classification method, discussed earlier, categorizes data and information as external public, internal public, confidential, regulated confidential, and restricted. Metadata can be used to indicate the level of confidentiality of data and information.

Regular, formal security audits are an essential element of a data and information security program. They can be performed by internal or external auditors. The auditors should not be directly responsible for the area being audited. Audits can identify vulnerabilities that need to be addressed and help ensure regulatory compliance.

---

[76] The DAMA Dictionary of Data Management, First Edition 2008, Mark Mosley Editor, Technics Publications LLC, New Jersey, copyright 2008 DAMA International, p. 123.

Security Controls

Organizations can implement a variety of controls to help ensure the security of their data and information. Administrative controls are policies and procedures that help ensure unintentional losses of data and information do not occur. Technical controls achieve the same outcome by using features in hardware and software. Administrative and technical controls can focus on limiting data and information losses resulting from either internal or external sources. Figure 8.1 provides examples of the various types of controls.

Controls	Administrative	Technical
Internal	e.g. data security training, computer use policies, employee background checks	e.g. passwords, relational database views, biometric identification, badge readers
External	e.g. visitors sign in and out with security guard, visitors restricted from computer areas	e.g. firewall for system access via the Internet, encryption of off-premises computers

Figure 8.1 Data security controls

Administrative and Technical Controls

Administrative control can often be best exercised through effective management. For example, an organization might stipulate that employees be given access only to the data and information they need in order to do their job, and that they receive regular, ongoing training in data security risks and best practices. Individuals using the organization's computers and mobile devices such as notebooks, tablets, and smartphones, should be prohibited from loading unauthorized software or personal items onto the device. Thorough background checks could be completed for all new employees who will have access to the organization's data and information. Visitors might be required to sign in and out with a security guard or be restricted from entering areas in which they could access a computer.

Technical controls protect data and information using the features of software and hardware. Examples of technical controls include the use of passwords to access systems and installing antivirus software or network security software.

Internal and External Controls

Internal controls can be either administrative or technical. They are primarily designed to prevent loss resulting from internal sources, although they can also help protect an organization from external threats. One approach is referred to as access control. A simple, administrative example of access control is the storage of confidential information, such as employee files, in a locked area. Technical access control can manage and limit user access to the network, applications, database management systems, servers, web pages, and other corporate resources. Technical access control includes user identity authentication through passwords, biometric identification (e.g. a fingerprint or retina scan), or the use of a hardware device such as a badge reader. A badge reader reads user identity badges and interfaces with a physical access control system, which in turn may control locked doors.

Generally, all computers permanently or intermittently connected to an insurance company network are password-protected or have a biometric identity authentication process. Multi-user systems employ user IDs and passwords unique to each user, as well as user privilege restriction mechanisms. User consoles have screen savers that lock automatically after a given period of time, requiring the user to re-authenticate his or her identity in order to continue working.

External controls are designed to protect against threats from outside the organization and they can be either administrative or technical. A firewall is an example of a technical external control. A firewall is a logical barrier that stops computer users or processes from going beyond a certain point in a network unless they pass a security check, for example, providing a password. Users accessing the insurance company's internal networks and systems from the Internet must typically pass through a firewall or network access control point before access is granted.

For mobile devices that leave the premises, employees may be required to use a cable locking system to secure the device to a large object, such as a desk, to prevent theft. Policy may require users to lock their mobile devices in a desk or file cabinet when not in use. Computers assigned to employees who have access to confidential or regulated information should have either full or partial disk encryption to protect the information if the computer is lost or stolen. The amount of confidential information that may be downloaded to mobile devices should be managed by policy.

Security audits can help identify exposures to both internal and external risks of data and information loss. They should be undertaken regularly by experienced IT professionals who are not directly responsible for the area being audited.

Backup and Recovery Procedures

If data are lost or corrupted as a result of a security breach or a disaster such as a fire, a recovery plan and appropriate backups are essential. **Backup and recovery** involves keeping a copy of programs, files, and databases so that they can be used for recovery in case something happens to the normal master production copy. It is a strategy to protect the existence of a physical database and to re-create or recover data when loss or destruction occurs. The *DAMA-DMBOK* specifies that database administrators "must make sure a recovery plan exists for all databases and database servers, covering all possible scenarios that could result in loss or corruption of data."[77]

---

[77] The DAMA Guide to the Data Management Body of Knowledge (DAMA-DMBOK) First Edition, DAMA International, Technics Publications LLC, New Jersey, copyright 2009 DAMA International, p. 132.

To protect an insurance company's data and information from loss or damage, the IT department is usually responsible for backing up corporate servers. Standard operating procedures for backups help ensure integrity, confidentiality, and availability of backup data. As a general rule, backups are stored offsite and policies dictate how long they are retained, for example:

- Daily backups for database servers will be retained for at least ____weeks.
- Daily backups for all other servers will be retained for at least ____weeks.
- Month-end full backups will be retained for a minimum of ___year(s).
- Year-end full backups will be retained indefinitely or for a time period defined by regulation.

There is a significant difference between backups intended for use when a single application or machine fails, and those created for the purpose of restoring full business capability after a disaster causes an entire facility to become non-operational. These differences are beyond the scope of this chapter, but backup and recovery plans for both situations need to be developed and instituted.

Data stored locally on an employee's computer may not be backed up by the central data backup system unless specific backup software is installed. As a general rule, any important data which requires backup should be stored in the user's home directory on the corporate network's server. All data critical to an employee's job should also be stored on the corporate network's server.

When an employee requires confidential information to be stored on a mobile device, the device should be both protected by encryption and backed up when it is connected to the corporate network. This policy typically applies to all personal devices that may hold confidential information as well as all communication devices that could receive corporate email.

Roles and Responsibilities

Ensuring that an organization's data and information are secure is not the sole responsibility of the IT department. Everyone within the organization has an important role to play. Although roles and responsibilities for data and information security may vary depending on the size, complexity, and culture of an enterprise, a variety of responsibilities need to be assigned.

The Data or Information Security Governance Committee

If an insurer has a data or information security governance committee, it is typically composed of managers from each of the company's major divisions and subsidiaries, or their delegates, as well as IT leadership, the security administrator, and an attorney with expertise in the area of intellectual property. If no security governance committee is in place, the data and/or information governance committee should fill that role. The committee typically meets regularly, and the purpose of these meetings is to:

- Periodically review the status of the company's computer and network security;
- Review and monitor remedial work related to computer and network security incidents and issues;

- Authorize major projects relating to computer and network security and evaluate their success;
- Approve new or modified information security policies, standards, guidelines, and procedures;
- Determine the best methods and practices to achieve information regulatory compliance;
- Review and approve security application development, acquisition, and implementation guidelines;
- Review policies and procedures for safeguarding information impacted by external standards and legal requirements; and
- Perform other high-level information security management activities.

The Chief Information Security Officer

Typically, the role of a chief information security officer (CISO) is to protect the insurance company's data and information by ensuring regulatory compliance and practicing effective risk management. Often, a CISO will partner with operations managers who understand the organization's security requirements from a business perspective. A CISO may also employ security engineers who focus on technical controls, forensic investigation, and resolving security incidents.

The Security Administrator

The security administrator is responsible for establishing, interpreting, implementing, and administering organization-wide IT security policies, standards, guidelines, and procedures. He or she performs or supervises information systems risk assessments; works with the business leadership to establish and enforce information security policies; prepares IT security action plans; evaluates information security products; and performs other activities necessary to assure a secure systems environment. The security administrator typically relies on a recognized information security framework to provide a benchmark for the corporation's security policies and practices. Appropriate metrics can help gauge the effectiveness of the organization's information security policies and practices. The security administrator is also responsible for conducting investigations into any alleged computer or network security compromises, incidents, or problems.

User Responsibilities

It is important that all employees receive appropriate training in data and information security, and that they clearly understand the implications of a breach in that security. Users of an insurer's data and information, particularly confidential information, are responsible for complying with the organization's security policies and administrative control measures. Employees should be trained to identify and promptly report any suspected security incidents, including intrusions and out-of-compliance situations, to the security administrator or to their supervisor.

Federal Trade Commission

In addition to data about customers, agents, brokers, claimants and others, there is other information insurers are required to keep confidential. For the insurance industry in the United States (US), there is a specific set of proprietary information that is not to be shared outside of the insurance company itself, its direct business associates, and regulators. To do so would be in violation of US antitrust laws. Antitrust laws prohibit certain practices such as price fixing or monopolies, which would restrain trade. The information insurers are prohibited from sharing includes:

- Rates presently charged or proposed to be charged by a company
- Restrictions proposed to be placed by a company on the availability of insurance
- Allocation of markets, territories or insureds
- Refusals to deal with third parties
- Profit levels
- Credit terms
- Costs of insurance coverage
- Determinations to quote or not to quote certain classes of business
- Insurance companies need to ensure that staff and management are properly trained so as to be in compliance with antitrust legislation.

Summary

Information can be categorized in a variety of ways: external public, internal public, confidential, regulated, and restricted. One of the most important types of confidential information for insurers is personally identifiable information (PII). It is essential that insurers and other organizations protect the confidential information in their possession. There are a number of laws and regulations related to PII. Breach laws, intended to prevent identity theft, require organizations to promptly inform affected parties when their PII has been exposed by a security breach. Privacy laws go farther than breach laws to protect individual's privacy. The Gramm-Leach-Bliley Act, the Health Insurance Protection and Accountability Act (HIPAA), and the NAIC's *Principles for Effective Cybersecurity: Insurance Regulatory Guidance* all outline how insurers are required to protect the security and confidentiality of the data and information they obtain.

Data and information can be disposed of intentionally; however, they can also be lost or corrupted unintentionally. An organization can help prevent unintentional losses by implementing a data and information security program. This involves identifying the organization's needs and the regulatory requirements with which it must comply; defining data security policies, standards, controls, and procedures; managing access to data and information; monitoring user authentication and access behavior; classifying data and information based on their level of confidentiality; and performing regular data security audits. Implementing effective security controls is an important element in ensuring data security. These controls can be administrative or technical, internal or external. Even effective controls do not negate the need for back-up and recovery plans. Various individuals and groups are involved in data security, including a governance body, a chief information security officer, security administrator, security engineers, business managers and all of the users of an organization's data and information.

Finally, US federal antitrust legislation prohibits insurers from sharing certain proprietary information outside of the insurance company itself, its direct business associates, and regulators. Companies need to ensure that staff is appropriately trained to ensure compliance.

Bibliography

The DAMA Dictionary of Data Management, First Edition 2008, Mark Mosley Editor, Technics Publications LLC, New Jersey, copyright 2008 DAMA International.

The DAMA Guide to the Data Management Body of Knowledge (DAMA-DMBOK) First Edition, DAMA International, Technics Publications LLC, New Jersey, copyright 2009 DAMA International.

Information Security Handbook, Restricted Confidential and Public/Internal Data, viewed at http://bit.ly/2rpPbde (accessed June 30, 2015).

Arvind Narayanan and Vitaly Shmatikov, Privacy and Security – Myths and Fallacies of "Personally Identifiable Information", Communications of the ACM, 06/2010 Vol. 53 No. 06, Association of Computing Machinery, p. 24.

Margaret Rouse, personally identifiable information, viewed at http://bit.ly/1j6kazZ (accessed July 1, 2015).

California CIVIL CODE SECTION 1798.80-1798.84 (accessed July 1, 2015).

Maine Revised Statutes, Title 10: COMMERCE AND TRADE, Part 3: REGULATION OF TRADE. Chapter 210-B: NOTICE OF RISK TO PERSONAL DATA, viewed at http://bit.ly/2rG7Rog (accessed July 1, 2015).

Summary of the HIPAA Privacy Rule, viewed at http://bit.ly/1HsSy8r (accessed July 1, 2015).

Security 101 for Covered Entities (accessed July 1, 2015).

NIST Publishes Final Guidelines for Protecting Sensitive Government Information Held by Contractors, From NIST Tech Beat: June 19, 2015, viewed at http://bit.ly/2rFTu3s (accessed July 2, 2015).

Ron Ross, Patrick Viscuso, Gary Guissanie, Kelley Dempsey, Mark Riddle, Nist Special Publication 800-171, Protecting Controlled Unclassified Information in Nonfederal Information Systems and Organizations, viewed at http://bit.ly/1qwFdoT (accessed July 2, 2015).

Regulations for NPI & PII, Intrusion, viewed at http://bit.ly/2txrxw3 (accessed July 2, 2015).

The Security Rule, U.S. Department of Health & Human Services, viewed at http://bit.ly/1FrxGIX (accessed July 2, 2015).

A Brief Background on the HIPAA Rules and the HITECH Act, viewed at http://bit.ly/2rBgVQ2 (accessed July 2, 2015).

Data Masking, Techopedia, viewed at http://bit.ly/2txtgRK (accessed August 10, 2015).

Cloud Tokenization Primer, Perspecsys, Tokenization: How it Works in The Cloud, viewed at http://bit.ly/1g6EQuo (accessed August 10, 2015).

Data Protection, viewed at http://bit.ly/1iUvjIH (accessed August 12, 2015).

Personal Data Protection Act, viewed at http://bit.ly/2skUI5Q (accessed August 12, 2015).

Robert Sheldon, Deleting Files in the Cloud, 23 September 2014, Simple Talk, viewed at http://bit.ly/2sIQCHi (accessed August 13, 2015).

Data Modeling Fundamentals

Data modeling is a way of graphically illustrating the relationships among the various entities that are important to an organization. Those relationships can be categorized in a variety of ways, and a data model can visually differentiate between those different categories. There are three levels of data modeling: conceptual, logical, and physical. A good data model will help an organization better understand and communicate its business processes and requirements. Data modeling is a collaborative, iterative process that involves a variety of stakeholders throughout an organization. There are several criteria against which the quality of a data model can be measured.

Educational Objectives

Upon completion of this assignment, you should be able to:

1. Explain the basic concepts underlying data modeling.
2. Define data modeling and describe its importance.
3. Describe the different relationships between entities: one-to-one, one-to-many, many-to-many, recursive.
4. Describe the building blocks of a data model.
5. Describe a database model and how relationships among entities are indicated.
6. Describe the criteria for judging data model quality.

Basic Data Modeling Concepts

A number of basic data modeling concepts were introduced earlier in the context of relational databases. However, data models do not have to be associated with relational databases. They can serve other purposes as well, and they can have value in and of themselves because they allow an organization to better understand its data requirements.

In data modeling, the first step is to identify and define the required entities, which are the things, processes, transactions, or concepts the organization wants to collect or create data about. Then, the required attributes of each of these entities need to be identified and defined, including how each attribute will be represented in the data. For example, an Employee entity may have the employee's name, job category, or the date he or she was hired as attributes. Data modelers then explore and document all of the various relationships among the required entities and create a graphical representation of those relationships.

In a relational database, every entity has a primary key, which serves as a unique identifier for that particular entity. A primary key can be a single field, for example a customer number, or it can be a combination of fields, such as brokerage name and brokerage address. When a combination of fields serves as a primary key, it is referred to as a **composite key**, or sometimes a structured or concatenated key. When the primary key from one entity appears in another entity, it is referred to as a foreign key. Foreign keys point, or refer, to data contained in other entities. The use of primary keys and foreign keys defines relationships between entities, reduces data redundancy, preserves data integrity, and supports data normalization.

Data normalization enhances the efficiency of a relational database. The goal is to store "one fact in one place"; to ensure that a specific attribute is assigned to only one entity. It focuses on including only attributes of the primary key in each entity. This often involves splitting a single entity into two or more entities. One approach to normalization uses reference data. Reference data are data in look-up or code entities that are read but not updated by business applications. For example, rather than including a sales commission rate for every row in a POLICY entity, the policy type could serve as a foreign key to read a value in a COMMISSION reference data look-up entity. If the commission rate for a particular policy type increases or decreases, only the COMMISSION entity would need to be updated.

This storing of "one fact in one place" might seem to create limitations in terms of accessing the data. However, in relational databases it is possible to extract selected data from multiple entities and combine them into a single consolidated view. This means that confidential or sensitive information can be excluded from the view presented to employees not authorized to see it, and that data from several different tables can be accessed together as needed. In order to find the required data in each table, a database may use an index. Just like the index in a book, a database index is an ordered set of pointers to the location of specific information, in this case one or more rows in a database table. Indexes accelerate data access.

Data Modeling

Data modeling is a method for determining what data, and what relationships among those data, should be stored in a database. It is also a way of graphically communicating database design. There are three levels of data modeling: conceptual, logical, and physical. Typically, database designers work sequentially through each of these stages as illustrated in Figure 9.1. Within each stage, development is generally an iterative process.

A **conceptual data model (CDM)** is created in consultation with business subject matter experts. The process involves determining what data an organization needs to capture or create, and identifying how those data are related to each other. Because it focuses on entity names and entity relationships, it is often referred to as **entity-relationship modeling** or E-R modeling. A conceptual data model forms the basis for a logical data model.

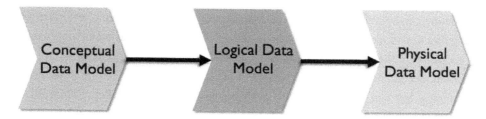

Figure 9.1 Creating data models

A **logical data model (LDM)** defines the structures that will be used by the database management system (DBMS). In a relational database, those structures are tables. A logical data model includes more detail than a conceptual data model. These details include entity names, entity relationships, the attributes of each entity type, and the primary and foreign keys that will be used in the tables.

A **physical data model (PDM)** is "a data model depicting relational tables, columns, foreign key relationships, and indexes. A physical data model is usually based on a logical data model (LDM) but may also be reverse engineered to describe an existing database design. A physical data model adopts the naming conventions and the physical data types specific to a particular DBMS."[78] The following table summarizes the elements of conceptual, logical, and physical data models.[79]

Item	Conceptual	Logical	Physical
Entity names	X	X	
Entity relationships	X	X	
Attributes		X	
Primary keys		X	X
Foreign keys		X	X
Table names			X
Column names			X
Column data types			X

Data modeling is important because it helps an organization achieve a number of goals:

- Understand the organization better
- Document and enforce business rules
- Facilitate program design
- Ensure data quality

[78] The DAMA Dictionary of Data Management, First Edition 2008, Mark Mosley Editor, Technics Publications LLC, New Jersey, copyright 2008 DAMA International, p. 95.

[79] Adapted from Data Modeling, Big Data Analytics, viewed at www.1keydata.com/datawrehousing/data-modeling-levels.html (accessed July 31, 2015).

Although data modeling can be a time-consuming activity, it is an essential element of effective data management. The process of creating a data model helps individuals and groups to better understand an organization's business requirements by focusing on the relationships between the entities that are important to its operations. It can also facilitate identification, documentation, and enforcement of business rules. For example, a customer can own one or more insurance policies, but can a customer exist with no policies? Can a policy exist without an associated customer? Can a policy be owned by more than one customer?

An organization's application systems work with the data in the database, updating them, viewing them, or sharing them. As a result, the design and structure of those systems can be influenced by the way in which the data are organized. A well-designed data model can facilitate system development and programming. It also has the advantage of being concise and comprehensible by non-technical staff as compared to a detailed functional specification.

Finally, poor quality data are often the result of a lack of clear definitions for each data element in each table in the database. Data modeling helps to create a common understanding of an organization's data, which in turn helps to ensure data quality.

Types of Relationships

A conceptual data model focuses simply on entities and the relationships between them. These relationships can be of several different types:

- One-to-one
- One-to-many
- Many-to-many
- Recursive

In a **one-to-one relationship**, there are only two entities involved. This chapter returns to ABC Insurance, introduced in an earlier chapter, to provide some examples. If ABC Insurance supplies company vehicles to its marketing representatives and some of its claims adjusters, each of those employees would be assigned a specific vehicle, and that vehicle would be assigned exclusively to that particular employee. That is not to say that, over time, an employee would never be assigned a new vehicle, or a vehicle would never be reassigned. But at any given time, one employee would have the use of one particular vehicle.

A single marketing representative would have responsibility for servicing a number of different insurance brokerages, and each of those brokerages would only be served by that one marketing representative. This is an example of a **one-to-many relationship**. The marketing representative may eventually leave the organization and be replaced, or brokerages could be reassigned to a different marketing representative, but the relationship would remain one-to-many.

A **many-to-many relationship** involves multiple entities on both sides. For example, many of the insurance brokerages with which ABC has entered into a brokerage agreement sell policies to many of ABC's customers.

In the one-to-one, one-to-many, and many-to-many relationships just discussed, there are two different entity types involved, for example, employees and vehicles, employees and brokerages, or brokerages and customers. This kind of relationship is sometimes referred to as **binary** because it involves two types of entities. A relationship between two instances of the same entity type is called a **recursive relationship**, or self-referencing relationship. Recursive relationships can be referred to as **unary** because they only involve one entity type. For example, Employee would be a common entity type for most organizations. Some employees are managers and some are not. Therefore, some members of the Employee entity type manage other members of the Employee entity type.

Understanding Relationships Among Entity Types

Data modelers first need to determine what entity types ABC Insurance needs to capture or create information about, and to understand the relationships among them. They meet with data stewards, operational staff, and subject matter experts and ask a variety of questions. Once they have answers to their questions, they can use that information to document those relationships graphically.

Question:	Answer:
"Is every employee at ABC Insurance assigned a company vehicle?"	"No, only the marketing representatives and the outside claims adjusters get company cars."
"Would a situation occur in which a company vehicle is not assigned to any employee?"	"Yes, there are three unassigned vehicles; they are temporary substitutes used when an assigned vehicle is in for maintenance or being repaired after an accident."
"Is it possible that a marketing representative might not be responsible for any brokerages?"	"Yes, a new hire would not be assigned any brokerages until after successfully completing his or her training."
"Is it possible that a brokerage might not be served by a marketing representative?"	"No, every brokerage contracted with ABC Insurance is served by a marketing representative."
"Might a brokerage be served by more than one marketing representative?"	"No, even the largest brokerages only deal with one marketing representative. It helps to avoid errors and confusion."
"Would every one of ABC's customers have	"Yes, at present ABC only markets through its

purchased a policy from a broker with whom ABC has a brokerage agreement?"

brokerage network, but that will change. We will be opening a call center for direct sales next year."

"Is it possible that a contracted broker might not have placed any business with ABC Insurance?"

"Yes, for a short period immediately after signing the brokerage agreement, a brokerage may not sell an ABC policy. Often they wait until their staff receives training in our underwriting guidelines."

"Is it possible that an ABC employee might not have a manager?"

"No, all employees have a manager. If a manager leaves the organization, his or her employees are temporarily assigned to another manager until he or she is replaced."

"Is it possible that an employee might be managed by more than one manager?"

"No, that is against ABC's Human Resources policies."

"Is it possible that a manager may not have any employees?"

"Yes, ABC has a number of technical specialists who are categorized and paid at a management level, but who have no direct reports."

Conceptually Illustrating Relationships Between Entity Types

There are a number of different notations used in data modeling. The basic building blocks in conceptual data modeling begin with boxes and lines. Boxes represent entities and lines represent relationships. Figure 9.2 illustrates one commonly used notation system for indicating the types of relationships among entities.

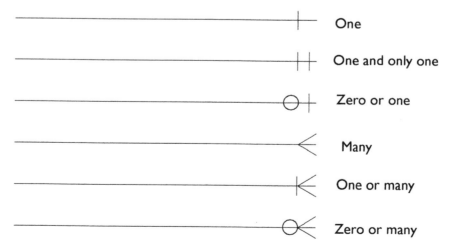

Figure 9.2 Illustrating relationships

Figure 9.3 shows how boxes, lines, and symbols are used in data modeling to document and define relationships.

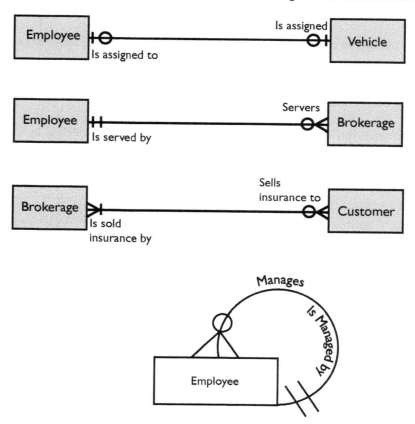

Figure 9.3 Documenting relationships

The appropriate symbol is added to each end of the line linking two entity boxes to indicate the type of relationship the entities have. Because there can be more than one relationship between the same two entity types, text is used to clarify the nature of each relationship.

Figure 9.3 returns to ABC Insurance and illustrates how the answers to some of the data modelers' questions can be documented:

- The first example indicates that an employee is assigned zero or one vehicle and a vehicle is assigned to zero or one employee. This can be read: Each employee <u>may</u> be assigned one vehicle, and each vehicle <u>may</u> be assigned to a single employee. This reflects the facts that not every employee is assigned a company vehicle, and there are vehicles in the fleet that are unassigned.

- In the second example, a marketing representative is a member of the Employee entity type. Each marketing representative services zero or many brokerages, and each brokerage is served by one and only one marketing representative. This can be read: Each employee <u>may</u> service many brokerages, but each brokerage <u>must</u> be served by a single employee. This notation clarifies whether a relationship is optional or mandatory. In this case, it reflects the fact that marketing representatives are not assigned brokerages until after completion of their training.

- In the third example, a brokerage sells insurance to zero or many customers, and a customer purchases insurance from one or many brokerages. This can be read: A brokerage <u>may</u> sell insurance to customers but a customer <u>must</u> purchase ABC insurance policies through one or more contracted brokerages. This, however, will change after the opening of the call center.

- In the final example, an employee may manage zero or many employees but each employee must be managed by one and only one employee. This can be read: An employee <u>may</u> or <u>may not</u> manage other employees, but each employee <u>must</u> report to a single manager. This reflects the fact that some technical specialists are classified and paid as managers but have no direct reports.

The relationships illustrated in Figure 9.3 are very simple. In reality, data modeling quickly becomes far more complex. Figure 9.4, on the following page, represents a small sample of the many tables in ABC Insurance's relational database. It includes the EMPLOYEE, BROKERAGE, VEHICLE, CUSTOMER, and POLICY entity types.

Figure 9.5, on the page following Figure 9.4, illustrates how slightly more complex relationships among entities at ABC Insurance can be documented using data modeling notation. It has been drawn to reflect the anticipated opening of ABC's direct sales call center. After the center opens, customers will have the option of purchasing ABC insurance from brokerages or directly from call center employees.

This conceptual data model, or entity-relationship model, illustrates a number of links:

- Each employee (i.e. marketing representative) may service many brokerages, but each brokerage must be served by one and only one employee (i.e. marketing representative). This may be the case with underwriters as well.

- Each employee may be assigned a single company vehicle and each vehicle may be assigned to one employee.

- Each employee may or may not manage other employees, but each employee must report to a single manager.

- Many brokerages might represent many customers, and many customers might be represented by more than one brokerage. Because customers will be able to purchase coverage through either a brokerage or the direct sales call center, they may deal with an employee to the exclusion of a brokerage, or with a brokerage to the exclusion of a call center employee. Alternatively, they may deal through a brokerage for some lines of business but deal directly with ABC for other lines.

- Many employees (i.e. call center employees) might sell insurance coverage to many customers and some customers might purchase coverage from more than one employee. As is the case with brokerages, there may be a short period after he or she is hired that a call center employee may not make any sales. In the longer term, that individual would probably be terminated, but in the short term a lack of sales might be considered acceptable.

- A customer must be covered under at least one policy and a policy must cover at least one customer. This implies that the definition of "customer" is "an insured" and reflects a business rule that has been created by ABC's operational managers.

- Each brokerage might sell many policies but each policy must be sold by one and only one brokerage. Policies may be transferred from one brokerage to another, but at any given time, each policy is associated with only one brokerage.

- A brokerage may earn commission income on many policies, but each policy must generate commission for one and only one brokerage.

ABC Insurance

EMPLOYEE

Employee ID Number	Employee Name	Employee Job Category	Employee Salary Grade
1234	Amanda Allen	Underwriter	B
2345	Brian Brown	Claims adjuster	C
3456	Calvin Chang	Marketing rep	C
4567	Denis Dubois	Marketing rep	B
5678	Elaine Ellsworth	Call Center Sales	D
6789	Frank Ferelli	Call Center Sales	D

BROKERAGE

Brokerage ID Number	Brokerage Name	Employee ID number
B145	Northwoods Ins.	3456
B197	Protectall Ins.	4567
B237	Neighborhood Ins.	4567
B315	Southside Ins.	3456

VEHICLE

Vehicle ID Number	Vehicle Description	Employee ID Number
A568	2014 Honda Civic	3456
A652	2013 Honda Civic	2345
A957	2012 Honda Civic	4567

CUSTOMER

Customer ID Number	Customer Name	Street Address	City	State	Zip Code	Brokerage ID Number
12345-01	Milton Mobrey	123 4th St.	Anytown	PA	12345	B145
98766-21	Nancy Newton	234 Willow St.	Homeville	IA	23456	B197
34567-12	Orton Oswald	19 Main St.	Fairtown	GA	34567	B237

POLICY

Policy Number	Customer ID Number	Inception Date	Lines of Business	Policy Type Code	Brokerage ID Number
123456	12345-01	03/15/2015	Property	01	B145
234567	34567-12	01/27/2015	Property	01	B197
345678	98766-21	07/15/2015	Auto	05	B237
456789	34567-12	08/15/2015	Property	02	B145
567890	12345-01	09/23/2014	Auto	06	B197
678901	98766-21	06/19/2015	Property	01	B237

Figure 9.4 Sample tables

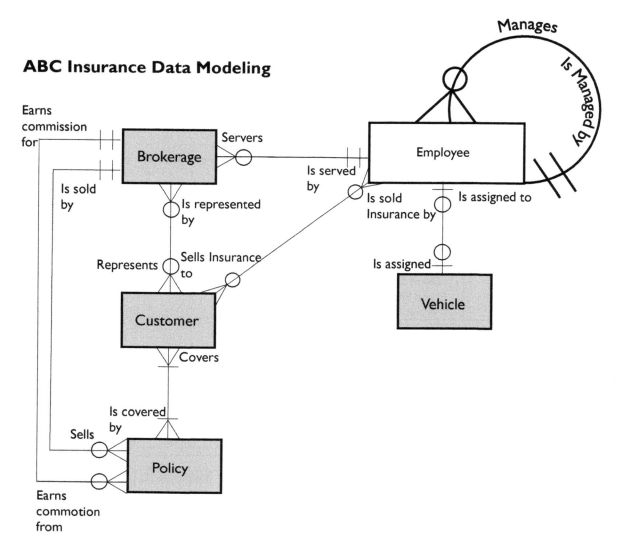

Figure 9.5 More complex relationships

The words used to describe the type of relationship a line represents are important, and they help to define or reflect the nature of the entity types. For example, in the relationship between the Customer and Policy entity types the terms used are "Covers" and "Is covered by". This indicates that anyone covered under the policy is considered to be a Customer. If, on the other hand, the terms used had been "Purchases" and "Is purchased by" that might imply that only the entity paying the premium, presumably the named insured or policyholder, would be considered to be a Customer. To avoid confusion or misunderstanding it is important to have clear definitions for each entity type or class included in a conceptual data model.

Logical Data Models use the same relationship indicators as conceptual data models, but they include additional detail, such as the entity's attributes, primary key, and foreign keys. Figure 9.6 shows how an entity type is often represented in logical data modeling. The attributes are those included in the EMPLOYEE entity illustrated in Figure 9.4.

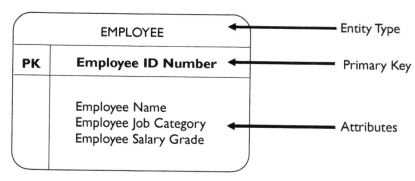

Figure 9.6 Entity on a logical data model

Figure 9.7, on the following page, illustrates how a variety of relationships could be documented in a logical data model.

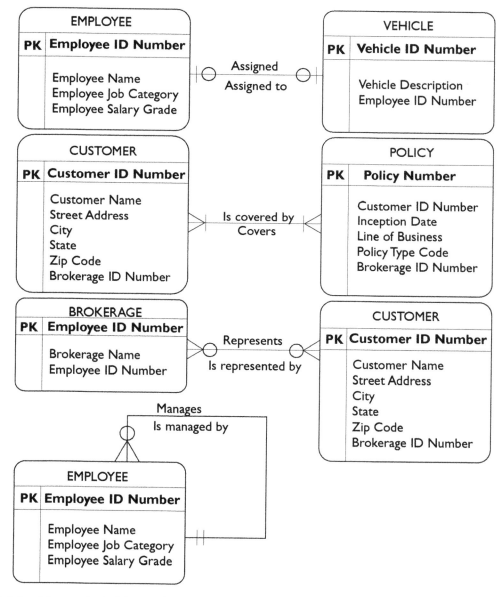

Figure 9.7 Relationships on a logical data model

Often, logical data modeling helps identify opportunities for normalization that may go unrecognized in conceptual data modeling. For example, in Figure 9.7, the representation of the CUSTOMER entity includes the attribute Brokerage ID Number. The POLICY entity also includes a column for Brokerage ID Number. This results in redundant data. Data redundancy is generally considered undesirable, although it is sometimes necessary to enhance system performance.

How to best normalize the entities depends on the situation. In the case of customers and policies, a customer may choose to deal with multiple brokerages, but a policy will only ever be written through a single brokerage. An insured may transfer a policy from the original brokerage to another brokerage, but at any given time, one policy will only be associated with a single brokerage. For example, Milton Mobrey, ABC Insurance Company's customer number 12345-01, purchased automobile insurance in September of 2014 through Protectall Insurance Brokerage. Milton subsequently relocated to another city and bought a home. He purchased ABC's homeowners coverage through a local brokerage there, Northwood Insurance. When his automobile policy came due for renewal, he transferred it to Northwood, but in the interim he was associated with two of ABC's contracted brokerages.

ABC Insurance needs to be able to link both policies and customers with the appropriate brokerages. The company needs to determine which brokerage should be paid commission for which policies and which office to contact if an issue arises with a customer. Because the data managers have created a business rule that a person or organization needs to have at least one policy in order to be considered a customer, it follows that there will always be at least one policy for each customer. ABC's systems can link customers to brokerages using the POLICY entity. In this case, the column Brokerage ID Number can be removed from the CUSTOMER entity to help normalize the database.

Figure 9.8 illustrates the relationship between ABC's call center employees and the policies the company writes through direct sales. One limitation of this relationship illustration is that there is no way to determine specifically which employee sold a particular policy. ABC's call center managers would want to be able to track the performance of individual employees in terms of the number of policies they sell and the premium volumes they generate for the organization.

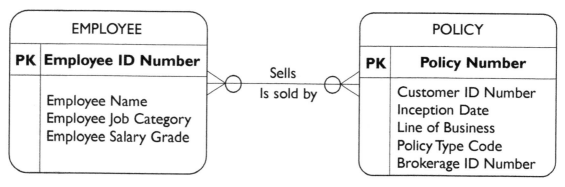

Figure 9.8 Call center sales relationship

One way individual call center employee performance could be measured involves creating an **associative entity**. An associative entity is an alternative way for dealing with many-to-many relationships by creating a separate entity to represent the association between two other entities. In this case, the data modeler has created an entity called SALE. The primary key for the SALE entity is a combination of Employee ID Number and Policy Number as shown in Figure 9.9. This combination creates a unique identifier for each insurance policy sale completed through the call center. By including the attribute Premium in the SALE entity, it will be possible for call center managers to monitor the premium volume generated by each employee.

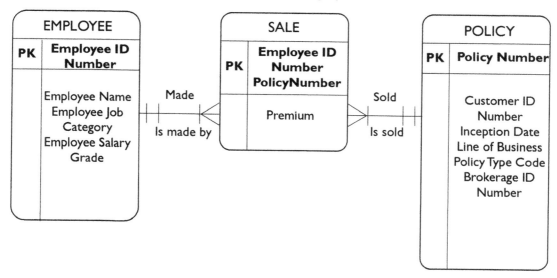

Figure 9.9 Associative entity

The relationship lines indicate that each sale involves one and only one call center employee and one and only one policy. In addition, it shows that each individual employee will be involved in many sales and that many policies will be sold. For call center sales, the Brokerage ID Number in the POLICY entity could be a unique code used to identify the call center.

Another type of relationship that can be described graphically is the relationship between **subtypes** and **supertypes**. Subtypes and supertypes essentially define a taxonomy, or an "is a kind of" relationship. In Figure 9.10, Policy is the supertype and Automobile and Homeowners are the subtypes. The half circle with an X is the notation used to indicate this type of relationship.

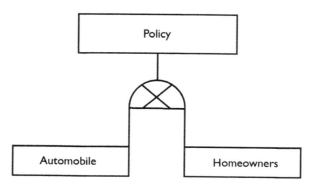

Figure 9.10 subtypes and supertype

Figure 9.11, on the following page, presents a portion of an insurance data model. It has been excerpted and adapted from a high-level conceptual data model developed by the Insurance Working Group of the Object Management Group (OMG). OMG is "an international, open membership, not-for-profit technology standards consortium. Founded in 1989, OMG standards are driven by vendors, end-users, academic institutions and government agencies. OMG Task Forces develop enterprise integration standards for a wide range of technologies and an even wider range of industries."[80] This conceptual data model was developed in consultation with 50 insurance organizations including insurers, system vendors, and insurance organizations. It is intended to accommodate all property and casualty lines of business.[81]

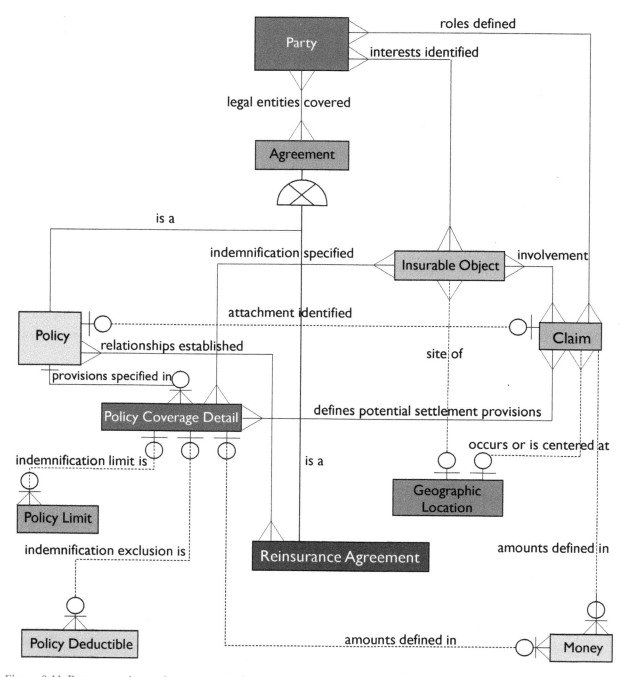

Figure 9.11 Property and casualty conceptual data model, excepted from Word Conceptual Data Model, document 13-04-08_p_c_conceptual_data_model_overview.docx, viewed at www.omgwikilorg/pcwg/doku.php?id=start (accessed August 4, 2015)

---

[80] About OMG, viewed at http://omg.org/gettingstarted/gettingstartedindex.htm, (accessed August 4, 2015).

[81] William Jenkins, Object Management Group, (email dated August 3, 2015).

Figure 9.11[82] illustrates a slightly different notation than the other figures in this chapter; optional relationships are indicated by dashed lines and the zero-to-many symbol used in previous figures is shown here as zero-one-or-many. There are several data modeling notations in common use and there are differences among them. However, once a data management professional understands the concept of data modeling, the differences in notation should not present a challenge.

The OMG data model includes clear definitions of the terms used. For example, Party is defined as "a Person, Organization, or Group playing a role in the insurance industry. In the data model, Party is a major entity that relates to almost all the other major entities as it defines how people, organizations, and groups are involved in the insurance and financial services business involving agreements, policies, claims, insurable objects, etc. With the use of party, many other data requirements can be made common and managed more efficiently."[83]

Judging Data Model Quality

Data modeling is as much of an art as a science; there are typically a variety of ways of defining entities and expressing the relationships among them. Even so, well-designed data models have a number of features:

- Perhaps most importantly, a good data model is complete. It comprises all of the entities and relationships required by the organization's operations and systems.

- Normalization is an important feature of a well-designed logical data model. While some de-normalization may occur in a physical data model to enhance system performance, the objective in data modeling is to reduce data redundancy as much as possible.

- A good data model highlights and helps to enforce an organization's business rules. For example, if an insurer has a business rule that a party must have at least one insurance policy to qualify as a customer, that rule should be integrated into the data model.

- In a well-crafted data model there is no ambiguity. Entities, attributes, and relationships are clearly defined and those definitions are documented and available for general reference.

- Adaptability is an important quality in a well-crafted data model. It should be both flexible enough and stable enough to respond to changes in the business environment, such as a change in regulations or the launch of a new product or service.

- Another feature of a good data model is sometimes referred to as "elegance". An elegant data model is one that is as simple and concise as possible, rather than highly complex. Elegant models can often result from rethinking existing business processes after data modeling highlights inefficiencies or redundancies.

---

[82] Excerpted from Word Publication Conceptual Data Model, document 13-04-08_p_c_conceptual_data_model_overview.docx, viewed at www.omgwiki.org/pcwg/doku.php?id=start, (accessed August 4, 2015).

[83] Ibid.

- A good data model communicates effectively. In order to be able to give the feedback required to ensure that the data model is accurate, operational staff have to be able to understand it. It needs to use terms and concepts with which they are familiar.

- A good data model takes into consideration how one database will integrate with the organization's other databases. Specifying an enterprise-wide data architecture helps to ensure that the various data models are integrated.

One term that is sometimes used to refer to a high quality data model is "high fidelity". Just as a high fidelity audio recording lacks distortion and accurately reproduces the original performance, a **high fidelity data model** accurately and completely depicts the realities of an organization's operations.

Summary

Data modeling is a method for determining what data, and what relationships among those data, should be stored in a database. It is also a way of graphically communicating database design. A data model can be conceptual, sometimes referred to as an entity-relationship model, logical, or physical. Conceptual data modeling focuses simply on entity types and relationships. Logical data modeling includes entity types and relationships with the addition of attributes, and primary and foreign keys. Physical data modeling deals with primary and foreign keys, table names, column names and column data types.

Data modeling is important because it helps an organization achieve a number of goals including understanding the organization better, documenting and enforcing business rules, facilitating program design, and helping to ensure data quality.

A conceptual data model focuses simply on entities and the relationships between them. These relationships can be one-to-one, one-to-many, many-to-many, or recursive. Data modelers use a variety of symbols to indicate the various types of relationships and whether those relationships are optional or mandatory. For example, a marketing representative may or may not serve one or more brokerages, but each brokerage must be served by a marketing representative. Another type of relationship that can be described graphically is the relationship between subtypes and supertypes. Subtypes and supertypes essentially define an "is a kind of" relationship.

Often, logical data modeling helps identify opportunities for normalization that may go unrecognized in conceptual data modeling. How to best normalize relational database tables depends on the situation.

A well-crafted data model is complete; is normalized to reduce data redundancy; highlights and helps to enforce an organization's business rules; is unambiguous; is adaptable; is simple and concise, often referred to as elegant; communicates effectively; and helps ensure that the database will integrate well with the organization's other databases. A particularly well-designed data model is sometimes referred to as "high fidelity".

Bibliography

The DAMA Dictionary of Data Management, First Edition 2008, Mark Mosley Editor, Technics Publications LLC, New Jersey, copyright 2008 DAMA International.

The DAMA Guide to the Data Management Body of Knowledge (DAMA-DMBOK) First Edition, DAMA International, Technics Publications LLC, New Jersey, copyright 2009 DAMA International.

Mark L. Gillenson, Fundamentals of Database Management Systems, 2nd Edition, Fogelman College of Business and Economics, University of Memphis, published by John Wiley & Sons, Inc., printed and bound by RR Donnelley, copyright 2012, 2005 by John Wiley & Sons, ISBN 978-0-470-62470-8.

Graeme C. Simsion and Graham Witt, Data Modelling Essentials, Third Edition, Morgan Kaufmann Publishers, Elsevier, 500 Sansome Street, Suite 400, San Francisco, CA 94111, © 2005 by Elsevier Inc. ISBN: 0-12-644551-6.

Data Modeling 101, Scott Ambler, viewed at http://bit.ly/2szQSIv (accessed July 13, 2015).

ER Diagram Symbols and Meaning, viewed at http://bit.ly/1O8YZLz (accessed July 17, 2015).

Crow's Feet Are Best, Posted on June 1, 2008 by Jim Stewart, The Data Administration Newsletter, viewed at http://bit.ly/2tcV3rE (accessed July 22, 2015).

Data Modeling, viewed at http://bit.ly/1FeShQ7 (accessed July 31, 2015).

Barry Williams, Data Modelling by Example, viewed at http://bit.ly/2sCEwjs (accessed August 4, 2015).

Object Management Group, Insurance Working Group, P & C Workgroup artifacts, Conceptual Data Model, viewed at http://bit.ly/2sl4q8y (accessed August 4, 2015).

Document and Content Management

Consider the amount and variety of data and information on the typical mobile device. Many individuals have so much information on their devices that they often cannot find the photo, message, or email they are looking for. Now consider the amount of data and information that resides outside of traditional databases at an insurance company. This would include, for example, word processing documents, emails, spreadsheets, and photographs. An insurer needs policies, processes, and tools to effectively manage this vast amount of data and information so that it generates the greatest value for the organization. Document and content management is the element of data management that focuses on data that reside outside of databases. It involves a number of activities that help an organization manage the lifecycle of its documents. An earlier chapter discussed the risks associated with data in databases; data outside of databases face the same types of risks, and organizations need effective management to avoid or mitigate those risks. Ensuring the security of documents, and complying with operational and regulatory requirements related to their appropriate retention and disposal, are important elements of a document and content management program. Periodic audits help ensure the effectiveness of an organization's document management practices.

Documents and content are referred to as **unstructured data**, and there are a number of synonyms in use for that term. Whatever terminology an organization elects to use, clear definitions are essential. While data mining extracts meaning from structured data in databases, text mining can discover information from textual documents. The unstructured data in documents are important because they represent a significant amount of an organization's data and they provide insights that cannot be gleaned from structured data. However, there are challenges associated with managing unstructured data and integrating them with structured data.

Educational Objectives

Upon completion of this assignment, you should be able to:

1. Define and describe document and content management.
2. Outline the document management life cycle.
3. Describe the activities involved in document management and content management.
4. Describe the methods used to index and retrieve content.
5. Describe the risks associated with document and content management and how they can be mitigated.
6. Describe the issues related to document and content retention and destruction.

7. Describe audit protocols in document and content management.

8. List the guiding principles of content and document management.

9. Define structured and unstructured data. Provide examples of each.

10. Define multi-structured data. Provide an example.

11. Define data mining and text mining.

12. Describe the importance of unstructured data to organizations.

13. Outline the challenges involved in managing unstructured data.

14. Describe the challenges of integrating structured and unstructured data.

Document and Content Management

Document and content management is "control over capture, storage, access and use of data and information stored outside structured databases."[84] These data and information may be in a variety of forms including paper documents, electronic word processing documents, emails, scanned copies of paper documents, spreadsheets, photographs, audio and video recordings, and intranet content. The *DAMA-DMBOK* lists the goals of document and content management:

1. To safeguard and ensure the availability of data assets stored in less structured formats.

2. To enable effective and efficient retrieval and use of data and information in unstructured formats.

3. To comply with legal obligations and customer expectations.

4. To ensure business continuity through retention, recovery, and conversion.

5. To control document storage operating costs.[85]

Document management and content management were introduced briefly in an earlier chapter. **Document management**, sometimes referred to as records management, is a collection of systems, either manual or electronic, used to maintain, classify, organize, and retrieve paper or electronic documents. It focuses on documents that have been designated as significant to the organization's business activities and regulatory compliance. Not all of an organization's documents are subject to document and content management.

For the purposes of data management, a document is any unstructured presentation of information. Document management focuses on the document as a whole rather than on the content elements it contains, and it has been practiced for centuries. Even the earliest libraries relied on some form of document management. For example, for over two hundred years, the Dewey Decimal system has been used in libraries to categorize and locate books, papers, and articles. For electronic documents, indexes and well-crafted metadata can facilitate discovery of, and access to, all appropriate resources for a specified purpose.

---

[84] The DAMA Dictionary of Data Management, First Edition 2008, Mark Mosley Editor, Technics Publications LLC, New Jersey, copyright 2008 DAMA International, p.54

[85] The DAMA Guide to the Data Management Body of Knowledge (DAMA-DMBOK) First Edition, DAMA International, Technics Publications LLC, New Jersey, copyright 2009 DAMA International, p.240.

Electronic document management systems (EDMS) store electronic documents and scanned copies of paper documents. EDMS, such as Microsoft SharePoint, typically support a variety of different functions:

- Creating and collaborating on documents
- Approving documents
- Checking out and checking in documents to lock them while they are being worked on
- Adding metadata when they are filed to allow for discovery and retrieval
- Distributing documents to the intended users
- Retrieving documents, for example, by using a keyword query
- Ensuring documents' integrity and security
- Allowing version control and reactivation of an earlier version if required
- Creating an audit trail for each document
- Enforcing the organization's document retention policies
- Archiving documents

Compared to document management, content management is a relatively new discipline that has tended to focus on the management of website and intranet content. However, the distinction between document management and content management is blurring as software vendors enhance their products, and the functions become more integrated. **Content management** is "the organizing, categorizing, and structuring of information resources so that they can be stored, published, and reused in multiple ways. A content management system is used to collect, manage, and publish information content, storing the content either as components or whole documents, while maintaining the links between components. It may also provide for content revision control. Content management is a critical data management discipline for non-tabular data found in text, graphics, images, video and audio recordings."[86]

As a simple illustration of the concept of content management, consider this book. Rather than managing it as a single word processing document, it could be broken down into a collection of components. For example, the text associated with each individual Educational Objective could be managed as a single content component, as could each Figure.[87] Content components could be combined into this text and published as a paper document or a pdf file. They could be recombined and packaged as a series of self-study courses on IDMA's website. Individual components could be posted on a Facts page and changed daily. Specific components could be extracted and packaged to create customized courses.

Individual content components can be updated and edited quickly and easily, thereby ensuring the accuracy and timeliness of the information they present. To access, use, and reuse content in these sorts of ways, it is essential that each component includes high-quality metadata that clearly defines such things as the module's creation date, the author, a brief description of its content, its version, the extent to which it is considered confidential or proprietary, and who is authorized to edit or delete it.

---

[86] Ibid, p. 29.

[87] To use the figures as content modules, the Figure Number would need to be removed because of the various ways in which they might be used outside a specific chapter in a book.

The Document Management Lifecycle

All documents and content have a similar lifecycle. Books, images, slide presentations, audio and video recordings – all unstructured presentations of information – are initially created by an author, graphic designer, videographer, or other originator, or as a collaborative effort. Typically, the document is edited to ensure quality, consistency, and compliance with, for example, a style guide or other such requirements. Once the document or content has been edited it is published. Publication makes it available to others in whatever form, or forms, the publisher chooses, for example on paper, digitally, or on a website. Many documents and content elements require maintenance in terms of updates to ensure that they are current and relevant. Finally documents and content are retired, which can involve archiving for future retrieval, or purging, depending on the type of information they include and any operational, regulatory or other retention requirements. Figure 10.1 illustrates the document lifecycle.

Figure 10.1 The document lifecycle

The *DAMA-DMBOK* expands on the simple lifecycle of an individual document. It outlines the document management lifecycle, which involves all of an organization's documents and includes a number of steps:

- Identification of existing and newly created documents/records.
- Creation, approval, and enforcement of documents/records policies, including retention policies.
- Classification of documents/records.
- Short and long term storage of physical and electronic documents/records.
- Allowing access and circulation of documents/records in accordance with policies, security and control standards, and legal requirements.
- Archiving and destroying documents/records according to organizational needs, statutes, and regulations.[88]

Document Management Activities

Document management involves a number of activities, which are outlined in the *DAMA DMBOK*:

- Planning;
- Implementing document management systems;
- Backing up and recovering documents;
- Retaining and disposing of documents; and
- Auditing.[89]

---

[88] The DAMA Guide to the Data Management Body of Knowledge (DAMA-DMBOK) First Edition, DAMA International, Technics Publications LLC, New Jersey, copyright 2009 DAMA International, p. 242.

As is the case with any type of management, planning is important. It is essential that organizations have document management policies and procedures in place, and ensure that they are followed. Proprietary information and information subject to privacy legislation, freedom of information legislation, or other regulatory or legislative requirements needs to be managed, retained, and disposed of appropriately.

Document management systems support the acquisition, storage, access, and security of documents. In traditional libraries these were manual systems, but EDMS software is commercially available that facilitates the creation or acquisition, classification, indexing, storage, maintenance, version control, access, security, retention, and archiving of documents.

Ensuring the security of an organization's documents is an important element of backup and recovery planning. A business continuity or disaster recovery plan should outline how an organization's documents are to be backed up and protected, and should include policies and procedures to mitigate the risk associated with such things as fires, natural disasters, hardware failures, cyber attacks, or simple carelessness in the retention or maintenance of documents.

Documents need to be retained for operational, legal, and financial purposes, and an organization may archive some documents of historical interest. Effective document management involves determining how long each document needs to be retained, and arranging for appropriate storage. Documents in current use are typically stored locally; archived documents may be stored off-site.

Although archiving is frequently given a low priority, its importance should not be underestimated. Often, an existing document is not in its final form; it is still in the process of revision. As a document is revised, each version should be dated and identified with a version number. When a new version is created, the older version should be archived to ensure that all users of the document are working from, or studying, the most current version. When documents no longer serve a useful purpose, and there is no regulatory or other reason to retain them, they should generally be disposed of securely.

Document management audits examine a variety of areas including the accuracy of the classification and indexing of documents; the ease with which users can identify, access and retrieve required documents; the compliance of document retention with operational, regulatory, legal, and other requirements; the security and confidentiality of documents; the appropriateness with which documents are discarded; and the extent to which employees understand the organization's document management policies and procedures.

Content Management Activities

The DAMA DMBOK outlines the activities that are essential to effective content management.

- Defining content architecture
- Developing effective metadata
- Providing content access

---

89 Ibid, p. 240.

- Governing for quality[90]

Data modeling techniques and the use of taxonomies help to define a content architecture. A **content architecture** is a logical way of organizing content so that the information it contains can be readily discovered, accessed, used and reused. High-quality metadata are essential. Without good metadata, content may go unrecognized and unused. Content management systems provide access to required content through the use of search engines or other tools. Finally, in order to make the best use of unstructured content, an organization needs to have an appropriate governance system in place, just as it has for its structured data.

Indexing for Retrieval

The index in a book helps the reader find information about a specific topic. Similarly, the index in an EDMS allows a user to find a specific digital document or documents. Google and other search engines provide familiar examples of the technique of indexing documents so that they can be retrieved when needed. "Google has three distinct parts:

- Googlebot, a web crawler that finds and fetches web pages;
- The indexer that sorts every word on every page and stores the resulting index of words in a huge database; and
- The query processor, which compares a search query to the index and recommends the documents that it considers most relevant."[91]

There are two approaches to indexing: full-text indexing and field indexing. Google's approach is an example of **full-text indexing**. The index includes every word on every page. Full-text indexing supports flexibility in search terminology. It also allows for the discovery of documents about which the individual initiating the search is unaware. However, it can result in the retrieval of a large number of documents that the searcher needs to review in order to find the information for which he or she is searching. One of the advantages of full text indexing is that it can be done automatically rather than manually.

Field text indexing includes a limited selection of metadata in the index. For example, digital images of scanned claims documents might be indexed using the claim number, policy number, insured's name, and the date the claim was opened. Alternatively, documents such as reports or presentations may be given a unique identifier for indexing and retrieval purposes. Additional information about each document can be indicated using a classification taxonomy based on a controlled vocabulary. A controlled vocabulary is simply a set of agreed upon terms that are clearly defined, consistently used, and formally managed with rules about how terms are added, modified, or deleted. Field text indexing has the advantage of efficiently retrieving a specific document, but it does not support discovery of documents about which the searcher is unaware. Some field text indexing can be automated, but often it is a manual process in which metadata are added, for example, when a paper document is scanned for digital storage.

---

[90] Ibid, p. 240.

[91] How Google Works, viewed at http://www.googleguide.com/google_works.html (accessed September 3, 2015).

Document and Content Management Risks

Documents and content are subject to the same sorts of risk as are data in a database, and the actions an organization can take to avoid or mitigate those risks are also similar. Unintentional loss or destruction of documents and content can be caused in a variety of ways:

- Employees may delete documents or content accidentally.
- Notebook computers, USB drives, and other mobile devices can be lost or stolen.
- System crashes and hard drive failures can occur.
- Viruses and malware can destroy documents and content.
- Power failures or disasters, such as building fires, can occur.
- Coffee or other liquids can be spilled on notebooks or other devices.
- Employees may intentionally steal documents or content.
- Unauthorized employees may access confidential or proprietary documents.
- Hackers may access documents and publish them inappropriately or illegally.

An organization needs to have policies and procedures in place to prevent these types of incidents and to respond effectively if an incident occurs. EDMS typically include security features and authorization levels for document access. Implementing appropriate administrative and technical controls, and instituting a robust backup and recovery program can also significantly reduce these risks.

Document and Content Retention and Destruction

An important element of document and content management is a plan for the appropriate retention, storage, and destruction of documents. Document retention policies categorize documents and specify:

- How long each type of document must be retained;
- How and where documents are to be stored; and
- How and when documents are to be discarded.

There are a variety of reasons for ensuring that effective document retention policies and procedures are in place. First, organizations need to retain those documents that are necessary for their business operations. For example, in the event of a coverage dispute, the insurer may need to examine the original insurance application and any subsequent endorsement requests. Retained documents are also useful in the event of litigation or an audit, or to demonstrate compliance with regulatory requirements.

There are a number of issues related to document retention. Retention requirements for certain types of documents are established by regulatory bodies. Organizations need to be aware of all applicable records-retention legislation and regulations, and ensure that they are in compliance. For example, in the State of New York, "an insurer must maintain a policy record for each insurance contract or policy for six years from the date the policy is no longer in force, or until after the filing of a report on examination, whichever is longer. A policy record includes the contract or policy forms, the application, the policy term, and basis for rating and return premium amounts, if any. Both the original policy that is issued and any subsequent renewals of the policy must be retained in the policy record for the retention period specified in Regulation 152."[92]

Insurers collect a large amount of personal information about insureds, agents and brokers, employees, claimants, and others. Personally identifiable information (PII) and personal health information (PHI), also referred to as individually identifiable health information, are subject to stringent regulatory requirements. It is important to ensure that this information is kept secure and confidential. It is also important that insurers not retain PII or PHI longer than is required or specified by law or regulation. These types of information should be disposed of in a secure manner.

In addition to PII and PHI, there is other information insurers are required to keep confidential. United States federal antitrust laws prohibit the sharing of specific proprietary information outside of the insurance company itself, its direct business associates, and regulators. Documents relating to any of these areas must be kept confidential and disposed of securely.

The volume of paper and electronic documents that an insurer receives and generates is significant. Storage of all of these documents, either physically or electronically, can be costly. Generally, a centralized storage system reduces the time and cost involved in retrieving retained documents. Documents that have been archived may be stored at a separate location.

Documents that are not subject to regulatory retention requirements and that are no longer of value to an organization should be disposed of in an appropriate manner. Depending on the type of document and the information it contains, shredding or re-cycling may be appropriate. This helps to make most efficient use of storage facilities and reduces maintenance costs. However, a document that no longer has value for one area of the organization may still have current or future value for another area. Determining which documents to dispose of can be challenging.

Audit Protocols

Periodic auditing is important to ensure the effectiveness and compliance of an organization's document and content management policies, procedures, and systems. An audit typically involves a number of steps:

- Planning
- Establishing responsibilities
- Selecting samples
- Performing the audit
- Reporting results

To be effective, audits should be carefully planned. It is important to define the objective of the audit, its scope, the method to be used, the number of samples to be tested, and the proposed start date. Audits can be conducted internally, or an external auditor may be used. In the case of an internal audit, the individuals responsible for the

---

[92] http://www.dfs.ny.gov/insurance/ogco2008/rg080905.htm (accessed September 13, 2015).

audit need to be identified. Audits typically do not examine all of an organization's records. Rather a representative sample of records is chosen. It must be large enough to give the audit team confidence in the validity of their findings. It is good practice to perform an audit in such a way as to disrupt operational activities as little as possible. Depending on the scope and purpose of the audit, auditors may examine a variety of areas. Once the audit has been completed, the audit team documents and reports their findings and recommendations to senior executives.

Guiding Principles of Document and Content Management

The *DAMA DMBOK* outlines the foundation for effective content and document management. "The implementation of the document and content management function into an organization follows three guiding principles:

- Everyone in an organization has a role to play in protecting its future. Everyone must create, use, retrieve, and dispose of records in accordance with the established policies and procedures.

- Experts in the handling of records and content should be fully engaged in policy and planning. Regulatory and best practices can vary significantly based on industry sector and legal jurisdiction.

- Even if records management professionals are not available to the organization, everyone can be trained and have an understanding of the issues. Once trained, business stewards, and others can collaborate on an effective approach to records management."[93]

Structured and Unstructured Data

An earlier chapter introduced the concept of structured and unstructured data. **Structured data** are data that are organized in a pre-defined manner. For example, the data contained in automobile insurance applications can be captured and stored in various tables in an insurer's relational database. In this case, the structured data are referred to as "tabular data". Structured data are often generated by transactions and each type of structured data has a consistent format.

In most organizations, a significant amount of data are referred to as "unstructured". These are the data that reside in an organization's documents. **Unstructured data** cannot easily be converted to a tabular form, and they cannot be stored in, or accessed from, traditional databases. Unstructured data can be classified as textual or nontextual. Examples of **textual unstructured data** include word processing documents, emails, and text messages. **Nontextual unstructured data** include such things as photographs, diagrams, X-rays, and audio or video recordings.

---

[93] The DAMA Guide to the Data Management Body of Knowledge (DAMA-DMBOK) First Edition, DAMA International, Technics Publications LLC, New Jersey, copyright 2009 DAMA International, p. 253.

Considering the examples of unstructured data just mentioned, it becomes clear that the adjective "unstructured" may be somewhat misleading. These types of data actually have structures that can be more complex than simple tabular data. For example, documents have structure in terms of organization, logical flow, grammar, and vocabulary. They are created and stored in a variety of structural formats such as word processing documents or PDFs. Graphics and photographs are also created, stored, and displayed in a variety of structural formats, for example, JPEGs.

One of the challenges practitioners face as the data management field evolves is settling on a consistent, common, and meaningful vocabulary. Although the term "unstructured data" continues in use, a variety of alternatives have been suggested; the discussion about appropriate terminology continues. In a December 2011 article, *What Are Unstructured Data?*, author Michael Brackett proposed categorizing data as follows:

- Unstructured
- Structured
- Highly structured
- Complex structured

Structured data have already been discussed. In his article, Mr. Brackett offered definitions for the remaining terms in this data categorization scheme. **Unstructured data** "are not structured, have few formal requirements, or do not have a patterned organization."[94] **Highly structured data** "are data that are more intricately structured than traditional tabular data, but are not as intricately structured as complex structured data."[95] **Complex structured data** "are any data that are composed of two or more intricate, complicated, and interrelated parts that cannot be easily interpreted by structured query languages and tools.[96] The complex structure needs to be broken down into the individual component structures to be more easily processed."[97] As examples of complex structured data, the author lists text, voice, video, images, and spatial data.

Another term that can be used to describe data is "multi-structured". **Multi-structured data** are data that are made up of two or more varieties of structured data. For example, a photograph would be categorized as complex structured data. However, that photograph may have an associated GPS location, date stamp, or time stamp, all of which are structured data. Some data management professionals consider multi-structured data to be a subset of complex structured data; others feel that the term "multi-structured data" more clearly describes this particular type of data.

Other terms have also been proposed, or used, to describe or categorize data, for example semi-structured data, super-structured data, fully-structured data, or poly-structured data. As organizations amass an increasing volume and variety of data, and as the sources from which those data are collected broaden, the need for a common, clearly defined vocabulary increases. Whatever terminology an organization chooses to use, it is essential that those terms are defined so as to be clearly and commonly understood by all of the organization's stakeholders.

---

[94] Michael Brackett, What Are Unstructured Data? December 13 2011, viewed at http://www.dataversity.net/what-are-unstructured-data/ (accessed August 26, 2015).

[95] Ibid.

[96] Structured query languages are used to.

[97] Ibid.

Data Mining and Text Mining

One method of obtaining business value from data is referred to as "data mining". **Data mining** is "the process of sifting through large amounts of data using pattern recognition and other knowledge discovery statistical techniques to identify previously undiscovered and potentially meaningful data content, relationships, and trends."[98] It emerged as a set of advanced analysis techniques for data captured by business transactions and gathered from other sources. Data mining focuses primarily on structured data.

Data mining is one step in the process of **knowledge discovery from data (KDD)**. In this process, data are typically cleansed, or "scrubbed", and integrated for storage in a data warehouse. Relevant data are selected depending on the type of analysis to be performed, and they may be transformed and consolidated to facilitate data mining. Data mining uses statistical techniques to identify patterns in, or relationships among, data. Those patterns and relationships can then be evaluated, and any knowledge discovered from that evaluation can be formatted and presented. Figure 10.2 illustrates the KDD process.

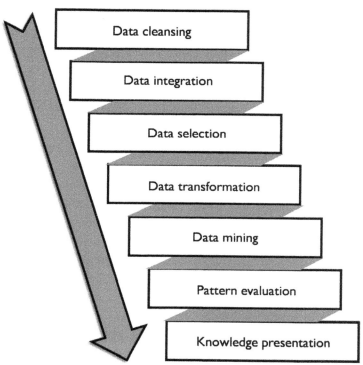

Figure 10.2 Knowledge discovery from data

Text mining is a relatively new type of data mining that focuses on the automated discovery of knowledge from large amounts of textual records, such as documents, emails, correspondence, or social media. It uses natural language processing (NLP) techniques that allow computers to analyze and understand human language, to categorize information, to establish links between otherwise unconnected documents, and to create summaries of content. When text mining is used to solve business problems it is referred to as **text analytics**, or textual analytics.

---

[98] The DAMA Dictionary of Data Management, First Edition 2008, Mark Mosley Editor, Technics Publications LLC, New Jersey, copyright 2008 DAMA International, p.41.

The Importance of Unstructured Data

It has been estimated that as much as 80 percent of business data and information are unstructured. As little as 20 percent of an organization's data might reside in databases that can be readily queried for analysis. It is far more challenging to efficiently analyze the data contained, for example, in word processing documents, emails, presentations, social media feeds, or photographs. But these unstructured data are important because they can offer insights far beyond those that can be gleaned from structured data alone. For example, consider an insurer's customer service call center. If calls are recorded and subsequently transcribed and analyzed, they could reveal a wealth of information about customers' attitudes, needs, and preferences. That information could enhance relationships with individual customers and lead to innovations in products and services that would give the insurer a competitive advantage.

Managing Unstructured Data

There are a number of challenges involved in managing unstructured data. Organizations are collecting and creating more and more unstructured data in a variety of formats, and the pace of that growth is accelerating. This ever-increasing volume and variety can be a challenge to manage. As well, unstructured data are typically distributed throughout an organization and it can be difficult to determine what data an organization actually has. Inefficiencies result when the same task, for example preparing a slide presentation or report, is performed multiple times because there is no effective way of determining that the presentation or report already exists, locating it, and accessing it. On the other hand, outdated or redundant data are often retained unnecessarily, taking up valuable storage space, because they cannot be readily identified. In addition, a large volume of unstructured data are created through interactions with customers and other stakeholders. These data need to be linked to the correct customer, transaction, process, or system. In a 2013 article entitled *How to win unstructured data management challenge?*, Nalaka Withanage wrote "Today 90% of unstructured data workload is handled manually. Understanding what the document is and what to do with it is heavily dependent upon information workers at the forefront of the organization. This manual processing of unstructured data causes delays and errors, and results in lower data quality."[99]

Probably the greatest challenge is determining which unstructured data an organization should collect, analyze, and keep. In a June 2015 article, *Solving the Unstructured Data Challenge*, Jaikumar Vijayan wrote, "Just because you can capture data from virtually any device or third-party resource doesn't mean you should."[100] Capturing too much data, in an unfocused manner, simply exacerbates the challenges inherent in unstructured data management. It is essential to create an enterprise-wide data strategy that supports the organization's business goals and strategies; to identify priorities in terms of the business need for data; and to determine which specific data best meet those needs. Those are the data on which the organization should focus.

---

[99] Nalaka Withanage, How to win unstructured data management challenge?, September 17, 2013, viewed at http://sloanreview.mit.edu/article/finding-value-in-the-information-explosion/ (accessed September 8, 2015).

[100] Solving the Unstructured Data Challenge, By Jaikumar Vijayan, June 25, 2015, viewed at http://www.cio.com/article/2941015/big-data/solving-the-unstructured-data-challenge.html (accessed September 9, 2015).

Integrating Structured and Unstructured Data

A number of surveys have indicated that executives and senior managers at many organizations are frustrated by their inability to derive meaningful business intelligence (BI) from their vast stores of unstructured data. If organizations are developing strategies and making decisions based only on the information that resides in databases, they may be relying on as little as 20 percent of the data in their possession. Clearly, integrating structured and unstructured data would allow for more informed decision making. If unstructured data could be included in a data warehouse and integrated along with structured data, they can be analyzed and even linked to structured data. However, there are challenges involved.

In their book *DW2 The Architecture for the Next Generation of Data Warehousing*, authors William Inmon, Derek Strauss, and Genia Newschloss write "While current technology is not yet able to handle nontextual data with much elegance, textual unstructured data are another story. Textual unstructured data can be captured and manipulated. Standard data base technology has a hard time with textual data because textual data are not repetitive like structured data. However, this does not mean that there is not great value in textual data. Indeed, there is great value in it. It is just that the textual data are not easily handled and manipulated by standard data base technology."[101]

In order to be able to analyze textual unstructured data, the data need to be transformed in a variety of ways. One challenge involves determining which data are of importance and value to an organization; much of them are not. As an example, consider email. Many of the emails that are sent on a daily basis are personal in nature or not of any significance to the organization. This extraneous content has been referred to as "blather". All of an organization's unstructured data needs to be screened to remove blather.

Another challenge in preparing unstructured textual data for analysis involves differences in vocabulary and expression. Different individuals express the same concept or idea differently. Natural language uses both general and specific terms, for example, "vehicle" versus "sedan" or "pick-up truck." These differences in terminology need to be rationalized in some way in order to allow for meaningful analysis of the textual data.

Once blather has been screened out and the terminology has been rationalized, textual unstructured data can be converted into a format used in text analytics. This process involves a variety of activities intended to impose structure on the text, to categorize it, and to optimize search capabilities. A further challenge relates to metadata. Traditionally, metadata have been associated with structured data. However, if textual unstructured data are to be included in data warehouses and used in analytics, high-quality metadata are essential.

There are technical challenges involved in integrating unstructured data with other enterprise systems. Organizations need enhanced storage and processing capabilities to deal with the huge additional volume of unstructured data. The tools available may not meet organizations' needs or may be perceived as too complex or costly. Finally, the business need for unstructured data may not be well understood or defined.

---

[101] William Inmon, Derek Strauss, Genia Neushloss, DW 2.0 The Architecture for the Next Generation of Data Warehousing, Morgan Kaufmann Publishers, USA © 2008 by Elsevier Inc., p. 38.

Summary

Document and content management focuses on managing the data that resides outside an organization's databases. It comprises two functions, although the distinction between them is blurring. Document management concentrates on documents as a whole whereas content management focuses on elements or components of content. While content management was originally limited to website and intranet content, that is no longer necessarily the case. Electronic document management systems store, manage, and allow access to electronic documents and scanned images of paper documents. They typically offer a variety of functions such as version control, enforcing document retention policies, or allowing document retrieval through a keyword query. The document management lifecycle involves a number of steps: identifying existing and new documents; implementing document control and retention policies; classifying documents; storing documents; allowing access in accordance with policies, standards, and regulations; and archiving and appropriately destroying documents.

Internet search engines are examples of how documents can be found using an index. There are two approaches to indexing: full text indexing and field text indexing. Full text indexing allows for discovery of documents, but can often result in the searcher having to review a large number of documents. Field text indexing efficiently retrieves the specified document, but does not support discovery of documents. While full text indexing can be done automatically, field text indexing may be a manual process.

Laws and regulations stipulate how long some documents must be retained. Organizations need to be aware of and in compliance with all applicable legislation. In addition, insurers must protect the confidentiality of the PII and PHI in their possession as well as other information the sharing of which is prohibited by antitrust laws. Because the volume of documents an organization has to manage is significant, and storage can be costly, documents not subject to retention requirements that have ceased to be of value to an organization should be disposed of in an appropriate manner. Shredding or recycling may be acceptable, depending on the type of document and the information it contains. Auditing helps to ensure the effectiveness of an organization's document management policies, procedures, and systems. The *DAMA DMBOK* offers three Guiding Principles for effective document management.

A significant amount of most organizations' data are unstructured. While the term "unstructured data" continues in use, a number of other terms have been proposed or used. Whatever terminology an organization elects to adopt, it is essential that the terms are clearly defined and commonly understood. Data mining can be an effective technique for deriving knowledge and value from a vast array of data. It is one step in the process of knowledge discovery from data (KDD) and it focuses on structured data in databases. On the other hand, text mining allows an organization to discover knowledge from its unstructured textual data.

There are a number of challenges associated with managing unstructured data. The volume of unstructured data that organizations acquire from a variety of sources is increasing exponentially. It can be difficult to determine what data an organization actually has. Unstructured data can require manual processing which is inefficient and results in errors and poor data quality. In addition, it can be challenging to decide what unstructured data an organization needs to capture, analyze and keep without exacerbating the challenges inherent in unstructured data.

Integrating unstructured data with structured data would allow organizations to make better-informed decisions but there are challenges involved. Standard databases do not handle or manipulate textual unstructured data well. Textual unstructured data need to be screened, rationalized, and transformed prior to use for text analytics. There are technical challenges associated with integrating unstructured data with an enterprise's other systems. The tools available may not be appropriate, or may be too complex or costly, and the business need for analyzing unstructured data may not be well understood or articulated.

Bibliography

The DAMA Dictionary of Data Management, First Edition 2008, Mark Mosley Editor, Technics Publications LLC, New Jersey, copyright 2008 DAMA International.

The DAMA Guide to the Data Management Body of Knowledge (DAMA-DMBOK) First Edition, DAMA International, Technics Publications LLC, New Jersey, copyright 2009 DAMA International.

Yanchang Zhao, R and Data Mining: Examples and Case Studies 1, April 26, 2013, viewed at http://bit.ly/2sD4QtW (accessed August 16, 2015).

A gentle introduction to text mining using R, Eight to Late, viewed at http://bit.ly/2fBGupj (accessed August 16, 2015).

Ingo Feinerer, Kurt Hornik and David Meyer, Text Mining Infrastructure in R, Journal of Statistical Software, March 2008, Volume 25, Issue 5, viewed at http://bit.ly/2rB9Qz3 (accessed August 16, 2015).

James Robertson, Is it DM of CM?, viewed at http://bit.ly/2sCMGIH (accessed August 27, 2015).

Jim Harris, Bridging the Divide between Unstructured and Structured Data, February 26th 2014, viewed at http://bit.ly/1jyPxYT (accessed August 31, 2015).

Paul Trotter, Component Content Management: What Is It and Why Does It Matter?, viewed at http://bit.ly/2sCKsZG (accessed September 2, 2015).

What is content management (CM)?, viewed at http://bit.ly/2mhoYtJ (accessed September 2, 2015).

Text mining (text analytics) definition, viewed at http://bit.ly/1kmZA01 (accessed September 3, 2015).

Margaret Rouse, data mining definition, viewed at http://bit.ly/1PMUYnE (accessed September 2, 2015).

The Importance of Managing Unstructured Data, By Paul Rubens, viewed at http://bit.ly/2rFWpsI (accessed September 7, 2015).

Managing Massive Unstructured Data Troves: 10 Best Practices, By Chris Preimesberger, 2013-07-03, viewed at http://bit.ly/1DMyVmn (accessed September 2, 2015).

Unstructured Data 101 - Defining unstructured data and its importance to organizations, by Lyndsay Wise, viewed at http://bit.ly/2rB8bcY (accessed September 7, 2015).

Unstructured Data is distracting Backup Administrators, December 1, 2014 by George Crump, viewed at http://bit.ly/1vxhhwl (accessed September 7, 2015).

Welcome to the Era of Unstructured Data, viewed at http://bit.ly/2rprykY, (accessed September 7, 2015).

The Four V's of Big Data, viewed at https://ibm.co/18nYiuo (accessed September 7, 2015).

A Single View: Integrating Structured and Unstructured Data/Information within the Enterprise, Unitas, viewed at http://bit.ly/2rFY9Cs (accessed September 9, 2015).

Solving the Unstructured Data Challenge, By Jaikumar Vijayan, Jun 25, 2015, viewed at http://bit.ly/2rpN3SO (accessed September 9, 2015).

Mariann Micsinai, 3 Key Capabilities Necessary for Text Analytics & Natural Language Processing in the Era of Big Data, November 04, 2014, viewed at http://bit.ly/1VtNCFc (accessed September 10, 2015).

What is document indexing?, viewed at http://bit.ly/1gzekX4 (accessed September 12, 2015).

Five Tips for Effective Indexing Across Your Enterprise: What your document management vendor should be telling you, viewed at http://bit.ly/2rAwWGd (accessed September 12, 2015).

Record-Retention Policy Helps Insurers, Brokers Avoid Exposures, Assure Clients, by Jennifer Vergilii (accessed September 13, 2015).

Business Analytics and Predictive Modeling Overview

Business managers evaluate the extent to which the organization is meeting its strategic goals through the use of metrics, and analysis of both internal and external data. Data warehousing and business intelligence (BI) allow managers access to large amounts of data. Data from various operational systems and external sources is collected and processed before it is loaded into the data warehouse for analysis. These data form the basis for strategic, tactical, and operational business intelligence.

The area of data warehousing and business intelligence is evolving rapidly as is the associated vocabulary. Analytics is a term sometimes used synonymously with business intelligence. Analytics includes tools and techniques for determining what is occurring now, and why; what is likely to occur in the future; and how best to respond. Predictive modeling is part of analytics. Analysts use software tools and formal methodologies to build and test a model designed to forecast potential future outcomes. This allows managers and executives to plan appropriate responses.

Educational Objectives

Upon completion of this assignment, you should be able to:

1. Describe business performance management (BPM).
2. Describe how data warehousing supports BPM.
3. Describe how to process data for business intelligence.
4. Define and contrast the concepts of strategic, tactical, and operational business intelligence.
5. Describe how the vocabulary of data warehousing and business intelligence is changing.
6. Define analytics.
7. Briefly describe the three disciplines of analytics.
8. Define business analytics.
9. Define predictive modeling.
10. List the five steps in building a predictive model.
11. Explain how business intelligence (BI) and predictive modeling impact the development of databases.

Business Performance Management (BPM)

Business performance management (BPM) is a set of methodologies and tools that help organizations optimize their performance and make better use of their financial, human, and data resources. The acronym BPM is also used to refer to business process management, which is essentially process optimization; this is not the focus of this chapter. BPM facilitates a systematic, integrated approach that aligns an organization's activities with its enterprise strategy. Core BPM processes include financial and operational planning, information consolidation and reporting, business modeling, analysis, and monitoring of key performance indicators.

A **key performance indicator (KPI)** is a metric used to measure an organization's effectiveness. KPIs help managers and executives evaluate how successfully the organization is achieving its strategic objectives. KPIs focus on what is most important to an organization. Examples of Key performance indicators in the insurance industry include new businesses written, written premiums, earned premiums, renewal retention rate, premiums per exposure, losses per exposure, loss ratios, expense ratios, combined ratios, and return on surplus. A KPI is an essential element of a measurable objective, which is typically made up of a direction, KPI, benchmark, target, and time frame. Figure 11.1 provides an example.

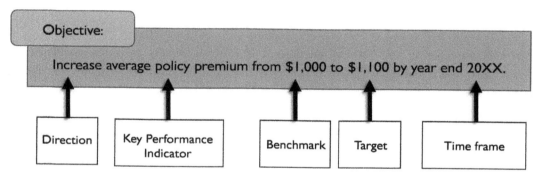

Figure 11.1 Key performance indicator

BPM allows managers to "run the business by the numbers" and it necessitates consolidating data from various sources. These sources include internal data such as financial data, production data, claims data, and operational data; and external data, such as industry benchmarks or third party data. The consolidated data can then be queried, analyzed, and made available to management either as a report or in another format, such as the graphical user interface of a dashboard. A **dashboard** is a "business intelligence application that consolidates, aggregates, and graphically presents performance measurements compared to goals, arranged so that information can be monitored at a glance."[102]

Many automated BPM environments are continuous and/or real-time. This enables managers to be proactive and to identify issues or shortfalls as they occur. Combined with forecasting tools, BPM allows organizations to anticipate where they will finish at the end of the analysis or reporting period, and to implement corrective or alternative initiatives as required to optimize performance.

---

[102] The DAMA Dictionary of Data Management, First Edition 2008, Mark Mosley Editor, Technics Publications LLC, New Jersey, copyright 2008 DAMA International, p. 33.

Data Warehousing

Data warehousing provides access to the high-quality information that facilitates business performance management. A data warehouse comprises two elements:

1. Software that collects, cleanses, transforms, organizes, and integrates specific data from internal operational systems and external sources; and
2. The resulting database.

Data warehousing enhances an organization's ability to access and analyze its data. Query and reporting tools, and advanced visualization tools, allow managers to request specific information from the database, organized in a particular way, and to generate reports or graphical representations of the data. This ability to analyze an organization's vast stores of data relatively quickly allows managers to gain greater insights into its operations and performance. This is referred to as business intelligence (BI).

As BI tools have become more sophisticated, they have begun to allow managers to use historical and current data to predict what is likely to happen in the future and to determine how best to respond. This enhances organizations' ability to practice effective business performance management.

The *DAMA-DMBOK* lists the activities involved in data warehousing and business intelligence management:

- Understand business intelligence information needs
- Define and maintain the data warehouse and business intelligence architecture
- Implement data warehouses and data marts
- Implement business intelligence tools and user interfaces
- Process data for business intelligence
- Monitor and tune data warehousing processes
- Monitor and tune business intelligence activity and performance[103]

Processing Data for Business Intelligence

Typically, the data in a data warehouse or data mart originate from a variety of internal and external sources and systems, and they exist in a variety of sometimes incompatible formats. In order to populate a data warehouse with these disparate data and to ensure that the data in the warehouse are of high quality, it is necessary to perform a process referred to as **extract-transform-load (ETL)**. Although the name implies three distinct steps, ETL is actually an integrated, iterative process. To keep the data in the warehouse current, after the warehouse is initially populated, ETL becomes a continuous and ongoing process. Depending on the organization and the specific data involved, ETL may occur periodically, daily, hourly, or in near-real time.

---

[103] The DAMA Guide to the Data Management Body of Knowledge (DAMA-DMBOK) First Edition, DAMA International, Technics Publications LLC, New Jersey, copyright 2009 DAMA International, p. 198.

Source-to-target mapping is "the documentation activity that defines data type details and transformation rules for all required entities and data elements, and from each individual source to each individual target."[104] It involves mapping data elements from the data sources to data elements in the data warehouse database. This is an important process in data warehousing because it documents the complete lineage for each data element in the warehouse.

Although the process is commonly referred to as "source-to-target", from a strict analytic standpoint it might be better named "target-from-source". First, the target should be determined. Then, the data from the various sources need to be analyzed to determine their precise meaning and what their relationship is to the target. Finally, a mapping should be laid out to develop the required target data from the elements in the source data.

Care needs to be taken since data elements from different sources may have similar names but different definitions. For example, "incurred loss" may be defined in one system as "net as to reinsurance", in another "net as to deductibles", and in a third "not reflecting deductibles or reinsurance". These distinctions need to be identified and thoroughly documented.

In the ETL process, data are extracted, or copied, from each of the sources, many of which will be transaction processing applications and databases. There are two extraction methods: full extraction and incremental extraction. In **full extraction**, all of the required data are copied from the data source. Part of the subsequent processing involves comparing the current extraction to the previous one to determine which data have changed. In **incremental extraction**, only those data that have changed since the last extraction are copied. Incremental extraction is more complex to perform than full extraction. Figure 11.2 offers a graphical representation of the ETL process.

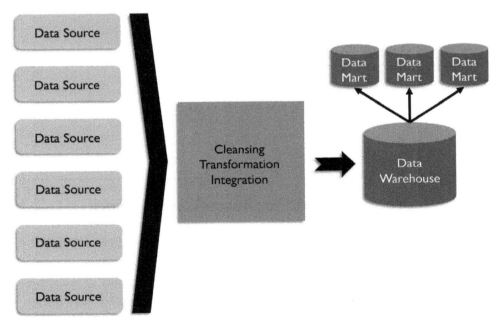

Figure 11.2 Extract, transform, and load (ETL)

After the data are extracted, they are transported either to an intermediate staging area or directly to the data warehouse database, depending upon where the subsequent transformation will take place. The data may be

---

104 Ibid, p. 230.

cleansed, or "scrubbed" to eliminate duplicate records and redundancies, and to enforce consistency and integrity. For example, different source systems may use different state or industry codes. All codes would be translated to a standard for consistency. Data are transformed from their original format to the format required by the data warehouse. These transformations can be relatively straightforward or extremely complex, depending on the situation.

Once the data have been cleansed and transformed they can be integrated and loaded into the warehouse database. From there, data can be exported to data marts. Data marts are subsets of the data warehouse that focus on a particular subject area enabling quicker response times for queries and facilitating use by limiting data selection options.

Strategic, Tactical, and Operational Business Intelligence

An earlier chapter introduced strategic, tactical, and operational planning. Strategic planning takes a long-term view, often three or more years into the future, and articulates senior management's vision for the organization at that point. It defines how the executives would like to see the organization positioned, and establishes objectives to help it reach that goal. Tactical planning involves identifying, selecting, and scheduling the activities middle managers must complete in order to achieve the organization's strategic objectives. Supervisors, unit managers, crew leaders, and other front-line managers are involved in operational planning. Just as tactical planning supports the goals established in strategic planning, operational planning facilitates completion of the activities identified in tactical planning.

There are three corresponding approaches to business intelligence (BI), which allow managers at every level to monitor actual performance relative to the organization's objectives:

- Strategic
- Tactical
- Operational

Strategic BI typically forms part of a formal business performance management (BPM) program. Strategic BI allows executives and senior managers to monitor key performance indicators such as loss ratio, expense ratio, or investment income, to determine the extent to which the organization is achieving its strategic objectives.

Tactical BI focuses on the activities identified and selected during tactical planning. It typically compares a metric from one period with that of the previous period or periods, or analyzes historical data, in order to identify trends. Tactical BI allows managers and analysts to measure the success of business initiatives and to identify where adjustments may need to be made in order to reach tactical objectives.

Operational BI allows an organization to manage and optimize its business operations or allocate resources. It provides managers and supervisors with daily or even real-time information about transactions or processes. Examples of operational BI would include a list of open claims or a list of pending policy applications.

Defining Terminology

In any field, particularly one that is evolving rapidly, it can be challenging for practitioners to reach agreement on a common vocabulary of clearly defined terms. In an October 2013 Association for Computing Machinery (ACM) *Tech Pack on Business Intelligence/Data Management*, committee members Pat Cupoli, Barry Devlin, Raymond Ng, and Stephen Petschulat wrote "Business Intelligence and data warehousing have spawned an extensive and specific set of terminology in the past 25 years. Unfortunately, many of the terms are vague or carry multiple meanings, often in the service of marketing various hardware and software solutions. In addition, the currently changing environment is creating a set of new terminology and repurposing the old."[105]

As an example, consider the word **analytics**. Merriam-Webster defines it simply as "the method of logical analysis."[106] Gartner's IT Glossary reflects the ACM Tech Pack comments: "Analytics has emerged as a catch-all term for a variety of different business intelligence (BI) and application-related initiatives.

For some, it is the process of analyzing information from a particular domain, such as website analytics. For others, it is applying the breadth of BI capabilities to a specific content area (for example, sales, service, supply chain and so on). In particular, BI vendors use the 'analytics' moniker to differentiate their products from the competition. Increasingly, 'analytics' is used to describe statistical and mathematical data analysis that clusters, segments, scores and predicts what scenarios are most likely to happen."[107]

The *DAMA Dictionary of Data Management* defines analytics as "Business intelligence procedures and techniques for exploration and analysis of data to discover and identify new and meaningful information and trends."[108]

In her book *Applied Insurance Analytics*, author Patricia L. Saporito provides another definition for the term. "Analytics includes the data, tools, and applications that support corporate strategic plans and business performance; they provide the ability to gather, store, access, and analyze corporate data for decision making."[109] This is the definition that will be used by IDMA.

A number of writers and theorists subdivide analytics into three disciplines:

- Descriptive analytics
- Predictive analytics
- Prescriptive analytics

Descriptive analytics presents a depiction of a past or current state. For example, it might describe the characteristics of different customer segments. Descriptive analytics can provide the information used in predictive

---

[105] Pat Cupoli, Barry Devlin, Raymond Ng, and Stephen Petschulat, ACM Tech Pack on Business Intelligence/Data Management, October 2013, © ACM 2013.

[106] www.merriam-webster.com/dictionary/analytics (accessed September 29, 2015).

[107] www.gartner.com/it-glossary/analytics (accessed September 28, 2015).

[108] The DAMA Dictionary of Data Management, First Edition 2008, Mark Mosley Editor, Technics Publications LLC, New Jersey, copyright 2008 DAMA International, p. 10.

[109] Patricia L. Saporito, Applied Insurance Analytics, © 2015 by Particia L. Saporito, Pearson Education Ltd., p. 20.

analytics. **Predictive analytics** focuses on determining what is likely to happen in the future based on historical trends and other data. For example, based on the characteristics of different customer segments, an insurer might predict which segments are likely to be most profitable in the future. **Prescriptive analytics** helps managers choose the best course of action when a decision needs to be made. Based on the likely scenarios developed in predictive analytics, prescriptive analytics helps managers determine how to mitigate risks, and capitalize on opportunities.

Gartner defines **business analytics** specifically in terms of tools used in analysis. "Business analytics is comprised of solutions used to build analysis models and simulations to create scenarios, understand realities, and predict future states. Business analytics includes data mining, predictive analytics, applied analytics and statistics, and is delivered as an application suitable for a business user. These analytics solutions often come with prebuilt industry content that is targeted at an industry business process (for example, claims, underwriting or a specific regulatory requirement)."[110]

Predictive Modeling

Gartner defines **predictive modeling** as "the process of analyzing data to create a statistical model of future behavior. Predictive modeling solutions are a form of data-mining technologies that work by analyzing historical and current data and generating a model to help predict future outcomes. These technologies can be used to generate a score (for example, a credit score), to assess behavior (for example, fraud detection or customer acquisition), or to analyze needed reserves. Insurers can apply this to key activities, such as customer service, pricing, actuarial, underwriting and claims, to improve outcomes."[111] Insurers have long used actuarial and statistical techniques to predict future losses based on historical loss data. This forms the foundation for ratemaking.

Different authors and theorists have proposed different approaches to building predictive models and there is a variety of software tools available to facilitate the process. However, using a tool is not sufficient to ensure the quality or reliability of a predictive model. It is also important to employ a structured methodology. One approach outlines a series of five steps:

1. Retrieve and organize the data
2. Understand the data
3. Split the data and build a model
4. Evaluate the model's performance
5. Iterate and choose a model[112]

The first step involves identifying what data are required. Depending on the focus and scope of the project, different data will be needed. The data need to be retrieved and organized in such a way as to facilitate the second step in the process. It is important to have an understanding of the nature and quality of the available data. The data

---

110 www.gartner.com/it-glossary/business-analytics (accessed September 28, 2015).

111 www.gartner.com/it-glossary/preductive-modeling-solutions/ (accessed October 1, 2015).

112 www.jesse-flores.com/a-five-step-process-for-predictive-modeling/ (accessed October 5, 2015).

are typically divided into two groups. One will be used to build the initial model and the second to test it. At this point, software tools are used to build an initial model. The model is evaluated using the test data. Typically, building a predictive model is an iterative process, involving several cycles of evaluation, modification, and evaluation before a final version of the model is selected for use.

Business Intelligence, Predictive Modeling, and Database Development

Traditional data warehouses were typically updated daily, in an overnight batch process. This approach resulted in a certain amount of data latency. **Latency** is "the time delay for data to be updated in a system. The term applies primarily to replicated data. When data are displayed in real time, data latency is eliminated."[113] Increasingly, business managers needed reduced data latency in the data warehouse and data marts in order to support operational business intelligence and other analytics. As a result, a variety of technical alternatives to the nightly batch extract, transform, and load (ETL) process have developed.

In addition, the development of **online analytical processing (OLAP)** has allowed managers to query the data warehouse and data marts in interactive sessions and to perform multi-dimensional analysis. For example, it can allow for simultaneous analysis of sales by region, by quarter, and product. Each of these categories for summarizing or viewing data (i.e., region, quarter, and product) is referred to as a **dimension**. There are several different technical approaches to implementing a database in support of OLAP.

The characteristics of a database used in a data warehouse or data mart differ from those of a database used by transactional applications. Transactional systems are used by front line staff to complete the organization's day-to-day operations. Each transaction typically involves only a few records and the amount of data processed per transaction is relatively small. Response times are short, generally a matter of seconds. These systems generally retain data for a limited amount of time, for example, 60 to 180 days.

Databases designed for use in data warehouses and data marts focus on facilitating analysis. Managers and analysts use these databases to gain an understanding of the business. Each analytic query can involve many records, in some cases millions, and the amount of data under analysis is generally quite large. Depending on the complexity of a query, the response time for these systems can range from seconds to hours. Because of the importance of historical data in analysis, data in these systems may be retained for a number of years.

Summary

Business performance management (BPM) aligns an organization's activities with its enterprise strategy and uses key performance indicators (KPI) to monitor performance to objectives. Core BPM processes include financial and

---

[113] The DAMA Dictionary of Data Management, First Edition 2008, Mark Mosley Editor, Technics Publications LLC, New Jersey, copyright 2008 DAMA International, p. 39.

operational planning, information consolidation and reporting, business modeling, analysis, and monitoring of key performance indicators. BPM allows managers to "run the business by the numbers".

Data warehousing provides access to the information that facilitates business performance management. It enhances managers' ability to analyze the organization's current and historical data to develop business intelligence (BI). As BI tools have become more sophisticated, they have begun to allow managers to predict what is likely to happen in the future and to determine how best to respond.

The *DAMA-DMBOK* outlines the activities involved in data warehousing and business intelligence management:

- Understand business intelligence information needs
- Define and maintain the data warehouse and business intelligence architecture
- Implement data warehouses and data marts
- Implement business intelligence tools and user interfaces
- Process data for business intelligence
- Monitor and tune data warehousing processes
- Monitor and tune business intelligence activity and performance[114]

Data in a data warehouse or data mart originate from a variety of internal and external sources and systems. To populate the database and keep it current it is necessary to perform an extract-transform-load (ETL) process. Depending on the organization and the specific data involved, ETL may occur periodically, daily, hourly, or in near-real time. Source-to-target mapping is an integral component of data warehouse development. It documents the complete lineage for each data element in the warehouse. There are two extraction methods: full extraction and incremental extraction. After the data are extracted, they are transported either to an intermediate staging area or directly to the data warehouse database. Once the data have been cleansed and transformed they can be integrated and loaded into the data warehouse and data marts. Data warehousing supports three levels of BI: strategic, tactical, and operational.

In any field it can be challenging to reach agreement on a common vocabulary, and this is the case in data warehousing and business intelligence. A term sometimes used synonymously with BI is "analytics". Writers and theorists subdivide analytics into three disciplines: descriptive, predictive, and prescriptive.

Predictive modeling is a subset of analytics. Different authors and theorists propose different approaches to building predictive models. IDMA's approach outlines a series of five steps:

1. Retrieve and organize the data
2. Understand the data
3. Split the data and build a model
4. Evaluate the model's performance
5. Iterate and choose a model[115]

---

114 The DAMA Guide to the Data Management Body of Knowledge (DAMA-DMBOK) First Edition, DAMA International, Technics Publications LLC, New Jersey, copyright 2009 DAMA International, p. 198.

115 www.jesse-flores.com/a-five-step-process-for-predictive-modeling/ (accessed October 5, 2015).

Traditional data warehouses were typically updated daily, in an overnight batch process. This approach resulted in a certain amount of data latency. As a result, a variety of technical alternatives to the nightly batch extract, transform and load (ETL) process have developed. In addition, the development of online analytical processing (OLAP) has allowed managers to query the data warehouse and data marts in interactive sessions and to perform multi-dimensional analysis. There are several different technical approaches to implementing a database in support of OLAP. Because the data in a data warehouse and data marts are used differently than data in transactional systems, the characteristics of the databases differ.

Bibliography

ACM Tech Pack on Business Intelligence/Data Management, Pat Cupoli, Barry Devlin, Raymond Ng and Stephen Petschulat, October 2013, Association for Computing Machinery.

Patricia L. Saporito, Applied Insurance Analytics, Pearson Education Ltd., © Patricia L. Saporito, Upper Saddle River, New Jersey 07458.

The DAMA Dictionary of Data Management, First Edition 2008, Mark Mosley Editor, Technics Publications LLC, New Jersey, copyright 2008 DAMA International.

The DAMA Guide to the Data Management Body of Knowledge (DAMA-DMBOK) First Edition, DAMA International, Technics Publications LLC, New Jersey, copyright 2009 DAMA International.

Business Intelligence Versus Business Analytics–What's the Difference?, By Rock Gnatovich, viewed at http://bit.ly/2rBalsV (accessed September 23, 2015).

Building a Predictive Model, Alex Lin, Senior Architect Intelligent Mining, viewed at http://bit.ly/2sD61tl (accessed September 23, 2015).

How Predictive Analytics Reveals New Business Insights, By Jesse Jacobsen, September 9, 2014, viewed at http://bit.ly/2rG2TYP (accessed September 29, 2015).

Defining Data Analytics Services in Support of Business Process Optimization, By David S. Linthicum, February 5, 2013, viewed at http://bit.ly/2sbfC9l (accessed September 29, 2015).

Predictive Analytics and Business Value, Fern Halper, TDWI Research, August 23, 2013, viewed at http://bit.ly/2sIPzas (accessed September 29, 2015).

Building a Predictive Model, Alex Lin Senior Architect Intelligent Mining, viewed at http://bit.ly/2sD61tl (accessed October 5, 2015).

A Five Step Process for Predictive Modeling, Jesse Flores, viewed at http://bit.ly/2sbrs2Y (accessed October 5, 2015).

Data Management Trends, Technologies, and Frameworks

Data managers use a wide variety of techniques, technologies, languages, and solutions that can be broadly categorized as tools. The type of tool a data manager may use depends on the data management function he or she is performing. Organizations typically have two options: to buy tools or to build them. The decision whether to buy or build depends on a number of factors including the functional capabilities that are needed, the cost involved, the degree of customization that an off-the-shelf product might require to meet the business need, and the organization's culture. Whichever option an organization chooses for a particular tool, the data manager has a significant role to play.

When evaluating tools, the first step is to determine the criteria upon which the evaluation is to be based. These would depend on the business need the tool is expected to fill, the type of tool under evaluation, the technical environment, the organization performing the evaluation, and whether the tool is being purchased or developed internally.

There is a variety of resources available to the data manager in this initial phase. There are organizations that evaluate and compare software tools based on their own internal criteria, and these evaluations may prove useful. Also, standards development organizations (SDO) publish software evaluation standards that organizations may elect to adopt.

Another resource that can be useful is frameworks. Frameworks provide an organized way of approaching and thinking about a complex situation or problem, and offer tools and methodologies to help resolve issues or develop new approaches. There are a number of frameworks in current use. The ACORD Framework, the Zachman Framework, and The Open Group Architectural Framework (TOGAF) are three examples.

An area in which frameworks are particularly helpful is in the development of enterprise architectures. Enterprise architectures evolve out of an enterprise data strategy, which is developed to help an organization optimize the use of its enterprise data assets.

Educational Objectives

Upon completion of this assignment, you should be able to:

1. Describe how tools facilitate the data management functions.
2. List general types of tools that would be of use to a data manager.
3. Describe the issues to consider when determining whether to build or purchase tools.
4. Describe the data manager's role in building or purchasing tools.
5. Describe the IDMA approach to evaluating tools.
6. Define XML.
7. Describe the impact of XML.
8. Describe how frameworks assist data managers.
9. Describe how a framework is useful in change management.
10. Describe some common frameworks.
11. Discuss enterprise data strategy and its objectives.

Facilitating Data Management

Earlier chapters introduced and discussed the various data management functions:

- Data governance
- Data architecture management
- Data development
- Data operations management
- Data security management
- Reference and master data management
- Data warehousing and business intelligence management
- Document and content management
- Metadata management
- Data quality management[116]

Each of these functions can be challenging, particularly in an insurance environment. The large volume of data and the interrelationships among those data add to the challenges inherent in data management. In the absence of useful tools, effective data management would essentially be impossible in today's complex, fast-paced business environment.

Tools facilitate data management in a variety of ways, depending on the data management function being performed. For example, in data governance, issues management tools can help an organization identify and prioritize data-related issues, determine their impact, and document their resolution. In data architecture

---

[116] The DAMA Guide to the Data Management Body of Knowledge (DAMA-DMBOK) First Edition, DAMA International, Technics Publications LLC, New Jersey, copyright 2009 DAMA International, p. 18.

management, data modeling tools can graphically illustrate the various relationships among entities. In data development, tools help data management professionals design, implement, and maintain solutions to meet the organization's data requirements. The data operations management function relies on robust database management systems (DBMS) and database administration tools to manage the lifecycle of the organization's structured data. Data security management uses a variety of tools, for example technologies that authenticate an individual's identity through biometrics (e.g., a fingerprint or retina scan). Effective reference and master data management requires data cleansing and integration tools. Data warehousing and business intelligence management use extract, transform and load tools, data discovery and visualization tools, and statistical analysis tools. Organizations use electronic document management system (EDMS) tools to manage the unstructured data in content and documents. Metadata management relies on metadata repositories and data modeling tools. Data quality management depends on data profiling tools that automate data quality analysis, and data cleansing and integration tools.

Although perhaps not properly termed a data management function, data managers are often involved in transferring data between systems or entities, within the organization or across the internet. The use of language tools such as extensible markup language (XML) can be of significant assistance in facilitating those transfers.

One of the challenges that data managers face is the fact that they operate in an environment that is continually changing. Businesses acquire, create, and analyze increasing amounts of data, from a widening variety of sources, and they use those data in a growing number of ways. Hardware and software vendors continue to enhance their products and services, offering a greater selection of tools. Professional data managers ensure that they keep current. New techniques, technologies, and solutions, designed to meet businesses' evolving operational, analytic, and data management requirements, emerge regularly. While not embracing every new option simply because it is new, effective data managers recognize those that may be of value to the organization. They identify those that may meet the organization's needs, evaluate them carefully, and make appropriate recommendations. The goal is to add value cost-effectively.

Categories of Tools

Tools to support data management and data quality best practices can be purchased from a vendor or developed in-house. Some are single-function and stand-alone, while others are integrated suites, or packages, of tools.

Data management tools can be categorized into six general types:

- Data modeling tools
- Database management systems
- Data integration and quality tools
- Business intelligence tools
- Document management tools
- Metadata repository tools

Here are some examples of data management tools:

- Analytic applications

- Application frameworks
- Backup and recovery tools
- Business intelligence tools
- Business process and rule engines
- Change management tools
- Collaboration tools
- Configuration management tools
- Data archiving tools
- Data cleansing tools
- Data development and administration tools
- Data dictionaries
- Data integration tools
- Data integrity tools
- Data mining tools
- Data modeling tools
- Data profiling tools
- Data quality tools
- Data security tools
- Data synchronization tools
- Database administration tools
- Database application development tools
- Database design tools
- Database management systems
- Database performance tools
- Document management tools
- Encryption tools
- Extract-transform-load tools
- Frameworks
- HTML tools
- Image and workflow management tools
- Issue management tools
- Log analysis tools
- Master data management applications
- Metadata repositories and associated tools
- Model management tools
- Object modeling tools
- Office productivity tools
- Performance management tools
- Process modeling tools
- Records management tools
- Reference and master data management tools
- Reference data management applications
- Report generating tools
- SGML tools

- Software development tools
- System management tools
- Testing tools
- Text mining tools
- XML development tools

Buying vs. Building Data Management Tools

An earlier chapter discussed the considerations involved in determining whether to buy or build a metadata repository. Those same considerations apply to essentially any data management tool. The principle considerations are:

- Capabilities;
- Cost;
- Customization; and
- Culture.

Capabilities

The first step before deciding whether to buy or to build any data management tool is to clearly define the organization's requirements from a business perspective. What does the organization need to accomplish? Understanding the organization's business needs is essential to defining the functional capabilities that a tool must have. In order to properly evaluate commercial off-the-shelf products, or to develop a tool in-house, it is important to understand both the organization's current and anticipated future business needs.

A particular tool will most probably need to be integrated with other tools or systems. It is important to identify any architectural requirements or organizational standards that must be met to ensure that a tool is capable of being integrated efficiently.

In addition, it is important to assess the capabilities of the organization's data managers and IT professionals. Do they have the expertise required to design, build, and maintain a tool in-house?

Cost

Depending on an organization's size and the complexity of its requirements, the cost of a commercial off-the-shelf tool can be significant. However, developing tools in-house can be costly as well.

In addition to the financial cost associated with in-house development, there is the opportunity cost, which is the loss of one option when another option is chosen. For example, the time employees spend building a new tool is time they are not able to spend maintaining or enhancing existing tools or systems. In addition, it might take longer to implement a tool developed in-house than a vendor's product. Implementing a vendor's product might allow the organization to begin using the tool more quickly and realizing the associated benefits sooner.

A cost-benefit analysis can often help determine whether buying or building would be the better approach for a particular organization or situation.

Customization

A vendor's product may not meet all of an organization's needs. It may require some degree of customization, which can increase the cost of both implementing and maintaining an off-the-shelf solution. Understanding the users' requirements, and mapping them to the capabilities of off-the-shelf products, help IT professionals identify the level of customization that would be required. That can then be factored into the cost of a vendor's product.

Alternatively, it may be possible to modify a tool the organization already has in order to meet the identified business need.

Culture

Some organizations simply have a preference for purchasing solutions while others prefer to develop them internally. An organization's culture can have a significant impact on the decision to buy or build a system.

In addition, some organizational cultures value investing in technical infrastructure to enhance operations. Other organizations place a high priority on expense control. Organizations with an investment culture are often more likely to purchase tools, while those with an expense control culture may choose to build tools in-house, perceiving that as a less costly alternative.

The Data Manager's Role

An organization relies on the expertise and skills of both its IT and data management professionals when buying or building data management tools. An individual data manager's role may vary depending on his or her particular skill set and the internal structure and culture of the organization. They may be involved in the initial decision as to whether buying or building would be the better option.

When selecting among a number of vendor's products and ultimately buying a tool, the data manager's role can include some or all of the following activities, completed in consultation with IT and operational staff:

- Plan and budget for software acquisition
- Work with operational staff to identify and document functional requirements
- Consult with IT staff to understand any technical requirements
- Review product comparisons
- Research software vendors
- Select several vendor products for evaluation

- Review product and pricing information from selected vendors
- Determine the evaluation criteria to be used
- Determine the evaluation method to be used
- Assemble an evaluation team of business and technical professionals
- Complete the evaluation and analyze the results
- Make a purchasing recommendation to the appropriate decision makers

If no vendor's product meets the organization's needs, or if an organization has a preference for developing tools in-house, the data manager's role is similar:

- Plan and budget for software development
- Work with operational staff to identify and document functional requirements
- Consult with IT as required during development and testing
- Determine the evaluation criteria to be used
- Determine the evaluation method to be used
- Assemble an evaluation team of business and technical professionals
- Complete the evaluation and analyze the results
- Make recommendations for modifications as required

Once the tool has been purchased or developed, the data manager would be involved in the launch of the tool, user training, monitoring usage of the tool, and resolving any issues that arise related to the tool.

Tool Evaluation

The first step in tool evaluation is to determine the criteria upon which the evaluation is to be based. Generally, the criteria would depend on the type of tool under evaluation. Theorists, authors, and tool vendors have suggested various evaluation criteria for different categories of tools, such as data governance tools, data quality tools, master data management tools, analytics reporting tools, email management tools, or data warehousing tools. However, even within the same category of tools, different sources suggest different evaluation criteria. Some approaches are relatively simple; others are quite complex and detailed. One organization markets a master data management software requirements checklist that includes 3,350 evaluation criteria.[117]

The criteria for evaluating a tool would also vary depending on the business need the tool is expected to fill, the technical environment into which it must integrate, and even the culture and methodologies of the organization performing the evaluation. There would be differences in evaluation criteria depending on whether a tool is being purchased or developed internally. For example, in the case of purchased tools, evaluation criteria would typically include such things as the technical support the vendor is prepared to offer and the quality of the documentation it provides.

---

[117] www.infotivity.com/data-management.html (accessed October 18, 2015).

There are organizations that evaluate and compare a variety of different software tools based on their own internal criteria and make the results of their research available for a fee. In addition, standards organizations develop and publish software evaluation standards that organizations may elect to use. For example, the International Organization for Standardization (ISO) publishes *ISO/IEC 25010:2011 Systems and software engineering – Systems and software Quality Requirements and Evaluation (SQuaRE) – System and software quality models*. The Institute of Electrical and Electronics Engineers (IEEE) publishes *P1062 – IEEE Draft Recommended Practice for Software Acquisition*, which is "designed to help organizations and individuals incorporate quality, including security, considerations during the definition, evaluation, selection, and acceptance of supplier software for operational use."[118]

When evaluating a tool, data management professionals typically consider a variety of factors including such things as the following:

- The extent to which the tool meets the identified business need and whether it can be customized.
- How easy and intuitive the tool is to use, particularly by non-technical staff.
- The total cost of ownership, including acquisition costs, licensing fees, support and maintenance.
- The tool's architecture and how it will integrate with the organization's other systems.
- Whether the tool includes a business rules engine that allows non-programmers to add or change business rules.
- Whether the tool can support the expected volume of data and number of concurrent users, and the extent to which it can scale up as needed.
- The types of data the tool can handle, for example highly structured or complex structured data.
- The maturity of the technology and any plans the vendor has for development or enhancement of the tool.
- The amount of training and technical support that the vendor is able to provide.
- The extent to which the vendor is well-established and financially stable.

When evaluating a number of competing products, organizations take a variety of approaches, some formal and others less so. In one approach, the decision criteria are first selected. Each is assigned a weight based on its relative importance. Evaluators use a scoring system to rate each vendor's product against the selected evaluation criteria. For example, for each criterion they could score two if the product fully meets all the organization's needs, one if it partially meets the needs, and zero if it does not meet the needs. The data manager can create a spreadsheet to tabulate the evaluator's scores, apply the weighting factors, and compare two or more tools.

Tools to Facilitate Data Exchange

As noted previously, data managers are frequently involved in transferring data between systems and entities. There are a variety of tools that can facilitate such transfers, with the most common being extensible markup language (XML). The *DAMA Dictionary of Data Management* defines **extensible markup language (XML)** as "a tag-based markup language (a subset of SGML) defined by W3C with a tag set that can be added to. The tags enable XML

---

118 http://standards.ieee.org/develop/project/1062.html (accessed October 19, 2015).

documents to be self-describing structures."[119] While this definition is accurate, it requires some additional explanation.

The organization that defined the XML standard, the World Wide Web Consortium (W3C), is an international organization that develops standards for the Web. XML uses **tags** contained in chevrons, also called angle brackets or pointy brackets (< >), like those used in HTML (hypertext markup language). In HTML, tags are used for formatting, for example specifying the headings and fonts used for web page content. In XML the tags serve a different purpose. XML tags focus on the content itself rather than the format. They act as metadata to "describe the content, structure and business rules in a document or a database."[120] For example, in XML the string <PolNumber>1234567</PolNumber> indicates that "1234567" is a policy number with the "/" tag identifying its endpoint.

The structure of an XML document can indicate the relationships among the data elements it contains. In addition, while HTML has a predefined and limited set of markup tags, XML is extensible, meaning that it allows users to create new tags to meet their specific content description needs. Each community or industry can develop XML vocabularies that meet its particular needs. The Association for Cooperative Operations Research and Development (ACORD), a recognized insurance data standards organization, took on the responsibility of establishing XML standards for the insurance industry.

Both HTML and XML are based on standard generalized markup language (SGML), which was developed by the International Organization for Standardization (ISO) as a standard for document representation. "SGML can be used for publishing in its broadest definition, ranging from single medium conventional publishing to multi-media data base publishing. SGML can also be used in office document processing when the benefits of human readability and interchange with publishing systems are required."[121]

The Impact of XML

Because XML offers a common format for expressing data content and structure, it facilitates the automated sharing of data among different applications and databases, either internally or with external stakeholders via the Internet. XML can be used to link legacy systems and newer systems, including intranets and the Web.

XML is independent of platforms, vendors, applications and database structures. Conceptually, it functions similarly to electronic data interchange (EDI). Data are converted from their original system format into XML format and sent to the receiving system, which can read the tags to identify the various types of data received and map those data appropriately. XML does not perform the conversion, transport, or mapping functions. Other tools

---

[119] The DAMA Dictionary of Data Management, First Edition 2008, Mark Mosley Editor, Technics Publications LLC, New Jersey, copyright 2008 DAMA International, p.62.

[120] Ibid, p. 251.

[121] ISO 8879:1986 Information processing – Text and office systems – Standard Generalized Markup Language (SGML) viewed at https://www.iso.org/obp/ui/#iso:8879:ed-1:v1:en (accessed October 22, 2015).

or software are required for those operations. XML is simply a language used to describe data so that they can be understood and manipulated by other tools.

Because XML can be used to define the structure and content of unstructured data, it allows for the integration of unstructured data, such as text reports or Web pages, with structured data, such as those in relational databases. This facilitates access to a large volume of data and information that was previously inaccessible, or difficult to access, for analysis and decision support.

The use of XML offers a number of benefits to businesses:

- Standardization
- Manageability
- Longevity
- Business-to-business (B2B) and business-to-customer (B2C) communication
- Freedom of extensibility
- Human and machine interfaces
- Internationalization[122]

XML is an accepted standard and as such it has done much to facilitate e-commerce, which has grown significantly over the past two decades. Because XML data are independent, they can be managed, used and reused in a variety of ways by a variety of systems. Because XML documents are simple text files, they may have a longer lifespan than platform-dependent data. As technology changes, text files continue to be accessible for use and reuse. In addition, older data from disparate systems can be converted to XML and integrated for analysis or other uses.

XML facilitates business-to-business communication because all that is required is a mutually agreed-upon set of markup tags. It can be used to create enterprise portals that offer customers and other stakeholder's access to a wide variety of information from a single access point. Because XML is extensible, as business requirements for data change, all that is needed are new tags. Even though XML documents can be read by machines, they remain comprehensible to humans. Finally, as a globally accepted standard, XML allows organizations to broaden their customer base internationally through the Web without having to maintain a physical presence in a targeted geographical market.

JavaScript object notation (JSON) is an alternative to XML. It is derived from JavaScript, which is the programming language used for the Web. It can be used to exchange data and it offers many of the same benefits as XML.

Frameworks

Frameworks are another category of tools that are invaluable to data managers. The term "framework" is widely used but it has a variety of context-dependent definitions. The *DAMA-DMBOK* offers a three-part definition:

---

[122] http://www.irt.org/articles/js215 (accessed October 23, 2015).

"framework"

1. A basic skeletal structure.

2. A classification scheme used to better understand a topic; a defined and documented paradigm, used as a lens to view a complex problem.

3. In software development a reusable object-oriented design, including a library of reusable classes and other components, along with standards for designing additional components and how they interact."[123]

Another definition, that highlights the various ways in which the term is used, comes from an IT standards and organizations glossary:

"In general, a framework is a real or conceptual structure intended to serve as a support or guide for the building of something that expands the structure into something useful.

In computer systems, a framework is often a layered structure indicating what kind of programs can or should be built and how they would interrelate. Some computer system frameworks also include actual programs, specify programming interfaces, or offer programming tools for using the frameworks. A framework may be for a set of functions within a system and how they interrelate; the layers of an operating system; the layers of an application subsystem; how communications should be standardized at some level of a network; and so forth."[124]

Frameworks can also be procedural guidelines. For example, a compliance framework could outline the processes and the internal monitoring and controls that an organization has in place to ensure and demonstrate that it is meeting all of its regulatory obligations.

Frameworks assist data managers by providing:

• An approach to conceptualizing complex situations or problems; and
• A structured way in which to manage complex situations or resolve problems.

Frameworks, Enterprise Architecture, and Change Management

An earlier chapter discussed enterprise data architecture. Enterprise data architecture is one element of an organization's overall enterprise architecture. **Enterprise architecture** is "an integrated collection of models and design approaches used to align information, processes, projects and technology with the goals of the enterprise."[125]

In many organizations, the growing number and complexity of information technology (IT) and related systems has resulted in three related issues:

---

[123] The DAMA Dictionary of Data Management, First Edition 2008, Mark Mosley Editor, Technics Publications LLC, New Jersey, copyright 2008 DAMA International, p. 66.

[124] Framework, Margaret Rouse, February 2015, viewed at whatis.techtarget.com/definition/framework (accessed October 25, 2015).

[125] The DAMA Dictionary of Data Management, First Edition 2008, Mark Mosley Editor, Technics Publications LLC, New Jersey, copyright 2008 DAMA International, p. 63.

- The cost of building and maintaining IT systems increases
- Timely access to high-quality data decreases
- The ability of the organization to be agile and innovative decreases

Developing and implementing an enterprise architecture would help to resolve all of these issues. However, doing so is a highly complex and iterative process, particularly in large organizations with many disparate systems that incorporate products from many different vendors. Frameworks are essential in that they help an organization take a structured, cohesive, and manageable approach to designing and deploying an enterprise architecture.

There are a variety of frameworks in general use, developed by standards organizations, government bodies, vendors, and consulting firms. Often different frameworks take very different approaches and they can sometimes be used in combination.

ACORD Framework

Framework is the name of one of the products and services that ACORD offers. Framework was developed in response to a recognized need for enterprise architecture within the insurance industry. ACORD's Framework includes five component parts:

- A Business Glossary
- A Capability Model
- An Information Model
- A Data Model
- A Component Model

The business glossary contains non-technical, business definitions of terms, and those same terms are used consistently across all of the Framework models. The Capability Model defines what insurance companies do. While it does not define workflows, it reflects the industry's usual way of doing business. The Information Model organizes and relates insurance concepts, and it forms the basis for the development of model-driven standards. The Data Model turns the concepts from the Information Model into formats that can be used, for example, to create physical data models for databases. Finally, the Component Model allows organizations to create systems using different component combinations and interfaces.[126]

The Zachman Framework

The Zachman Framework supports a structured way of thinking about and describing virtually anything, including an enterprise and its architecture. It is typically represented as a labeled six-by-six matrix. Figure 12.1 provides an example.

---

[126] The ACORD Framework – An Insurance Enterprise Architecture, viewed at http://www.acord.org/resources/framework/Presentatinos/Framework.pdf, (accessed October 25, 2015).

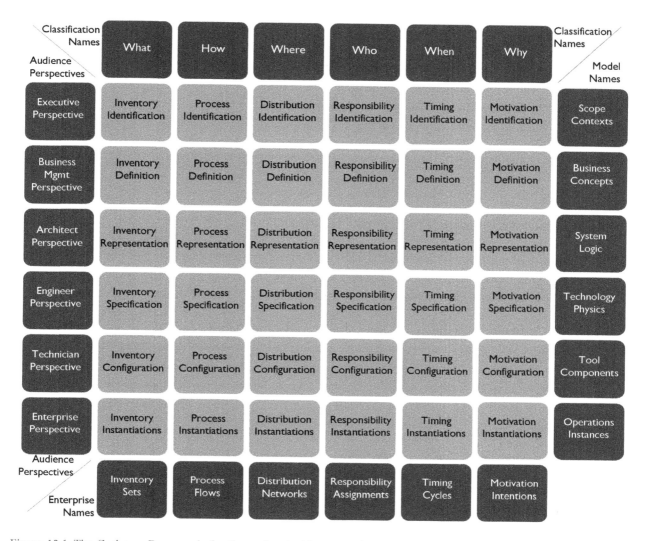

Figure 12.1 The Zachman Framework for Enterprise Architecture, adapted from The Zachman Framework for Enterprise Architecture, The Enterprise Ontology viewed at www.zachman.com/about-the-zachman-framework (accessed October 24, 2015)

The developer, John Zachman, describes the function of the framework. "The Zachman Framework ™ IS NOT a methodology for creating the implementation (an instantiation) of the object. The Framework IS the ontology for describing the Enterprise. The Framework (ontology) is a STRUCTURE whereas a methodology is a PROCESS. A Structure is NOT a Process. A Structure establishes definition whereas a Process provides Transformation."[127]

An **ontology** is "a semantic data model defining structure and meaning typically used to model non-tabular data."[128]

The Zachman Framework is widely used for a number of reasons:

- It is relatively simple and easy to understand.

---

[127] John Zachman's Concise Definition of the Zachman Framework ™, by John Zachman, 2008, viewed at www.zachman.com/about-the-zachman-framework (accessed October 25, 2015).

[128] The DAMA Dictionary of Data Management, First Edition 2008, Mark Mosley Editor, Technics Publications LLC, New Jersey, copyright 2008 DAMA International, p. 91.

- It can be widely or narrowly applied, to the entire enterprise or individual areas.
- It helps people think and communicate more clearly using non-technical language.
- It can be used to conceptualize a wide variety of situations and issues.
- It can help focus on details within the context of the whole.
- It can be used in teaching data management concepts.
- It can be used as a planning tool by providing context.

It is independent of specific tools or methods and can be used in conjunction with them

The Open Group Architecture Framework (TOGAF)

The Open Group is an international information technology standards organization. The Open Group Architecture Framework (TOGAF) comprises a set of tools and methodologies that can be used to develop a range of IT architectures including an enterprise architecture. The Open Group makes TOGAF available for use free-of-charge.

TOGAF divides enterprise architecture into four components: business architecture, data architecture, application architecture, and technology architecture. Business architecture relates to such things as strategy, organization, and business processes. Data architecture describes logical and physical data assets and the resources used in data management. Application architecture details such things as how individual applications are used, and how they integrate with other applications. Technology architecture specifies the hardware and software required to meet the organization's needs.[129]

TOGAF is designed as a practical approach to developing an enterprise architecture and it includes three elements:

- An Architecture Development Method (ADM)
- An Enterprise Continuum
- A Resource Base

The Architecture Development Method (ADM) explains how to design an enterprise architecture that best meets an organization's needs. The ADM describes an architectural development process. The Enterprise Continuum and the Resource Base include a variety of tools and resources that an architect can use in conjunction with the ADM. The Enterprise Continuum is a "virtual repository of all the architecture assets – models, patterns, architecture descriptions, and other artifacts – that exist both within the enterprise and in the IT industry at large, which the enterprise considers itself to have available for the development of architectures for the enterprise."[130] The Resource Base includes resources, guidelines, templates and background information.[131]

---

[129] Welcome to TOGAF – The Open Group Architecture Framework, viewed at pubs.opengroup.org/architecture/togaf8-doc/arch/ (accessed October 25, 2015).

[130] Introduction to the Enterprise Continuum, viewed at pubs.opengroup.org/architecture/togaf8-doc/arch/chap17.html (accessed November 24, 2015).

[131] TOGAF Standard Courseware 8.1.1 Edition, Module 2 The TOGAF 8 Components, viewed at www.togaf.com/togafSlides/TOGAF-V8-M2-TOGAF8-Components.PDF, (accessed November 24, 2015).

Enterprise Data Strategy

The development of a strong data management culture begins at the executive level. Effective management of the organization's data assets needs to be integrated into executives' strategic vision for the enterprise as a whole. The foundation is an enterprise strategic plan that includes a well-formulated enterprise data strategy. An **enterprise data strategy** is a plan for improving the way an enterprise leverages its data, allowing the company to turn data into information and knowledge which, in turn, produce measurable improvements in business performance.

An enterprise data strategy focuses on achieving a number of objectives:

- Enhancing strategic and tactical decision making at the enterprise level
- Enhancing operational focus on enterprise-wide strategies
- Supporting flexibility and agility in a rapidly changing environment
- Consolidating data architecture to optimize information delivery
- Increasing integration and alignment among the functional areas
- Providing timely access to high quality data across the entire enterprise
- Eliminating information silos
- Improving data quality in terms of accuracy and consistency
- Standardizing processes and guidelines for ensuring data security

Implementation of an enterprise data strategy can require a significant commitment in terms of both financial and human resources. Some executives may be disinclined to expend resources on something that they may not recognize as an essential part of the organization's core business. "What do metadata and data warehousing have to do with our combined ratio or policyholders' surplus?" Data management professionals may need to convince executives of the value of the organization's data assets, and to demonstrate how an enterprise data strategy can help the organization leverage its data while at the same time reducing risk.

The scope of developing and implementing an enterprise data strategy can be daunting, particularly in large multi-national organizations. An enterprise data strategy could focus on a variety of areas including the following:

- Data standardization and integration
- Data quality
- Metadata management
- Data ownership and stewardship
- Balancing data security and availability
- Sharing and reuse of data

Implementing an enterprise data strategy involves dealing with complex technological issues. It may also require significant organizational and cultural changes. Selecting the appropriate individual to spearhead the initiative is important. It should be the business side of the organization that drives its enterprise data strategy, rather than the IT side.

Above the strategic foundation, effective governance is essential. Data and information governance can do much to engender a strong data management culture. In particular, data and information governance can help align operational functions and data management functions more closely, which in turn can offer significant benefits to the organization.

Summary

Data management can be challenging, particularly in an insurance environment. Techniques, technologies, and frameworks facilitate data management in a variety of ways, depending on the data management function being performed. Data management tools can be categorized into six general types: data modeling tools, database management systems, data integration and quality tools, business intelligence tools, document management tools, and metadata repository tools. The decision whether to buy or build a tool depends on a number of considerations including the required capabilities, the cost of ownership, the degree of customization required for a vendor's product, and the organization's culture.

Data transfer languages like XML are important tools for data managers. XML facilitates the sharing of data among different applications/databases, internally and externally, as well as the integration of unstructured data with structured data. XML offers a number of benefits including standardization, manageability, longevity, B2B and B2C communication, the ability to create and customize tags as required, support for both human and machine interfaces, and internationalization. JSON is an alternative to XML.

Frameworks are another category of tools that are invaluable to data managers. Frameworks assist data managers by providing an approach to conceptualizing complex situations or problems; and a structured way in which to manage complex situations or resolve problems. There are a number of frameworks in current use including the ACORD Framework, the Zachman Framework, and TOGAF.

An organization needs a robust enterprise data strategy in order to develop cohesive enterprise data architecture. An enterprise data strategy focuses on achieving a number of objectives including enhancing strategic and tactical decision making; supporting flexibility and agility; consolidating data architecture; increasing integration; providing timely access to high quality data; eliminating information silos; improving data quality; and ensuring data security. However, developing and implementing an enterprise data strategy can be challenging in that it can involve both complex technical issues and significant organizational and cultural change.

Bibliography

Patricia L. Saporito, Applied Insurance Analytics, Pearson Education Ltd., © Patricia L. Saporito, Upper Saddle River, New Jersey 07458.

The DAMA Dictionary of Data Management, First Edition 2008, Mark Mosley Editor, Technics Publications LLC, New Jersey, copyright 2008 DAMA International.

The DAMA Guide to the Data Management Body of Knowledge (DAMA-DMBOK) First Edition, DAMA International, Technics Publications LLC, New Jersey, copyright 2009 DAMA International.

Data Management and Data Management Tools, R. Stephen Richard, viewed at http://bit.ly/2sbai5z (accessed October 12, 2015).

Tools to Facilitate Efficient Data Management, Data and Technology Today, viewed at http://bit.ly/2szLOUr (accessed October 14, 2015).

Buy vs. build: Six steps to making the right decision, by Dan Oliver, viewed at http://tek.io/2rpTTY9 (accessed October 15, 2015).

Software Evaluation: Criteria-based Assessment, by Mike Jackson, Steve Crouch and Rob Baxter, Software sustainability Institute, viewed at http://bit.ly/29L6n7s (accessed October 16, 2015).

Big Data: Ten Criteria for Evaluating Analytics Reporting Tools (Part 1), By Dave Beulke, on July 30th, 2013, viewed at http://bit.ly/2sJ11mG (accessed October 17, 2015).

P1062 - IEEE Draft Recommended Practice for Software Acquisition, viewed at http://bit.ly/2rpQ5GE (accessed October 18, 2015).

Quantitative Methods for Software Selection and Evaluation, Michael S. Bandor, September 2006, viewed at http://bit.ly/2sl57Pc (accessed October 20, 2015).

Insurance Integration Tools for Risk Free Implementation of EDI and XML Standards, viewed at http://bit.ly/2rBhSb4 (accessed October 20, 2015).

Anatomy of the ACORD TXLife XML standard - Under the covers of the insurance industry's primary XML standard viewed at https://ibm.co/2tcGynl (accessed October 20, 2015).

3 On SGML and HTML, W3C, viewed at http://bit.ly/2slqIqz (accessed October 21, 2015).

Perspectives of XML in E-Commerce, Internet Related Technologies, viewed at http://bit.ly/2slqKyH (accessed October 23, 2015).

The Data Management Framework: From Conceptual to Tactical, viewed at http://bit.ly/2txxRUa (accessed October 24, 2015).

John Zachman's Concise Definition of The Zachman Framework™, by John A. Zachman, viewed at http://bit.ly/1KBVXDu (accessed October 24, 2015).

A Comparison of the Top Four Enterprise-Architecture Methodologies, Roger Sessions, ObjectWatch, Inc., May 2007, viewed at http://bit.ly/1UWzOoY (accessed October 24, 2015).

Introduction to the Enterprise Continuum, viewed at http://bit.ly/1esoR9U (accessed November 24, 2015).

TOGAF Standard Courseware 8.1.1 Edition, Module 2 The TOGAF 8 Components, viewed at http://bit.ly/2slkKpU (accessed November 24, 2015).

Data Strategy, by Larissa Moss, viewed at http://bit.ly/2tcChQV (accessed November 24, 2015).

What We Learned From IDMA 201

This text, *Introduction to Data Management Functions and Tools*, has introduced a wide variety of data management concepts. This final assignment provides a review intended to allow the reader to step back and see the "big picture".

Educational Objective

The objective of this final assignment is to provide a high-level overview of the prior twelve assignments. It is intended to allow the reader to step back and see the "big picture".

The Data Management Environment

Organizations are facing significant data-related challenges today and may need to make fundamental changes to respond successfully. The volume of data that organizations acquire, create, use, and rely on has increased significantly and continues to do so. Part of the reason that the volume of data are increasing is because the sources of data are increasing. For example, organizations are mining social media to discover consumer preferences and unmet consumer needs. As another example, insurers are using telematics in automobiles to gain greater insights into the driving habits of individual insureds. Telematics is "the use of wireless devices and 'black box' technologies to transmit data in real time back to an organization."[132]

"Big data" is a popular topic and has been so for a number of years. There are many definitions of big data, but a common one is the "Three Vs" definition: Big data is "high-volume, high-velocity and/or high-variety information"[133]. Other definitions include additional "Vs", such as validity, veracity, value, visibility, and volatility. IDMA uses the "Three Vs" definition.

---

132 Gartner, IT Glossary, viewed at www.gartner.com/it-glossary/telematics/ (accessed January 28, 2016.

133 Gartner, IT Glossary, viewed at http://www.gartner.com/it-glossary/big-data/, (accessed January 28, 2016).

The speed at which data enter an organization is accelerating, and the variety of data to which organizations have access is expanding. Organizations that have appropriate technology in place, and that have a data management culture and a mature data management program, will be best able to exploit big data to gain a competitive advantage.

An Enterprise Data Management Culture

In the past, data and information were not typically considered assets. Today, they are recognized as among the most valuable of an organization's assets because of the potential benefits they provide. Organizations that are best able to collect, organize, access, and analyze high quality data in order to create accurate, useful information have a significant competitive advantage.

The development of a strong data management culture begins at the executive level. Data management needs to be integrated into executives' strategic vision for the enterprise as a whole. The foundation is an enterprise strategic plan that includes a well-formulated enterprise data strategy. For example, an insurer may devise strategies in the areas of pricing, marketing, underwriting, or product innovation, but it should also develop a strategy for optimizing the value and productive use of its data. An enterprise data strategy is a plan for improving the way an enterprise leverages its data, allowing the company to turn data into information and knowledge that can produce measurable improvements in business performance.

Implementation of an enterprise data strategy can require a significant commitment in terms of both financial and human resources. Some executives may be disinclined to expend resources on something that they may not recognize as an essential part of the organization's core business. "What do metadata and data warehousing have to do with our combined ratio or policyholders' surplus?" Data management professionals may need to convince executives of the value of the organization's data assets, and to demonstrate how data management can improve the organization's performance, while at the same time reducing risk.

Because data are a valuable corporate asset, it should be governed in the same manner as other corporate assets. Corporate governance is the next level above the strategic foundation. It encompasses the principles and policies the organization develops and implements in an attempt to balance the various interests of its many stakeholders. Data and information governance are essential elements of overall corporate governance. An effective data and information governance program can do much to engender a strong data management culture. In particular, data and information governance can help align operational functions and data management functions more closely, which in turn can offer significant benefits to the organization.

Enterprise architecture is "an integrated collection of models and design approaches used to align information, processes, projects, and technology with the goals of the enterprise."[134] An enterprise data architecture is an important part of the overall enterprise architecture. The implementation of an enterprise data architecture can help

---

[134] The DAMA Dictionary of Data Management, First Edition 2008, Mark Mosley Editor, Technics Publications LLC, New Jersey, copyright 2008 DAMA International, p. 63.

promote a data management culture because it requires IT and operational staff to learn to communicate more effectively about data.

Data Information and Knowledge

Data are facts about, or attributes of, entities. Information is data that have been analyzed, processed, or organized for a particular purpose and presented in a form and context that are relevant and meaningful. Knowledge is the ability, based on experience and understanding, to use information in a competent, productive way.

Managers' Use of Information

Executives, middle managers, and front line supervisors rely on detailed, accurate, and timely information in all of their leadership activities: planning, organizing, leading, and controlling. Executives use information when developing or realigning an organization's business model and during the strategic planning process. Middle managers require information for tactical planning, and front-line managers use information for operational planning.

Enterprises can be organized in a variety of ways—centralized, decentralized, or a mix of the two. Senior executives determine the overall structure of an organization, but middle managers and even front-line managers also make decisions about organizational design, job design, and resource allocation within their region, department, office, or team. To make these decisions they require information about both their internal and external environments.

One important aspect of management is the ability to lead. They need sufficient information to clearly understand the organization's strategic vision, its objectives, processes, and the environment in which it operates, so that this can be communicated to staff. They also need detailed information about the actual performance of both the organization and its employees.

Controlling is an important aspect of managing. Controls are needed to ensure that an organization meets its goals. Managers establish performance benchmarks, compare actual performance to those benchmarks, and take action to correct shortfalls in performance. Accurate information, provided in a timely manner and appropriate format, helps managers determine the reason for any deviation from objectives and decide on appropriate corrective action.

Organizational Change

Organizations operate in dynamic environments. To remain viable, or to take advantage of opportunities, organizations need to be able to change. Organizational change is the process of using an organization's resources, people, technology, and financial assets to reach a desired future outcome or state. To do so successfully, organizations need information to help identify gaps between desired and actual performance, to establish goals that are challenging but realistic, and to determine how best to close any gaps between actual and desired performance.

Information provides a catalyst for organizational change. As an organization acquires more data and uses them more effectively, it becomes more agile. It is better able to understand its environment and to adjust its focus, structure, processes, and relationships to respond to environmental changes.

Data Quality

Information is essential to all of an organization's activities. Because information is derived from data, the quality of those data is critical. Data quality is the degree to which data are fit for their intended use in operations, decision making, or planning.

The cost of bad data can be significant. It has been estimated that the consequences of poor data quality cost businesses in the United States more than $800 billion a year. "Dirty data" can also lead to increased scrutiny by regulators, particularly in industries that are highly regulated such as the insurance industry.

In manufacturing, quality professionals use the 1-10-100 rule to describe the increasing cost of correcting errors as a product moves from initial design through manufacturing and on to the customer. The 1-10-100 rule applies to data quality as well. The cost of correcting a data entry error at the moment it is made is small. The cost increases if that same error needs to be corrected downstream. The cost of not correcting the error is greater still.

There is a variety of reasons why it is difficult to maintain a high level of data quality. Inaccurate data entry or typographical errors can be common. If data are not clearly defined, inconsistencies result. Input fields may not be long enough, resulting in truncation of the data. Fields may not accept the type of data that needs to be entered. Carelessness in selecting the correct record to update can cause data quality problems. The passage of time is another source of bad data. Many organizations have multiple systems that are not well-integrated; when a change occurs several systems need to be updated; this does not always occur. Increasingly, organizations obtain data from outside sources and it can be difficult to verify the quality of those data. As organizations update systems, they move existing data from an older system to the new one. This can be challenging because the two systems may require different data in different formats. Another consideration with respect to data quality relates to the processes they undergo. Data are acquired, stored, selected and retrieved, transformed and manipulated, aggregated, and presented. Errors can occur in any of these processes.

The Data Lifecycle

The data lifecycle includes the following steps: plan, specify, enable, create and acquire, maintain and use, archive and retrieve, and purge. Planning is the first step in any successful project or undertaking. Specification involves deciding on, and documenting, such things as what the sources of data will be; how they will be formatted, organized and stored; who will have authority to enter, access, change, or delete data; how data will be shared; and how they will be kept secure and confidential. Enabling involves overlaying these specifications onto a technological platform that allows the organization to complete the next two steps in the data lifecycle: create and acquire data, and maintain and use data. These two steps are the operational portion of the data lifecycle. Archiving and retrieval occur when data are no longer required operationally, but are still necessary for query, analysis, reporting, or compliance purposes. When it is no longer necessary to retain data, they should be purged from the system.

Data Architecture

When developing systems, data architects work closely with business analysts and operational staff. They identify all of the entities about which the organization wishes to collect or create data, and the attributes of those entities. Data architecture identifies what data are needed; how they should be collected, organized and stored; and how they will be used. It highlights the interactions and relationships among data from different sources, and the various users of those data. It develops a comprehensive framework for defining and organizing data and information efficiently within the organization as a whole.

Many insurers continue to use and maintain legacy systems for a variety of reasons. However, legacy systems present challenges. They were typically developed for a single purpose and were not generally designed to integrate with other systems. Often, when they were developed there was no cohesive data architecture, resulting in the creation of business information silos. Information silos cause duplication of effort, reduced data quality, and a lack of coordinated decision making among the various functional areas. In addition, there is a risk of reporting contradictory or inaccurate information to external regulatory and non-regulatory bodies based upon disparate data from different internal sources.

Attempts to automate the connections between legacy systems or to integrate them with more current technology can be expensive and are often focused on simply meeting basic functional needs. A comprehensive architecture for all of an organization's applications would allow insurers to use their data more effectively.

Organizational Memory

Organizational memory is essentially any place in which an organization can store knowledge. While many different theoretical classifications of knowledge have been proposed, three types are commonly recognized today, and they form the components of organizational memory. Explicit knowledge is knowledge that has been codified or documented in some way. Tacit knowledge is largely undocumented knowledge that individuals develop through personal experience. Embedded knowledge is knowledge that may have been forgotten but that remains as an artifact within processes, routines, or cultures.

Some of an organization's knowledge is in a structured format that is readily accessible, for example data and information stored in databases. However, the majority of an organization's data and information is unstructured—some estimate up to 80 percent. Capturing and tapping the tacit knowledge of an organization's human assets, and the knowledge embedded in its processes and culture, is challenging. Yet this knowledge has significant value. The ability to access organizational memory makes an enterprise more efficient and flexible, helps it respond better to change, and helps avoid "reinventing the wheel" when a previously solved problem or issue resurfaces.

Introduction to Data Management

Data management is the process of planning, defining, organizing, maintaining, and managing access to digitally created, stored, and transmitted data. Data managers focus on understanding an organization's data needs, enhancing data quality, ensuring data security, maintaining data integrity, increasing data integration, and improving access to information.

Data management roles can vary, even among similar organizations. Data management professionals include data architects, data modelers, business intelligence analysts, data analysts, database administrators, and data security administrators. There may be external relationships with collaborators and data brokers. In addition to these more technical functions, individuals throughout an organization may participate in data stewardship activities. Several formal groups are commonly involved in an organization's data management and data stewardship activities including data management services, a data governance council or committee, a data stewardship committee, and a data governance officer.

Although a structured framework for data management is essential, insurers with a strong data management culture go beyond these formal roles and responsibilities. They ensure that all of their employees receive appropriate training in data management concepts and best practices.

Enterprise Data Management

Enterprise data management, often referred to as enterprise information management (EIM), can help eliminate information silos, lead to increased integration and alignment among functional areas, and enhance operational focus on enterprise strategies. Effective EIM initiatives can improve data quality, enhance decision making, consolidate data architecture, and increase the enterprise's flexibility and agility. However, there are challenges associated with EIM. Successful implementation of an EIM strategy requires careful planning, strong leadership, a considerable investment, and significant technical expertise. It may also require the organization to restructure itself, its business processes, and its internal and external relationships.

Data Managers

Data managers are individuals whose primary day-to-day role is to provide business managers with the information they need to accomplish the objectives of the organization. A data manager is a professional who specializes in one or more of the data management functions. Depending on the size, structure, and culture of an enterprise, data managers may be located in a variety of areas. Because of their role as a technical facilitator, data managers interact with a wide variety of individuals within the organization.

Effective data managers have a variety of skills and abilities. They understand the organization's strategic and tactical focus, business operations, and the environment in which it operates. They have comprehensive technical knowledge and keep current with new technologies. In addition to technical skills, successful data managers have well-developed interpersonal skills. Finally, successful data managers maintain a level of professionalism. IDMA publishes *Standards for Professionalism for Insurance Data Managers* and Insurance Services Office (ISO) publishes *Data Management Best Practices* specifically targeted at the insurance industry.

Data Standards

A standard is a specification to which materials, products, processes, or services should conform. Standards help to facilitate product development, enhance service delivery, reduce costs, improve quality, ensure health and safety, accelerate communication, support innovation, provide ready-made solutions, protect the environment, and promote international trade.

There are a variety of standards within the insurance industry. Some are imposed by regulators; some reflect traditional business practices; some have been developed by industry groups through open discussion and consensus. Areas in which standards exist include terminology, coverage and forms, accounting practices, solvency requirements, market conduct, rating and pricing, business processes, data quality and consistency, and data exchange.

Standards Development Organizations (SDOs)

Standards development organizations (SDOs) create standards in an open, consultative manner. There are thousands of SDOs operating globally. Some important SDOs include the International Organization for Standardization (ISO), the American National Standards Institute (ANSI), the Association for Cooperative Operations Research and Development (ACORD), the International Association of Industrial Accident Boards and Commissions (IAIABC), and the Workers Compensation Insurance Organizations (WCIO).

SDOs are not the only developers of standards. Individual organizations, professional membership groups, industry associations, labor unions, consumer groups, regulators, and international organizations all create standards. There is a variety of standards that should be of interest to data management professionals working in the insurance industry.

Insurance Regulation

The insurance industry is more highly regulated than most other industries. The primary reason for insurance regulation is to protect consumers. Regulators focus on insurer solvency, market conduct, and ratemaking. They review insurers' financial statements and perform tests to identify those with potential solvency problems. They periodically review insurers' underwriting and claims settlement procedures, and verify that the rates and forms used are those that have received regulatory approval where such approval is required. They attempt to ensure that rates are adequate, not excessive, and not unfairly discriminatory. In order to properly evaluate rates across the industry, regulators require insurers to submit detailed statistical information at regular intervals. Data collection organizations (DCOs) are authorized to collect and submit the required data on behalf of insurers.

Electronic Data Interchange (EDI)

One implementation of a data standard is in electronic data interchange (EDI). In an EDI-based transaction, different systems at different organizations, or within the same organization, can "talk" to each other in a common format, automating data sharing and eliminating the need for human involvement. This reduces errors and inefficiencies. A variety of EDI standards exist.

Standards for naming and defining data elements support EDI as well as other data sharing and data management activities. Each data element is given a unique name, usually based on the common or business term for that piece of data. Data element names often include three parts: an object, a property, and a representation. However not all data elements conform to this standard as they can contain only two words, or more than three words. Data element names should be recorded in data dictionaries.

Information Integrity

Data integrity is the extent to which data are trustworthy, meaning that they are complete, accurate, consistent, and uncorrupted. Information integrity is the extent to which information is accurate, complete, consistent, and valid. At best, information is only as good as the data from which it is derived. If the data are of poor quality or lack integrity, then the information will also be of poor quality and lack integrity.

Introduction to Relational Databases

A relational database is a collection of tables. Each row in a table contains information about an individual entity and is referred to as a record. A collection of similar entities is an entity set, or data set. The columns in a table represent specific attributes of the entities. The point at which a row and column intersect is a field. Each field contains a single data element.

Each entity has a unique identifier, called a primary key. Sometimes, a combination of two or more of an entity's attributes serves as a primary key. When a primary key from one table appears in another table, it is referred to as a foreign key. Foreign keys point, or refer, to data contained in other tables. The use of primary keys and foreign keys helps define relationships between entities, reduce data redundancy, and can enhance data integrity. While foreign keys often protect against loss of data integrity, in some cases they can actually expose a database to integrity issues, for example when they point to a record that has been deleted from another table. Data integrity issues are often difficult to recognize and resolve.

In the absence of careful database design, and implementation of tools and techniques to help ensure data integrity, "dirty data" can cause system crashes, downtime, silent data corruption, lost credibility, inappropriate business decisions, lost confidence in the organization's data, and even regulatory intervention. An objective of data management is to prevent or mitigate these risks as much as possible.

Transaction Management

In an insurance company environment, transactions occur constantly. All of these involve reading from, or writing to, the organization's applications or databases. In this process data can be added, deleted, or changed. Whenever data are changed, there is a possibility that they might become corrupted. To prevent this, database designers have for years employed a variety of transaction management principles and techniques. One common technique is to apply the ACID Principles, in which transactions have four properties: atomicity, consistency, isolation, and durability.

Atomicity requires that all steps in a transaction must complete successfully; otherwise, none of them is reflected in the database. Transactions move through a number of states: active, partially committed, and committed or failed and aborted. Consistency requires that a database be as consistent, or reconcilable, after a transaction as it was before the transaction. This requires that each transaction completes as if it were processed in isolation. One transaction cannot inadvertently affect another. One method of ensuring isolation is the use of locks. Durability ensures that once a transaction has completed successfully, when it is in the committed state, the associated changes are stored until the database or application update has been confirmed.

Maintaining Data Integrity

There are a number of techniques data management professionals can use to help ensure data integrity including normalizing, defining business rules, validating data, using constraints, imposing referential integrity, and using generation data groups.

The goal of data normalization is to store "one fact in one place"; to ensure that a specific attribute is assigned to only one entity. Business policies and guidelines can be ambiguous, so data management professionals translate them into formally stated business rules. Business rules are expressed as "if-then" statements, tables, or decision trees. Business rules allow processes to be automated, which helps to preserve data integrity. Data validation involves verifying that the data in each field are as expected—it is not necessarily a method for determining whether the data are accurate. Data validation techniques can be implemented in several different ways: data type validation, allowed character checks, range checking, and code checking, as well as more complex validation routines. Constraints help to preserve data integrity by controlling or limiting the values that can be inserted into columns in a table. There are several types of constraints in general use: check constraints, not null constraints, unique constraints, primary key constraints, and foreign key constraints. Foreign key constraints help ensure referential integrity. Referential integrity helps maintain the accuracy of a database, by ensuring that relationships between entities remain intact, and that records are not inadvertently "orphaned" when associated records are deleted. A generation data group is essentially a collection of sequential automatic backups of a particular data set. Each backup, or "snapshot" of the data set, is referred to as a generation. Any of the generations in the group can be accessed as required.

Integrated Data Resource and Common Data Architecture

Many organizations have vast quantities of data in different formats, in different systems, implemented in different ways on different platforms. The result is referred to as disparate data. The problem with disparate data is that they perpetuate a spiraling cycle of increasingly disparate data. People are uncertain about the quality of the available data, so they create their own. Because these new data are often not documented or integrated, other people cannot find them or access them and this adds to people's general distrust of the organization's data. The data manager's goal is to consolidate disparate data as much as possible. One effective way is through the development of an integrated data resource that has a common data architecture.

Data resource integration is the process of making disparate data across an enterprise homogeneous and ensuring that they remain so. Formal data resource integration involves taking inventory of all of an enterprise's current data; developing a thorough understanding of the data; deciding on a preferred enterprise data architecture; and transforming the disparate data into homogeneous data using formal data transformation rules.

Metadata and Metadata Management

Metadata put data in context, reveal their meaning, and make them accessible and useable. Metadata management is the preparation, definition, organization, managed access, and maintenance of an organization's metadata. Metadata management includes understanding requirements; defining the metadata architecture; developing standards; implementing the metadata environment; creating, maintaining, and integrating metadata; managing metadata repositories; distributing metadata; and analyzing metadata.

Theorists have categorized metadata in a number of ways. One method includes business metadata, technical metadata, operational metadata, process metadata, and data stewardship metadata. These categories are associated with structured data. In the case of unstructured data, metadata are categorized as descriptive, technical/structural, or administrative.

Using metadata, it is possible to trace the lineage of data from the original producer, and determine where they flow and how they are transformed. Data lineage helps organizations demonstrate the accuracy and integrity of the information contained in their statutory and financial reports. When data accuracy or integrity issues occur, data lineage can help identify the source of the problem. Data lineage can be used to identify the impact of systems or process changes on downstream systems or processes. It is also useful in creating business intelligence (BI), and it can help an organization to better protect sensitive or confidential data.

To make best use of its metadata, an organization requires a metadata strategy that is integrated into the enterprise data management strategy. The organization's business needs should drive a metadata strategy. The sheer volume of an enterprise's metadata can be daunting, so scoping is an essential element of a well-crafted metadata strategy.

Reference and Master Data Management

Standardized reference data are important in data integration efforts and they facilitate the sharing of information. Reference data management (RDM) attempts to reduce or eliminate variances and inconsistencies in reference data, and to accurately map those system-specific reference data that cannot be standardized. There are several approaches to reference data integration. In some cases, a single source can be identified and selected as the system of record for many reference data sets. The system of record provides the content for a database of reference data.

This becomes the source of reference data for online transaction processing (OLTP) systems and their associated databases. The application or database of record is also the source of reference data for data warehouse, and BI applications.

Master data are data about those things that are essential to an organization's operations. Master data are typically used by multiple systems within an organization and they can differ from system to system. The goal of master data management is to determine which data in each system are most correct and create a consolidated "golden record" of the most accurate and complete data. Those data are then integrated for use by all systems.

Master data management (MDM) is the process of defining how master data will be created, maintained, and integrated for general use; implementing appropriate governance, technologies, and procedures; and maintaining ongoing master data quality. Any organization initiating an MDM program needs to determine which master data should be managed, how they will be used, who their creators and consumers are, what the most appropriate architecture would be, and in which functional area to begin the MDM implementation.

Data and Information Governance

While some treat data and information governance as a single function, or simply refer to data governance on its own, others consider data and information governance as separate but complimentary. Some organizations have a data governance group and an information governance group; others have a single group that performs both roles. However, the governance function is implemented within a particular organization, its purpose is to establish corporate policies with respect to data, and monitor and enforce compliance with those policies. It guides all other data management activities. Information technology governance is a separate function that works to align IT strategy with business strategy to maximize the value of IT investments.

When the data and information governance functions are separated, data governance typically focuses on such things as metadata, data quality, data security, data lineage, the timeliness and synchronization of data, the impact of system changes on data quality and integrity, and accountability for data stores. Information governance generally focuses on compliance with regulatory requirements, the security and privacy of sensitive information, providing tools to facilitate analysis and interpretation of information, sharing and managing information, enhancing productivity, appropriate retention and disposal of information, and appropriate e-mail usage.

Effective data and information governance involves individuals from across the organization including executives, a data governance council or committee, data managers, IT professionals, business and technical data stewards, coordinating data stewards, and information stewards.

Successful implementations typically concentrate on carefully identifying, planning, and managing the organizational and cultural changes necessary to effectively implement the governance strategy. It is important to establish channels and procedures for identifying and resolving issues related to data. For the ongoing success of an enterprise governance program, it is essential to communicate and promote the value of data assets and the importance of effective data governance.

Data and Information Security

Insurers, their service providers, and data collection organizations collect confidential information about insureds, agents and brokers, employees, claimants, prospects, and others. It is essential that insurers protect the confidential information in their possession, particularly personally identifiable information (PII) and individually identifiable health information. In addition, organizations must comply with government privacy, confidentiality, and security regulations, as well as federal antitrust laws that prohibit the sharing of certain information.

Data security management is the process of developing, implementing, and monitoring the effectiveness of policies and procedures that protect data and information. It ensures that data and information are accessible for appropriate use and inaccessible for inappropriate use.

An organization can help prevent security breaches, or the loss or corruption of data and information, by implementing a robust security program. This involves first identifying the organization's needs and the regulatory requirements with which it must comply. Next, data security policies, standards, controls, and procedures should be developed and implemented. Some security controls are administrative, and others are technical. Data and information should be classified based on their level of confidentiality. Access to data and information should be managed, for example using passwords or views, and user access behavior should be monitored. Regular data security audits should be performed.

Various individuals and groups are responsible for data security, including a governance body, a chief information security officer, security administrator, security engineers, business managers and the users of an organization's data and information.

Data Modeling Fundamentals

Data modeling is a method for determining what data, and what relationships among those data, should be stored in a database. It is also a way of graphically communicating database design. There are three levels of data modeling: conceptual, logical, and physical.

A conceptual data model (CDM), sometimes called an entity-relationship model (ERM), is a high-level model, created in consultation with business subject matter experts, which focuses simply on the required entities and their relationships. These relationships can be one-to-one, one-to-many, many-to-many, or recursive. A CDM forms the basis for a logical data model. A logical data model (LDM) defines the actual structures that will be used by the database management system (DBMS). A physical data model (PDM) is more detailed than an LDM and it adopts the conventions specific to the particular DBMS.

Judging Data Model Quality

Data modeling is as much an art as a science. There are typically a variety of ways of defining entities and expressing the relationships among them. Even so, well-designed data models are complete; normalized as much as possible; enforce business rules; are unambiguous, adaptable and elegant; communicate effectively; and take into consideration how a database will integrate with other databases.

Document and Content Management

Document and content management focuses on managing unstructured data and information that are stored outside structured databases. Document management is a collection of systems used to maintain, classify, organize, and retrieve paper or electronic documents that are important to the organization's business activities or regulatory compliance. Document management deals with the document as a whole rather than the content elements it contains. Electronic document management systems (EDMS) facilitate the creation or acquisition, classification, indexing, storage, maintenance, version control, access, security, retention, and archival of documents.

Although document management and content management were initially seen as two separate disciplines, there has been convergence as software vendors have enhanced their products. Content management categorizes and organizes content elements so that they can be used and reused in various ways. Individual content components can be updated and edited quickly, ensuring the accuracy and timeliness of the information they present. Data modeling techniques and the use of taxonomies help to define a content architecture so that the information it contains can be readily discovered, accessed, used and reused.

As much as 80 percent of business data and information are unstructured. Unstructured data can offer insights far beyond those that can be gleaned from structured data alone. However, there are a number of challenges involved in managing unstructured data. Organizations collect and create more and more unstructured data in a variety of formats and the pace of that growth is accelerating. It can be difficult to determine what data an organization actually has. Outdated or redundant data are often retained unnecessarily because they cannot be readily identified. Probably the greatest challenge is determining which unstructured data an organization should create, collect, analyze, and keep.

Business Analytics and Predictive Modeling Overview

Business performance management (BPM) is a set of methodologies and tools that help organizations optimize their performance. Key performance indicators (KPI) help managers and executives evaluate how successfully the organization is achieving its objectives. BPM consolidates data from various sources so that they can be queried, analyzed, and made available to management. Many automated BPM environments are continuous and/or real-time.

Data Warehousing

Data warehousing enhances an organization's ability to access and analyze its data. This ability allows managers to gain greater insights into its operations and performance. These insights are often referred to as business intelligence (BI).

Typically, the data in a data warehouse or data mart originate from a variety of internal and external sources and systems. In order to populate a data warehouse, it is necessary to perform an extract-transform-load (ETL) process. ETL is a process that needs to be continuous in order to keep the data in the warehouse current. Source-to-target mapping documents the complete lineage for each data element in the warehouse. There are two extraction methods: full extraction and incremental extraction. After the data are extracted, they may be cleansed to eliminate duplicate records and redundancies, and to enforce consistency and integrity. Once the data have been cleansed and transformed they can be integrated and loaded into the data warehouse.

Strategic, Tactical, and Operational Business Intelligence

Strategic BI typically forms part of a formal BPM program. It allows executives to monitor KPI to determine the extent to which the organization is achieving its strategic objectives. Tactical BI allows managers and analysts to measure the success of business initiatives. Operational BI provides managers and supervisors with daily or even real-time information about transactions or processes.

Analytics

In any field it can be challenging for practitioners to reach agreement on a common vocabulary, and the term "analytics" has been defined in a variety of ways. IDMA defines analytics as "the data, tools, and applications that support corporate strategic plans and business performance; they provide the ability to gather, store, access, and analyze corporate data for decision making."[135] Descriptive analytics presents a depiction of a past or current state. Predictive analytics attempts to determine what is likely to happen in the future. Prescriptive analytics helps managers determine how to mitigate risks and capitalize on opportunities.

Developing a predictive model is an iterative process. The approach adopted by IDMA has a series of five steps: retrieve and organize the data; understand the data; split the data into development data and test data and build a model; evaluate the model's performance; iterate and choose a model.[136]

---

[135] Patricia L. Saporito, Applied Insurance Analytics, ©2015 by Patricia L. Saporito Upper Saddle River, New Jersey 07458, Pearson Education Ltd., p. 20.

[136] www.jesse-flores.com/a-five-step-process-for-predictive-modeling/ (accessed October 5, 2015).

Data Management Trends, Technologies, and Frameworks

Data management can be challenging, particularly in an insurance environment. The large volume of data and the interrelationships among those data add to the challenges inherent in data management. In the absence of useful techniques, technologies, languages, and solutions—broadly categorized as tools—effective data management would be hard to achieve and harder to maintain. Tools facilitate data management in a variety of ways, depending on the data management function being performed. Some are single-function and stand-alone, while others are integrated suites, or packages, of tools.

One of the challenges data managers face is that they operate in an environment that is continually changing. Professional data managers ensure that they keep current. New techniques, technologies, and solutions, designed to meet businesses' evolving operational, analytic, and data management requirements, emerge regularly. The goal is to add value cost-effectively.

Deciding to Buy or Build Tools

Tools can be purchased from a vendor or developed in-house. The principle considerations when determining whether to buy or build are the required capabilities, the cost, any customization that is required for a vendor's system, and the organization's culture.

When determining whether to buy or build it is important to confirm that an actual need exists for a tool, identify core business requirements, identify architectural requirements, evaluate existing systems, evaluate the in-house ability to build a custom solution, and determine whether a vendor's product meets the identified requirements. Whether buying or building, an organization relies on the expertise of both its IT and data management professionals. An individual data manager's role may vary depending on his or her particular skill set and the internal structure and culture of the organization.

Tool Evaluation

The first step in tool evaluation is to determine the criteria upon which the evaluation is to be based. The criteria for evaluating a tool varies depending on the business need the tool is expected to fill, the technical environment into which it must integrate, and the culture of the organization performing the evaluation. External resources are also available. Some organizations evaluate software tools and make the results of their research available for a fee. Standards organizations develop and publish software evaluation standards.

When evaluating a tool, data management professionals typically consider a variety of factors including such things as the extent to which the tool meets the identified business need and the maturity of the technology. When evaluating competing commercial off-the-shelf products, organizations take a variety of approaches, some formal and others less so. A preferred approach is to select the decision criteria and assign a weight to each based on its relative importance. Then, evaluators use a scoring system to rate each vendor's product, and the data manager creates a decision support spreadsheet to tabulate the scores.

Frameworks

Frameworks are another category of tools that are invaluable to data managers. Frameworks assist data managers by providing an established approach to conceptualizing complex situations or problems, and a structured way in which to manage complex situations or resolve problems.

In many organizations, the growing number and complexity of information technology (IT) and related systems has resulted in increased IT costs, decreased access to information, and a reduced ability to be agile and innovative. Developing and implementing an enterprise architecture helps to resolve all of these issues. However, doing so is highly complex. Frameworks help an organization take a structured approach to designing and deploying an enterprise architecture.

There is a variety of frameworks in general use developed by standards organizations, government bodies, vendors, and consulting firms. Often different frameworks take very different approaches and they can sometimes be used in combination. Some commonly used frameworks include the ACORD Framework, the Zachman Framework for Enterprise Architecture, and The Open Group Architecture Framework (TOGAF).

Bibliography

The DAMA Dictionary of Data Management, First Edition 2008, Mark Mosley Editor, Technics Publications LLC, New Jersey, copyright 2008 DAMA International.

The DAMA Guide to the Data Management Body of Knowledge (DAMA-DMBOK) First Edition, DAMA International, Technics Publications LLC, New Jersey, copyright 2009 DAMA International.

Fast Data hits the Big Data fast lane, By Andrew Brust for Big on Data | April 16, 2012, Guest Post By Tony Baer, viewed at http://zd.net/2sbiFOJ (accessed January 28, 2016).

What Is Big Data?, Lisa Arthur, Aug 15, 2013 viewed at http://bit.ly/1a8yGI7 (accessed January 28, 2016).

Big Data, IT Glossary, Gartner, viewed at http://gtnr.it/1rP0ANn (accessed January 28, 2016).

The 7 Vs of Big Data, By Rob Livingstone, June 21st 2013, viewed at http://bit.ly/2rq31fJ (accessed January 28, 2016).

How Fast Is Our Data Volume Growing? by Steve Mackie, viewed at http://bit.ly/2rpLK67 (accessed January 29, 2016).

Beyond Volume, Variety and Velocity is the Issue of Big Data Veracity, by Kevin Normandeau, September 12, 2013, viewed at http://bit.ly/1y2xlZ6 (accessed January 29, 2016).

Volume, Velocity, Variety: What You Need to Know About Big Data, By Edd Dumbill, viewed at http://bit.ly/2sbqSSV (accessed January 29, 2016).

To Build a Data-Driven Organization, Executives Must Create a Data-Centric Culture, Don Campbell, 9/29/2014, viewed at http://ubm.io/1vpZFXf (accessed January 29, 2016).

The PDSA Cycle, The Deming Institute, viewed at http://bit.ly/1O8lnuv (accessed January 29, 2016).

Index